michael bateman

the world of spice

kyle cathie limited

Author's acknowledgements

First I must thank my wife Heather Maisner, who
has effectively co-authored this book, putting a
brake on her writing of children's books to help me
get it on its feet.

There's never been a more exciting time to
explore a subject like spice and no country is more
open to enjoying the world's treasures than the
UK. I'm grateful to my publisher Kyle Cathie
who recognises this better than anyone. Thanks,
too, to my editor Sarah Epton for her enthusiastic
encouragement, to designer Paul Welti, to
photographer Steve Baxter, food stylist Linda Tubby
and props stylist Penny Markham who together
conjured up the wonderful photographs, and to
my supportive agent Abner Stein.

I've been lucky to have so many friends among
food writers, who share my passion for travel, and
I'd like to thank them all. Where to begin? I owe
a special debt to friends, chefs, writers and
colleagues such as Caroline Conran and Robert
Carrier (Europe), Elizabeth Lambert Ortiz (Mexico,
Latin America and the Caribbean), Susanna
Palazuelos and Susana Trilling (Mexico), Elizabeth
Luard (Latin America and Spain), Maria Jose Sevilla
(Spain), Anna del Conte and Antonio Carluccio
(Italy), Claudia Roden and Anissa Helou (the Middle
East), Jamie Jones (Egypt and Lebanon), Paula
Wolfert (Morocco and the Mediterranean),
Vatcharin Bhumichitr and David Thompson
(Thailand) and Paul McIlhenny (Louisiana).

Thanks also to Peter Gordon (New Zealand),
Tetsuya Wakuda and Vic Cherikoff (Australia), Deh-
Ta Hsiung and the late Kenneth Lo (China), Kimiko
Barber, Hirohisa Koyama (Japan), Madhur Jaffrey,
Camellia Panjabi, Meena Patak, Lesley Forbes, Pat
Chapman and Julie Sahni (India), T. Pubis Silva (Sri
Lanka), Renata Coetzee, Myrna Robbins and Topsy
Ventor (South Africa), Violet Oon (Singapore), Sri
Owen (Indonesia) and Marc Miron (Bali), Andrew
Dolby and the late David Wolfe (Korea).

Among the many rich sources I've consulted
are Alan Davidson's momentous *Oxford Companion
to Food*, the *Cambridge World History of Food*
(Kiple and Ornelas), Maguelonne Toussaint-Samat's
History of Food and Tom Stobart's *Cook's*

Encyclopaedia; also works by Margaret Shaida
and Nada Saleh (Middle East), Ghillie Basan, and
Artun and Behan Unsal (Turkey), Charmaine
Solomon (Asia), Bruce Cost (Far East), Diana
Kennedy (Mexico), Dorinda Hafner (Africa) and
Marc Millom (Korea); and finally, as fresh a source
of inspiration today as when they were alive, the
works of Elizabeth David and Jane Grigson.

First published in Great Britain in 2003 by
Kyle Cathie Limited, 122 Arlington Road
London NW1 7HP
general.enquiries@kyle-cathie.com
www.kylecathie.com

ISBN 1 85626 472 6

Project editor: Sarah Epton
Copy editor: Becky Alexander
Editorial assistant: Vicki Murrell
Designer: Paul Welti
Maps by ML Design
Production by Sha Huxtable and Claudia Varosio

A CIP catalogue record for this book is available from
the British Library.

Colour separations by Colourscan, Singapore
Printed and bound in Singapore by Star Standard

contents / contents / contents / conte

introduction / introducti

We all love spices in our food. Their heady aromas alert the senses and arouse the appetite; their perfumes may lodge in the nose – as do vanilla, cardamom or cloves – creating anticipation of pleasures to come; or they may mask some of the less appealing odours of cooked food, for example, saffron or bay leaf can transform a fish soup.

On the tongue, spices set a challenge for the palate with their picquancy: sweet, sour, bitter and salty. Or they may simply be hot, such as ginger and peppercorns and chilli, mustard and horseradish and wasabi paste.

Spices often evoke exotic notions of faraway countries and other food cultures. They excite and exalt. You only have to think of Indian food and the way it orchestrates dozens of spices in infinite combinations.

Sugar and spice and all things nice – how would our food today be without them? Palaeolithic man, with his stone implements, eating roots and fruits, small animals, fish and birds, was grateful merely for survival. It took many thousands of years for him to master the use of fire and learn to indulge his palate, refining the plainness of his fare, introducing aromatic leaves and seeds and barks.

Flavour was only part of the story. Salt and sugar, as well as herbs and spices, were soon found to play a vital role in human subsistence, both as medicines and preservatives. Many herbs, such as thyme and rosemary, contain oils which are bacteriocidal – they kill germs.

The understanding and use of spices has evolved gradually. Salt sharpens flavour but, when it was found to be a preservative, it became the most essential resource on the planet. Salt draws out moisture from food and inhibits spoilage from airborne bacteria, so you can brine down meat, fish and vegetables for long storage.

The Chinese were the first to appreciate the medical characteristics of plants, seeds, barks and roots, skills explored by Indian (ayurvedic) and Greek healers.

But it was the luxurious qualities of spices that appealed to gourmets and led to the steady increase in trade from East to West. Eventually, some highly perfumed spices, such as cinnamon, nutmeg, cloves, ginger and peppercorns, became symbols of conspicuous consumption among the wealthy. Peppercorns were worth a king's ransom – they were actually traded by one Roman emperor

to spare Rome from being sacked by the Goths, when they were at the gates of the city.

Centres such as Baghdad, Cairo, Venice, Genoa and Lisbon grew rich in turn, through the centuries, as they became hubs of the spice trade, spices being as precious as exotic perfumes (ambergris, incense and myrrh) or gold and silver and rare stones. The search for them and the profits they generated have shaped history, from Marco Polo opening up the East to Columbus discovering the Americas, and the East India Company establishing India as the 'Jewel in the Crown' of the British Empire.

Before the world-wide search for precious spices, though, medieval monasteries, the seats of learning in their day, all had herb gardens, or physic gardens as they called them. They studied herbal remedies as medicines long before cooks began to use spices and herbs to enhance and improve the flavour of dishes.

Nicholas Culpeper's *Complete Herbal*, published in the seventeenth century, lists over 400 herbs and their uses, and cooking is not one of them. Not even saffron, today the world's most expensive spice, which was then grown in Cambridgeshire is recommended for culinary use. 'It refreshes the spirits,' says Culpeper. 'It guards against fainting fits and palpitation of the heart, it strengthens the stomach, aids digestion, cleanses the lungs, is good for coughs. It is good in hysteric disorders. But some who have taken too large a dose,' he adds, 'have fallen into inveterate convulsive laughter which ended in death.' Nothing about food.

Paprika, the national spice of Hungary, was initially introduced by the church as a plant which they hoped might have medicinal properties. It didn't but it looked pretty in the garden, so it stayed. People began to cook and eat it. It wasn't until the occupying Turks tried to place a ban on it that it started to have unrealistic value. Grown in secret, it developed into the ingredient so essential to Hungarian cooking that they use 5kg per head per year.

My own interest in spices, and in food in general, began when I lived in Hong Kong for 18 months. I wondered how it was possible that the Chinese, working with similar ingredients to our own, could produce such different-tasting and delicious food. The answer was by adding masses of fresh ginger, spring onions and garlic, and lots of

A second-generation spice seller grinds his own produce for sale in his shop in Amsterdam, Holland – where specialist spice stores have existed for hundreds of years.

Chinese five-spice powder with its powerful anise flavour, soy sauce, chilli and *hoisin* sauces.

Over the years, thanks mostly to my life as a food writer, I've been able to travel and enjoy most of the world's gastronomies – first in France, Italy, Spain, China, Morocco and Turkey, and then in the Americas, India and Sri Lanka, Southeast Asia, Indonesia, Japan, Africa and Australasia.

Hunting down spices became an obsession, whether it was hot and fruity chillies in the Mercado de Abastos in Oaxaca, Mexico, or cardamoms in the 'spice trail' of Kerala, still a world centre for exotic spices.

My latest adventure was a trip, with my wife Heather, to Zanzibar, once a world hub of spice trading, where Arabians, Indians and Africans have fused into one identity under the banner of spices. As part of the Oman Empire it became the leading source of cloves in the world. The islanders brought seeds from the Dutch East Indies, captured slaves from the Congo to work the plantations, then sold the produce to European traders.

We spent a day on a spice farm, under the shade of towering coconut palms and dense evergreen clove trees, whose scented pink flower buds had not quite opened (and were thus ready for harvesting). Our guide cut the rhizomes (thickened underground roots) from bamboo-like ginger and turmeric bushes. And we saw cardamom bushes with similar leaves, but with orchid-like flowers close to the ground.

We fingered the slim, young, upright branches of cinnamon trees, which would be peeled to make the quills. We picked nutmegs – and saw that each was wrapped in a red lace jacket, which would be dried in the sun to sell as mace.

We marvelled at the climbing peppercorn vines with their lush deep-green heart-shaped leaves and tiny bunches of berries like so many miniature grapes. In dense shade, we found a vanilla vine, thick-leafed, with its 'beans' like French beans, tough and green. They had no aroma at all – the beans have to picked from the vines and processed for months before the colour, texture and haunting flavour of vanilla develops.

By now our hands were perfumed and stained. We bought bags of spices from the spice shop and returned to the hotel for dinner. From the kitchen came the unmistakable aroma of the spices of Zanzibar sizzling on fresh grilled fish.

In most people's minds, India represents the summit of cooking with spice. No country uses a wider range of fragrant spices, but heat is the quality most associated with India's food. Given the oven-heat of the subcontinent (which in some parts rises to 40°C in the height of summer), this is sensible, since chilli's constituent chemical capsaicin opens the pores and activates the body's own cooling system to provide relief.

Even before chillies were introduced by the Portuguese in the fifteenth century, India had already discovered a piquant heat source in the peppercorn; in its day the world's most sought-after spice, and still essential in Indian cooking. Today both peppercorns and chillies are important exports. India is the world's leading grower of chillies, producing some 80,000 tonnes a year, of which over a quarter is exported.

As a result of the British occupation of India, a story which dates back to the early seventeenth century, the subtleties of Indian cooking are well understood in the UK. From the eighteenth and nineteenth centuries the British kitchen has never been without curry powder, mango chutneys and bottled fruit sauces such as HP and Worcestershire Sauce, made with tamarind, chilli and other spices, all of which originate in the Raj. It was Captain William Hawkins, employed by the East India Company, who opened up this vast continent for Britain in 1608, landing at the north-western port of Surat to begin talks with the ruling Moghul emperors; he wrote back home describing the food, 'a mess of rice with meat, chicken and vegetables served with a mixture of bruised spices and turmeric called "masala"'.

The British moved by stealth initially, and certainly not by force, establishing bases in Madras, Bombay (then little more

than a fishing village), and Calcutta. How the country came to be Britain's proudest possession, the 'Jewel in the Crown' of Queen Victoria, who was made Empress of India in 1877, is fascinating history. And no aspect is more interesting to food scholars than a study of the riches of its food cultures. If the Moghuls, heirs of Genghis Khan, created a rich, meat-eating food culture in the northwest, it is to the south, and Kerala in particular, that one must look for the subtlety that the skilful use of spices brings.

A garden of eden

Kerala is fertile, green, subtropical land, with vast inland waterways fringed with coconut palms. It is rich in rice, seafood and vegetables, and is a Garden of Eden of spices. Cochin is the main port, a former Dutch trading post, with many great spice warehouses to store the spices grown in the nearby hills. All the exotic spices grow here, including ginger, cinnamon, nutmeg,

Pulses and spices being sold at the kerbside in Calcutta, India.

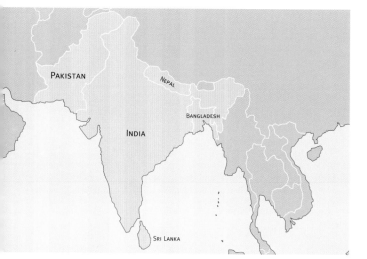

PAKISTAN

NEPAL

BANGLADESH

INDIA

SRI LANKA

cloves and peppercorns. The spice palate is a keyboard that the skilled chef plays like an instrument. Cumin seed, for example, offers at least three flavour options: the seed ground before roasting is musty and mild; the seed ground after roasting is pungent and biting; and the whole seed tossed into hot oil and cooked until it pops will taste sweet and nutty.

The Indian cook distinguishes between pungent and mild curry mixtures. A pungent mixture will be used to start a curry, and must be cooked in oil to temper and moderate the raw taste. Warm spice mixtures, such as *garam masala* (containing sweet spices such as cinnamon), are added at the end to give an aromatic finish.

Indian use of spices is the most subtle and well-balanced in the world. Where we in the West prepare many dishes without the addition of any spice, in India, by contrast, there is a barely a single dish that does not have a rich and delicate infusion of spice.

Although Indian restaurants have had a place in every high street in England since the 1950s, it wasn't until the 1980s, through the medium of television, that the home cook began to learn the mysteries and subtleties of cooking with spices, thanks to the educational programmes presented by the charismatic Indian actress Madhur Jaffrey.

First of all, she discouraged the use of curry powder because once spices have been ground, they stale quickly, as their oils, exposed to the air, oxidise and turn bitter. Spices for curries, such as coriander seed, cumin, cardamom and fenugreek, should be bought whole, kept in airtight containers, and ground only when needed.

What is vindaloo?

Today Indian food is one of the most popular foods in the UK, eaten up to three times a month by 75 per cent of families. Our knowledge of Indian spicing increases by the day; you'll even hear people claiming that vindaloo is entirely a British invention a dish never eaten in India and unknown there. There's some logic behind this claim and, given that the population of India is 800 million, with many subdivisions, regions, cultures and at least fifteen languages, it's hardly surprising that few of them know vindaloo. In fact, India's most notorious dish originates in Goa, the small port in southwest India, which had been an important trading centre for the Portuguese. Vindaloo evolved from the Portuguese way of preparing stews after marinating meat in wine with garlic to flavour and tenderise it. The name of the dish is a combination of the Portuguese words for wine and garlic, *vinho* and *alho*, giving, perhaps, '*vin'd'alho*'. The addition of chilli was a necessary local improvement, although the

combination of vinegar and chilli has the explosive effect of intensifying the spice's heat.

The cookery style of Sri Lanka (formerly Ceylon), historically a renowned spice island, is not so different from that of south India. Rice and curry is the most common food and it is usually hot and quite sour. A lot of coconut, green mango, *amchoor* (mango powder), tamarind and an acidic fruit called *gamboge* are also used.

Breakfast usually includes *hopper*, a pancake cooked in a semi-spherical pan like a small wok, in which an egg may be steam-cooked, or it may be served with a curried vegetable filling – you can be sure it will be hot. There is also string hopper, a pancake of tangled noodles, cooked to the same shape.

Hotels aiming to attract Western customers tend to modify the very strong spiced curries enjoyed by most Sinhalese, but you can track the real thing down if you ask for it. And the hot, sour flavours of the kitchen can be replicated at home, bringing to life the sounds, scents and scenery of this magical island.

Fiery red chillies are the soul of Indian cooking.

spiced paratha flatbread (INDIA)

In India there are many versions of flatbread. This one uses simple ingredients, laced with spices, to create a light, nourishing meal. Ghee is clarified butter and it doesn't burn when you fry with it.

SERVES 4

FOR THE DOUGH
450g whole-wheat flour
300ml lukewarm water

FOR THE FILLING
500g potatoes
Ghee **or sunflower oil, for frying**
1 onion, finely sliced
2.5cm ginger, grated
1 tablespoon chopped coriander leaves
1 teaspoon ground cumin
½ teaspoon chilli powder
1 teaspoon *garam masala* **(see page 31)**
Salt
Flour, for dusting

Put the flour in a mixing bowl and add the water, a little at a time, mixing well to make a soft dough. Knead with the hands for at least 10 minutes until the dough is soft and pliable. Cover with a damp cloth and leave to rest for ½–1 hour. Knead again for about 3 minutes. Cover once more.

Meanwhile, prepare the filling. Boil the potatoes in their skins for 20–25 minutes, then peel and slice finely. Heat 2 tablespoons of the *ghee* or sunflower oil and fry the onion for 5–10 minutes, until golden. Add the potato slices, ginger, chopped coriander, cumin, chilli and *garam masala*. Fry for a few more minutes, stirring to coat the potatoes with the spices. Add salt to taste and leave to cool.

Knead the dough for about 3 minutes. Break off a small piece of the dough and roll into a small ball about the size of a large coin. Flatten the ball slightly and, using a little flour, roll out thinly to make a *chapatti* about 5cm across. Roll out another *chapatti* of the same size.

Spoon a tablespoon of the potato mixture into the centre of one *chapatti*, cover with the second *chapatti* and press down the edges to seal. Sprinkle a little flour on top and roll out to about 18cm across. Heat a frying pan until very hot. Gently place the *paratha* in the hot pan and cook for about 3 minutes. Turn it over

and smear the upper side generously with *ghee* or sunflower oil. Repeat on the other side. The *paratha* is ready when it is golden brown and speckled. Repeat until all the dough and potato mixture are used up.

Serve hot with natural yoghurt.

ghee

Heat 225g butter until it melts and froths up. Pour through a cloth over a sieve. Store in a jar and keep in the fridge for use as required.

potato samosas (INDIA)

These tasty parcels are eaten at any time of the day but especially with afternoon tea.

MAKES 20–30

FOR THE PASTRY
250g plain flour
50g *ghee* **(see above) or sunflower oil**
5 tablespoons warm water

FOR THE FILLING
225g potatoes
50g *ghee* **or sunflower oil**
1 teaspoon cumin seeds
1 onion, finely chopped
1 green chilli, chopped
2.5cm ginger, grated
2 teaspoons coriander seeds
1 teaspoon *garam masala* **(see page 31)**
½ teaspoon chilli powder
2 tablespoons chopped coriander leaves
1 teaspoon dried mango powder, if available
   (from specialist stores)
Sunflower or groundnut oil, for deep-frying
Salt

To make the pastry, put the flour and a pinch of salt in a large mixing bowl. Using the fingertips, rub in the *ghee* or sunflower oil until the mixture resembles fine breadcrumbs. Add the water, a little at a time, to make a soft dough. Knead for at least 10 minutes. Cover with a damp cloth and set aside.

Meanwhile, prepare the filling. Boil the potatoes in their skins for about 25 minutes, then peel and cut into small cubes. Heat the *ghee* or sunflower oil in a frying pan, add the cumin seeds and, when they start popping, add the onion, green chilli and ginger. Fry for about five minutes or until the onion starts to brown.

Add the potato cubes, coriander seeds, *garam masala*, chilli powder, chopped coriander and mango powder, if using. Fry for a few minutes until the potatoes are coated with the spices. Add salt to taste, and leave to cool.

Knead the dough for about 3 minutes. Pull off a small piece of dough and flatten it into a disc about 5cm across. Cut it in half. Wet the edges with water and make an envelope using the second half. Half-fill with the potato mixture and press to seal. Set aside on a plate and cover with a damp cloth while you prepare the rest of the *samosas*.

Heat the sunflower or groundnut oil to 180°C/356°F – check with a thermometer. Drop in several *samosas* at a time. Turn them once and fry for a few minutes until golden brown. Remove, and drain on kitchen paper. Check the oil temperature again before dropping in the next batch of *samosas*. If the temperature is too low, they will soak up too much oil and will taste greasy. Serve hot, preferably.

spiced cauliflower and potato (INDIA)

Cauliflower assumes a new distinction in this spicy dish. Serve as a main course or as a side dish.

SERVES 4 AS A MAIN COURSE

500g potatoes, peeled
2 tablespoons sunflower or groundnut oil
1 teaspoon cumin seeds
1 cauliflower, cut into florets
1 green chilli, finely chopped
1 tablespoon curry powder (see page 31)
100ml water or chicken or vegetable stock
Pinch of chilli powder, to taste
Salt and freshly ground black pepper

Boil the potatoes for about 20 minutes, removing them from the heat while still slightly firm. Cut into bite-sized pieces and set aside.

Heat the sunflower or groundnut oil in a pan over a medium heat and add the cumin seeds. Cook for a few minutes until they start to pop. Add the cauliflower florets and cook for 2–3 minutes until they start to brown. Stir in the green chilli and curry powder and cook for a few minutes more, stirring well.

Add the water or stock and bring it to the boil. Lower the heat, cover the pan and cook for 5–10 minutes until the cauliflower is nearly tender.

Stir in the potatoes, mixing gently with a wooden spoon. Finish cooking, with the lid off, until the potatoes are heated through. Season to taste with the chilli powder, salt and pepper.

Drying chillies on a mass scale in the mountainous region of Khas, Nepal.

indian risotto with chilli prawns

This is an example of new wave cooking from Britain's most innovative cook, Vineet Bhatia, based on the disciplines of the classical Indian kitchen. It is a twist on Italian risotto, enhanced by ginger, cumin, coriander and turmeric.

SERVES 4 AS STARTER OR 2 AS A MAIN COURSE

FOR THE RISOTTO
50ml corn oil
1 teaspoon cumin seeds
3 cloves garlic, chopped
1cm ginger, grated
1 green chilli, chopped
1 red onion, chopped
1 teaspoon turmeric powder
250g basmati rice
600ml shellfish stock (use ground lobster, langoustine and/or prawn shells)
4 tablespoons natural yoghurt, whipped
1 tablespoon butter
1 tablespoon chopped coriander leaves
Salt

FOR THE CHILLI PRAWNS
2 eggs
½ teaspoon chilli powder
1 tablespoon cornflour
Sunflower oil, for deep-frying
8 medium-sized prawns, cooked, peeled and veins removed

To prepare the risotto, heat the corn oil to medium heat in a frying pan. Add the cumin seeds and cook briefly until they start to pop. Add the garlic and cook for 1 or 2 minutes. Add the ginger, chilli and onion, and cook for 2 minutes. Add the turmeric and rice, and stir for two minutes until heated through.

In a separate pan, heat the stock until warm, then pour it into the rice mixture. Bring to the boil, reduce the heat and cook for 12–15 minutes until the rice is three-quarters done and the stock is absorbed.

Meanwhile, prepare the prawns. Beat the eggs, chilli powder, cornflour and a pinch of salt together to make a batter. Heat the sunflower oil to 180°C/356°F – check with a thermometer. Dip each prawn in the batter, then fry for 1 or 2 minutes until golden. Drain on kitchen paper while you finish the risotto.

Add the yoghurt to the risotto and continue cooking for 2–3 minutes until the rice is cooked. Stir the butter and coriander into the rice, and season to taste with salt. Serve the risotto garnished with the prawns.

potatoes stuffed with almonds (INDIA)

This is an unusual, crispy snack that you can also serve as an appetiser.

SERVES 4 AS AN APPETISER

1 litre sunflower or groundnut oil, for deep-frying
225g small new potatoes, scrubbed
50g blanched almonds, cut into slivers
1 teaspoon ground coriander
1 teaspoon ground cumin
½ teaspoon chilli powder
2 tablespoons chopped coriander leaves
Salt

Heat the sunflower or groundnut oil in a deep pan to 180°C/350°F – check with a thermometer. Dry the potatoes well, then slip them into the oil and fry for about 10 minutes until coloured and soft all through. Drain and leave to cool.

Pierce one hole in the top of each potato using a skewer and slide a few almond slivers (depending on the size) into the hole.

Reheat the oil and fry the potatoes again for a few minutes until golden brown and crispy.

Place the potatoes in a bowl and sprinkle with the ground coriander, cumin, chilli powder, salt and coriander leaves. Season with salt and shake the bowl to spread the spices evenly, but be careful to keep the potatoes whole.

aubergine in tomato sauce

(INDIA)

This pungent dish from north India uses a variety of spices and makes a delicious first course or side dish. Leave overnight for the flavours to develop, or serve immediately hot or cold with naan, chapattis or pitta bread.

SERVES 4–6

6 cloves garlic
3cm ginger, cut into chunks
2 green chillies
1kg aubergines
300ml sunflower oil
1 teaspoon cumin seeds
1 teaspoon fennel seeds
2 teaspoons ground coriander seeds
2 large tomatoes, peeled and chopped
1 tablespoon tomato purée
½ teaspoon turmeric powder
2 teaspoons salt
Coriander leaves, to garnish

Using a blender, whizz the garlic, ginger and chillies with just enough water to make a thin paste.

Cut the aubergines lengthways into four thick slices, then cut across into 3cm thick chunks. Heat the sunflower oil in a wide pan and fry the aubergines in batches until completely tender and reddish-brown on both sides. Lift out using a slotted spoon and place in a sieve over a bowl. Leave for 30 minutes to drain off the surplus oil.

In the same pan, use 2 tablespoons of the drained oil and heat through. Add the cumin, fennel and coriander seeds and fry for a few seconds. Add the tomatoes, tomato purée, garlic, ginger and chilli paste, turmeric and salt. Cook gently, stirring well, for about 10 minutes until the mixture thickens.

Add the drained aubergines to the tomato sauce. Cover the pan and cook gently for about 15 minutes.

Serve at once or leave overnight in the fridge for the flavours to develop. Serve cold or warm with the coriander leaves sprinkled over.

spiced okra (INDIA)

In this simple dish okra (*bhindi*) retains its flavour and unique gooey texture, enhanced by a light sprinkling of spices.

SERVES 4 AS A SIDE DISH

450g okra, washed
2 tablespoons sunflower oil
1 teaspoon cumin seeds
3 onions, thickly sliced
½ teaspoon turmeric powder
½ teaspoon chilli powder
Salt

Dry the okra completely using kitchen paper. Top and tail and cut into slices about 0.5cm thick.

Heat the sunflower oil in a frying pan, add the cumin seeds and fry until they start to pop. Add the onions and fry until golden.

Add the okra, turmeric, chilli powder and a little salt. Mix well together and cover the pan. Simmer for about 15 minutes so that the mixture cooks in its own steam. Stir from time to time.

peas and cottage cheese (INDIA)

These two ingredients blend well in this classic Indian recipe, known as *mattar paneer*. You can use ready-made cottage cheese (*paneer*) or make it yourself a day in advance (see recipe right).

SERVES 4

3 tablespoons sunflower or groundnut oil
2 onions, finely grated
1 green chilli, finely chopped
2.5cm ginger, grated
1 clove garlic, finely chopped
1 teaspoon turmeric powder
1 teaspoon ground coriander
½ teaspoon chilli powder
125g fresh or canned tomatoes, peeled and chopped
Salt
225g cottage cheese
450g peas, fresh or frozen
2 tablespoons chopped coriander or parsley leaves

Heat 2 tablespoons of the sunflower or groundnut oil in a frying pan and add the onions, green chilli, ginger and garlic. Stir-fry for about 10 minutes until the onions are golden. Add the turmeric, ground coriander and chilli powder, and stir-fry for a further 2–3 minutes.

Add the tomatoes and a pinch of salt. Cook, stirring and adding a little water at a time, until the tomatoes become puréed. Continue to cook for about 5–10 minutes, until the oil separates on to the surface.

Meanwhile, fry the cottage cheese in the remaining oil for 3–5 minutes. Add the peas and fried cottage cheese to the tomato mixture and cover with water to about 2.5cm above the top of the mixture.

Cover the pan and simmer for about 10 minutes if using fresh peas or 5 minutes if using frozen. Garnish with the chopped coriander or parsley.

cottage cheese (INDIA)

2 pints milk
2 tablespoons lemon juice

Heat the milk until boiling and add the lemon juice. The milk will curdle into curds (cheese) and whey (liquid). Pour the mixture into a piece of muslin and tie it up. Hang it up from a hook so the whey can drip over a bowl. When the liquid has drained off, put a weight on the cheese to press out any excess whey.

When most of the moisture has drained away, cut the cheese into dice, about 5mm across, ready for use.

spiced potato cakes (INDIA)

This classic deep-fried, batter-coated delicacy from Gujarat, known as *bateta vada*, can be eaten as a snack or starter.

MAKES 20–25 CAKES

4 potatoes
1 teaspoon turmeric powder
1 teaspoon *garam masala* (see page 31)
1 teaspoon chilli powder
1 teaspoon salt
2 teaspoons sugar
1 tablespoon sesame seeds
Flour for dusting
1 litre corn oil, for deep-frying
1 tablespoon chopped coriander leaves, to garnish

FOR THE BATTER

225g gram flour (yellow lentil flour)
¼ teaspoon ajowan seeds
½ teaspoon chilli powder
1 teaspoon sesame seeds
2 tablespoons vegetable oil
300ml water

Boil the potatoes in their skins for about 20 minutes, until soft. Peel and mash them. In a large bowl mix the potato with the turmeric, *garam masala*, chilli powder, salt, sugar and sesame seeds. Using a spoon, scoop out small mounds of the potato mixture, and roll into balls on a floured surface. Flatten into patties.

To make the batter, sift the gram flour into a bowl and add the ajowan seeds, chilli powder and sesame seeds. Heat the vegetable oil and whisk it in, then stir in the water to make a smooth batter as thick as cream.

Heat the corn oil in a deep-fryer or in a large frying pan to 180°C/356°F or until fine blue smoke appears (check with a thermometer if you have one). Dip the potato patties in the batter, place in the fryer or pan about five at a time, and fry until golden. Transfer each batch on to kitchen paper to drain. After each batch, raise the heat to 180°C/356°F again. Repeat until all the potato cakes are cooked.

Serve hot with the coriander sprinkled over. These cakes are delicious with Special Coconut Raita (see page 29), Tamarind and Date Chutney (see page 30) or Fresh Mango Chutney (see page 30).

chickpeas and potatoes (INDIA)

Chickpeas, combined with potatoes and seasoned with a medley of spices, are a frequent one-dish meal in the Punjab. If you are using dried chickpeas, soak them overnight first.

SERVES 4–6

500g dried chickpeas, soaked overnight (or 2 x 400g cans of chickpeas), drained
½ teaspoon bicarbonate of soda (if using dried chickpeas)
350g potatoes
4 tablespoons sunflower oil
1 teaspoon cumin seeds
250g tomatoes, peeled and chopped
1 teaspoon salt
1 teaspoon turmeric powder
2.5cm ginger, grated or finely chopped
2 teaspoons curry powder or *garam masala* (see page 31)
½ lemon, to squeeze
150ml water
2 tablespoons chopped coriander leaves, to garnish

If using dried chickpeas, place them in a saucepan, discarding any hard, dark ones, and cover with fresh cold water. Add the bicarbonate of soda. Bring to the boil and cook until tender, adding more water if necessary. Skim off any scum that rises to the top. They will take from 1–2 hours, depending on the quality. Canned chickpeas will take 5 minutes to heat through – you do not need to add the bicarbonate of soda.

Boil the potatoes in their skins for about 20 minutes, but don't overcook. Peel and cut into dice.

Heat the sunflower oil in a frying pan, add the cumin seeds and fry until they start to pop. Add the tomatoes and cook on a low heat for 10 minutes. Add the salt, turmeric, ginger, curry powder or *garam masala* and a squeeze of lemon juice, and stir to form a thick sauce.

Add the chickpeas, diced potatoes and water, and simmer on the lowest heat for 15–20 minutes. Garnish with the coriander leaves.

Serve with a raw, sliced onion salad and naan bread.

dhal lentils (INDIA)

A large number of India's vast population eat rice, lentils
(*dhal*) and vegetables daily. The use of infinite permutations
of spice, however, means that the diet need never be
monotonous. As well as ginger, turmeric and chilli, this
dish contains *garam masala* – a mixture of ground spices
(see page 31). Often several kinds of lentils are cooked
together, each different in colour and texture, each adding
a slightly different quality to the dish. Some remain firm,
others break into a pulp. This recipe suggests five varieties,
but you can vary them as you wish.

SERVES 4–6

**300g dried mixed lentils such as yellow (*toovar* or *arhar*),
    pink (*masar*), green (*mung*), black and white (*urad* with
    and without skins) and yellow split peas (*channa*)**
1 litre water
1 onion, chopped
1 teaspoon turmeric powder
1 green chilli, finely chopped
3cm ginger, grated
1 tablespoon *garam masala* (see page 31)
Salt
3 tablespoons sunflower oil
2 cloves garlic, finely sliced
2 teaspoons cumin seeds
Chopped coriander, mint or parsley leaves, to garnish

Spread the lentils on a plate and pick out any stones. Rinse well,
then place in a saucepan and cover with the water. Add the onion
and turmeric and bring to the boil. Lower the heat, cover and
simmer for 35–45 minutes, stirring from time to time to prevent
sticking. When you have a soft, soupy purée, add the chilli, ginger
and *garam masala*. Add salt to taste.

Place the *dhal* in a warmed serving dish. Heat the sunflower oil
in a pan and fry the garlic and cumin seeds until brown. Pour this
sizzling mixture over the *dhal*. Garnish with the coriander, mint or
parsley leaves.

Serve with rice or as a side dish.

red chicken curry (SRI LANKA)

This recipe is by the most eminent chef in Sri Lanka, T. Pubis
Silva of the Mount Lavinia Hotel, Colombo. Pubis uses the
many spices of the island, including cinnamon, peppercorns,
cloves, ginger and many flavourings still unknown outside the
island. These include the *rampe* leaf, a sour fruit called
gamboge used like tamarind, and powdered dried *maldive*
fish. The renowned curries of the island are black, using dry-
roasted spices; red, using fiery chilli; and white, which includes
usually fish or seafood with lemongrass. In this red chicken
curry you can use paprika instead of the chilli powder to
reduce the heat.

SERVES 4

8 chicken thighs
500ml water
Salt and freshly ground black pepper
2 onions, finely sliced
3 tablespoons sunflower or groundnut oil
5cm ginger, grated
6 cloves garlic, grated
2 red chillies, finely chopped (or 2 teaspoons chilli powder)
12 curry leaves, if available
1 teaspoon jaggery (palm sugar) or brown sugar, optional

Skin the chicken thighs but leave them on the bone. Cover with the
water, add a pinch of salt and a dozen turns of freshly ground
pepper. Bring to the boil, lower the heat and simmer for 45 minutes
until the chicken is tender.

Remove the chicken thighs and set aside, continuing to cook
the liquor until it is reduced to about 150ml.

Fry the sliced onion in the oil for about 10 minutes until brown,
and add the ginger, garlic, chilli and curry leaves, if using. Lower
the heat and cook for 1 minute before adding the chicken. Cook
for a further 5 minutes.

Add the cooking liquor and cook until it bubbles and
thickens, adding a little boiling water, if necessary. Simmer for
5 minutes longer.

Chef Silva sometimes adds a teaspoon of jaggery (palm sugar)
or brown sugar at the end; check for taste before adding. Also, add
more salt if necessary.

Serve with plain boiled rice.

spicy crab in filo pastry (INDIA)

This is an example of modern Indian cooking, influenced by the West, but retaining the savoury essence of piquant Indian spicing. It was conceived by Vivek Singh, a classically trained chef from New Delhi, now head chef at London's Cinnamon Club.

MAKES 24 PARCELS

2 tablespoons sunflower oil
Pinch each of turmeric powder, chilli powder and cumin seeds
1 clove garlic
1cm ginger, chopped
1 onion, finely chopped
½ teaspoon chopped green chilli
1½ tomatoes, chopped
400g crab meat
1 teaspoon chopped coriander leaves
Juice of 1 lemon
Salt
24 filo pastry sheets (approximately 20 x 30cm each)
25g butter, melted

Preheat the oven to 190°C/350°F/gas 5.

Heat the sunflower oil and add the turmeric, chilli powder and cumin seeds and fry for a minute or two until the cumin seeds start to pop. Add the garlic and ginger and cook for 1 minute, then add the onions and green chilli and cook for 2–3 minutes. Add the tomatoes and cook until soft.

Add the crab meat and stir through until well mixed. Stir in the coriander and lemon juice, season to taste with salt and set aside to cool.

Brush each filo sheet with melted butter, then fold each sheet in half lengthways. Place a ball of the crab mixture at one end and fold up each sheet to make a triangle. Arrange the triangles on a buttered baking tray and bake in the preheated oven for 10 minutes until golden and crisp.

Serve hot with chutney.

spiced fish kebab (INDIA)

Firm white fish, such as cod, haddock or monkfish, absorb spices well and taste wonderful in this Indian tikka-style dish.

SERVES 4

875g firm white fish, filleted and cut into 4cm cubes
Sunflower or groundnut oil, for brushing
2 lemons, cut into wedges

FOR THE MARINADE

1 teaspoon ground cumin
1 teaspoon chopped coriander leaves
1 teaspoon *garam masala* (see page 31)
2 tablespoons natural yoghurt
1 green chilli
3 cloves garlic, crushed
1 teaspoon chilli powder
1 teaspoon salt

Mix all the ingredients for the marinade in a bowl. Add the fish cubes and turn the fish carefully, coating each cube in the marinade. Set aside to marinate for at least 1 hour, preferably longer.

Lift out the fish cubes and thread them on to eight skewers, leaving space between each cube. Brush with the sunflower or groundnut oil and cook under a hot grill for about 5 minutes on each side until golden brown.

Serve hot with the lemon wedges to squeeze over.

crusted lamb biriani (INDIA)

In its authentic form, *biriani* is one of the world's finest rice dishes, resembling the Persian *polows*. It appears regularly on Anglo-Indian menus in a debased form, often like fried rice with chopped-up leftover meat. In this version, Vineet Bhatia, the first Indian restaurateur to win a Michelin star in the UK, uses the authentic technique, preparing spice-marinated cooked lamb with layers of part-boiled spiced basmati rice, placed in a casserole and baked in a hot oven. Vineet's sophisticated extra touch is to cover the dish with a spiced pastry crust, which seals in the aroma. Contrary to belief, there are Indian recipes without chilli and this is one of them. Marinate the lamb a day in advance.

SERVES 3–4

300g lean tender lamb (preferably from the upper leg)
3 tablespoons sunflower oil
350g basmati rice
½ teaspoon turmeric powder
½ teaspoon fennel seeds
3 star anise
6 cardamom pods
2 Litres water
1 blade of mace
½ onion, finely sliced
2 tablespoons chopped coriander leaves
2 tablespoons chopped mint leaves
A few drops of rose water, optional
375g ready-made puff pastry, rolled to overlap the top of a
    casserole dish (about 25–30cm in diameter and 5cm deep)
Pinch each of melon seeds, fennel seeds and
    ground cardamom
Melted *ghee*, for brushing

FOR THE MARINADE
1 teaspoon ground coriander
2 teaspoons ground roasted spices (including star anise,
    fennel seeds, green cardamom seeds and mace)
2 tablespoons chopped mint leaves
4 tablespoons chopped coriander leaves
1 tablespoon tomato purée
30g *ghee* (see page 14)
Pinch of salt

Mix together the ingredients for the marinade. Cut the lamb into thin, bite-sized pieces. Mix with the marinade and leave for 4–6 hours or overnight for the flavours to infuse.

To cook the lamb, pour 2 tablespoons of the sunflower oil into a pan and bring to a medium heat. Add the marinated lamb and cook for 5 minutes until it starts to brown. Add enough boiling water to cover the lamb and simmer for 1 hour, adding more water from time to time to keep it moist and prevent it from burning.

Preheat the oven to 200°C/400°F/gas 6.

To cook the rice, put the rice, turmeric powder, fennel seeds, star anise, cardamom pods and mace in a large pan with the water and bring to the boil. Cook for about 8 minutes until the rice is three-quarters done. Drain and cover to keep warm.

Pour the remaining sunflower oil into a pan and heat until sizzling. Add the onion and fry for about 5 minutes until crisp and brown. Mix the onion, coriander leaves, mint leaves and rose water, if using, into the rice.

Fill the casserole (or four smaller individual dishes) with alternating layers of rice and meat, starting and ending with the rice. Seal the casserole with the pastry. Stud the surface with a few melon and fennel seeds, and sprinkle with the ground cardamom. Brush with the melted *ghee* and bake for 20 minutes. Serve at the table, cutting the pastry top in a wide circle to release the aromas.

chicken tikka masala (INDIA)

This speciality of the Punjab in the north of India uses a mixture of spices to transform chicken into delicious tikka morsels. Marinate the chicken at least 4–6 hours in advance for the best flavour.

SERVES 4–6

1 chicken, cut into 8 pieces
Juice of ½ lemon
1 teaspoon salt
500ml natural yoghurt
½ onion, chopped
2 cloves garlic, chopped
2.5cm ginger, chopped
1 green chilli, chopped
2 teaspoons *garam masala* (see page 31)
2 teaspoons paprika
Sunflower oil, for brushing

Skin the chicken pieces and prick all over with a fork. Make a few slashes with a knife, cutting to the bone. Place in a bowl, sprinkle with the lemon juice and salt and leave for 30 minutes.

Meanwhile, place the yoghurt, onion, garlic, ginger, chilli and *garam masala* into a blender and whizz to a cream. Strain through a sieve.

Pat the chicken pieces dry with kitchen paper and rub each piece with the paprika. Place in a bowl, cover with the yoghurt marinade and leave for 4–6 hours.

Preheat the grill to very high or the oven to 230°C/450°F/gas 8.

Transfer the chicken pieces to a baking sheet, shaking off the excess marinade. Brush the chicken with sunflower oil. Grill for 20 minutes on one side, then turn the chicken and grill for a further 10 minutes. Alternatively, roast in the oven for 25–30 minutes. To test that the chicken is cooked, insert a skewer into the largest piece to see if the juices run clear.

Serve with rice, salad and wedges of lemon to squeeze over.

lamb in a creamy yoghurt sauce (INDIA)

While India is renowned for the variety of its vegetarian dishes, there is a long tradition of luxurious meat-eating in the northwest, the legacy of the Moghuls, who invaded in the eighth century. The Hindu population found the eating of beef offensive and, as Muslims, the Moghuls could not eat pork. So the lavish court cooking of the Moghuls revolved around chicken and lamb, enriched by creamy sauces and the more expensive spices, such as saffron and cardamom.

This dish, known as *badam gosht*, is one you'd expect to find at a wedding feast or an elaborate family party.

SERVES 6

1kg boned lamb shoulder or leg, with surplus fat removed
1 tablespoon *garam masala* (see page 31)
500ml natural yoghurt
2 tablespoons *ghee* (see page 14) or sunflower oil
2 onions, finely chopped
4 cloves garlic, chopped
5cm stick of cinnamon or piece of cassia bark
2 cloves
1 teaspoon chilli powder
6 cardamom pods
100g almonds, ground and mixed to a paste with
**   2 tablespoons water**
400ml coconut milk
Salt

Cut the lamb into 2–3cm cubes, toss in a bowl with the *garam masala* and yoghurt and leave in the fridge for 1 hour to marinate.

Heat a pan and add the *ghee* or sunflower oil. Fry the onions for about 10 minutes until soft and yellowing. Add the garlic and cook for 30 seconds more. Stir in the cinnamon or cassia bark, cloves, chilli powder and cardamom pods, and heat through.

Remove the lamb from the marinade using a slotted spoon, and add the lamb to the onion mixture. Turn up the heat and stir-fry for about 5 minutes until the meat begins to change colour.

Add the yoghurt marinade and almond paste, and simmer for 10 minutes, stirring well. Pour in the coconut milk and simmer for a further 45 minutes or until the lamb is tender. Do not let it dry out completely. Taste for seasoning, adding salt if necessary.

Serve with plain boiled rice and chutneys.

special coconut raita (INDIA)

SERVES 4 AS AN ACCOMPANIMENT

1 tablespoon coriander seeds
1 tablespoon cumin seeds
500ml natural yoghurt
4 tablespoons grated fresh coconut (or desiccated coconut)
Juice of ½ lime
Large pinch of salt

In a dry pan, heat the coriander and cumin seeds for about 3 minutes until they start to release an appetising aroma. Grind them in a spice or coffee grinder or with a pestle and mortar.

Place the yoghurt in a bowl and stir in the coconut, lime juice and salt. Sprinkle the coriander and cumin mix over to serve.

spicy gram cake (INDIA)

Eat this hot spicy cake, made from chickpea flour, with morning coffee or afternoon tea. You need to prepare the batter a day in advance. Eno's health salts are available in chemists and large supermarkets.

SERVES 8–10

125g gram (chickpea) flour
250g natural yoghurt
2.5cm ginger, grated
1 green chilli, deseeded and finely chopped
50g sugar
Sunflower or groundnut oil, for brushing
1 teaspoon Eno's health salts or bicarbonate of soda
1 tablespoon desiccated coconut
1 teaspoon mustard seeds or sesame seeds
1 teaspoon chopped coriander leaves

Mix the gram flour with the yoghurt, cover with a cloth and leave overnight to develop and fluff up. When ready to use, stir in the ginger, chilli and sugar.

Stand a small saucepan inside a larger pan, half-filled with water, and heat over a low flame until simmering. Brush the inside of the smaller pan with oil and the Eno's health salts or bicarbonate of soda.

Spoon 2 tablespoons of the batter into the small saucepan, cover and leave to cook for 10–15 minutes, until the batter rises.

Spoon the risen batter into an oiled mould, 2.5–5cm deep, and set aside to cool. Repeat this process until the batter is used up. When cooled, brush each cake with a little oil and sprinkle with the coconut, mustard seeds or sesame seeds and chopped coriander. Cut into 2.5cm squares to serve.

cardamom dessert (INDIA)

Sweets are very important in India. They are served as an offering to the Gods and offered to friends and family at religious and other festivals. Most sweets are based on a full-milk preparation. Cardamom adds a distinctive flavour to this syrupy dessert, known as *gulab jamun*. It can be served hot or cold.

MAKES ABOUT 20 SWEETS

300ml full-cream powdered milk
150g plain flour, sifted
½ teaspoon baking powder
75g *ghee* (see page 14) or sunflower or groundnut oil
3 tablespoons cold milk
Cardamom seeds, scraped from 4 pods
1 litre sunflower or groundnut oil, for deep-frying
225g sugar
600ml water

In a large bowl, mix together the powdered milk, flour, baking powder and ghee, sunflower or groundnut oil. Using your fingertips, rub the mixture until it resembles fine breadcrumbs. Add 2 tablespoons of the milk, a little at a time, to make a soft dough. Leave to rest for about 15 minutes.

Break off small pieces of the dough and roll into smooth balls. Press down in the centre of each and place one cardamom seed in the indentation. Smooth into a ball again until the cardamom pod is hidden.

Heat the litre of sunflower or groundnut oil to 180°C/350°F – check with a thermometer. Add the balls and fry for 5 minutes or until golden brown. Drain on kitchen paper.

In a separate pan, bring the sugar and water to the boil and add the remaining cold milk. Strain off the froth as it rises to the surface. Boil the syrup for about 15 minutes, then lower the heat and leave to simmer.

Add the *gulab jamuns* and cook for 45 minutes, pressing them down into the syrup with a spoon from time to time.

aachar pickle (INDIA)

A well-flavoured pickle from north India, using the country's characteristic deep yellow, spicy mustard oil which you can find in Indian stores.

MAKES 4 JARS

1kg carrots, cut into 5mm rounds
1kg cauliflower, cut into florets
2kg turnips, cut into 5mm rounds
600ml mustard oil
250g onions, minced or grated
2 cloves garlic, minced or grated
125g ginger, minced or grated
2 tablespoons chilli powder
1 tablespoon ground mustard seeds
1 tablespoon *garam masala* (see page 31)
1 teaspoon turmeric powder
1 teaspoon salt
400ml malt vinegar
1kg dark brown sugar

Cook the carrots, cauliflower and turnips in boiling water for about five minutes. Drain, and pat dry using kitchen paper.

Heat about 150ml of the mustard oil in a saucepan until it is almost smoking, then add the onions, garlic and ginger and fry until golden, stirring to prevent sticking. Add the chilli powder, mustard seeds, *garam masala*, turmeric and salt, and fry for a few minutes, stirring continuously. Add the vegetables, take off the heat and mix well.

In a separate pan, heat the remaining mustard oil until it is almost smoking and pour this over the vegetables, shaking the saucepan to mix well. Spoon the vegetable mixture into large, sterilised glass jars with tight-fitting lids. Place in the sunshine or in a warm, dry place for about 3 days, shaking the jars each day.

On the third day, heat the vinegar in a saucepan with the sugar until it dissolves and boil rapidly for a few minutes. Set aside to cool completely, then add this to the vegetables. Continue to keep the vegetables in the sun or a warm, dry place until the mixture matures, which will take about 2 weeks.

fresh mango chutney (INDIA)

SERVES 4 AS AN ACCOMPANIMENT

1 unripe mango
Juice of ½ lime
2.5cm ginger, grated
1 tablespoon grated fresh coconut (or desiccated coconut)
1 fresh red chilli, deseeded and finely chopped
Pinch of salt
1 teaspoon brown sugar
Pinch of *garam masala* (see page 31)
Coriander leaves, to garnish

Peel the mango with a sharp knife and ease the flesh from the stone. Chop into small dice. Place in a bowl with any juice that runs off. Add the lime juice, ginger, coconut, chilli, salt, sugar and *garam masala*. Mix together thoroughly and leave to rest in the fridge for 30 minutes.

Garnish with coriander leaves to serve.

tamarind and date chutney (INDIA)

SERVES 4 AS AN ACCOMPANIMENT

50g dried tamarind
200g dates, stoned and finely chopped
1 tablespoon jaggery (palm sugar) or brown sugar
1 teaspoon *garam masala* (see page 31)
½ teaspoon chilli powder
Large pinch of salt

Tear the tamarind into lumps and pour over enough boiling water to cover. When cooled, push the tamarind through a coarse sieve, to remove stones and coarse fibres.

Add the dates, jaggery or brown sugar, *garam masala*, chilli powder and salt, and whizz together using a hand blender. The mixture should be runny. Chill in the fridge for 1 hour before serving.

coconut sambal (SRI LANKA)

Coconut features in much of Sri Lanka's cooking – coconut milk is mixed with rice flour to make the characteristic pancakes (*appam*), which are served with hot *sambal* sauces and curried vegetables. Grated coconut is the basis of this regular table condiment, a more or less instant chutney.

SERVES 4 AS AN ACCOMPANIMENT

100g fresh coconut, grated (or desiccated coconut)
½ red onion, chopped
4 cloves garlic, chopped
Juice of 2 limes
½ teaspoon chilli powder
1 teaspoon jaggery (palm sugar) or brown sugar
6 black peppercorns, ground (or a dozen turns of the pepper grinder)
1 teaspoon salt
Mint, parsley or coriander leaves, chopped, or 1 spring onion, chopped, to garnish
1 teaspoon paprika, to garnish

Place all of the ingredients (apart from the garnish) in a food mixer and whizz until well mixed.

Garnish with the mint, parsley or coriander leaves or spring onion and sprinkle with the paprika to serve.

curry powder (INDIA)

In India most families make their own curry powder, although commercial mixes can be bought. A homemade mix may contain up to 20 spices, with some piquant and some mild. This curry powder contains several key savoury spices. You can add others to taste, such as ground asafoetida and 'warm' spices like cinnamon, nutmeg, cloves and allspice. As a counsel of perfection, not only should whole spices be lightly roasted or heated in a non-stick pan until they begin to give off their aromas, but each should be done separately as the burning point of each is different. For example, if fenugreek burns, it has such a bitter taste that you will want to throw it away.

MAKES 1 SMALL JAR

25g coriander seeds
1 teaspoon cumin seeds
½ teaspoon mustard seeds
½ teaspoon fenugreek seeds
½ teaspoon black peppercorns
4 small dried red chillies
½ teaspoon turmeric powder
½ teaspoon ground ginger

In a dry pan, gently heat all the seeds, the peppercorns and chillies separately for a few seconds until they start to release an appetising aroma. Remove from the heat and leave to cool.

When cool, grind in a spice or coffee grinder or use a pestle and mortar. Store in a sealed jar in a cool, dark place.

garam masala (INDIA)

Every Indian home has a preparation of this mild spice mix, which is usually added at the end of cooking.

MAKES 1 SMALL JAR

2 teaspoons cumin seeds
4 teaspoons coriander seeds
Cardamom seeds, scraped from 2 pods
½ teaspoon ground black peppercorns
1 teaspoon cinnamon
½ teaspoon ground cloves

In a dry pan, heat the cumin, coriander and cardamom seeds for about 3 minutes until they start to release an appetising aroma. Grind them in a spice or coffee grinder or use a pestle and mortar. Add the remaining ingredients, then transfer to a sterilised jar.

ical Indian
cart offering
eric powder
lyes.

Much of the food of the Far East remains an enigma to the Western cook. The cooking of Japan, China, Korea and Vietnam is among the most sophisticated and exotic on the planet, but the West has made some huge strides towards understanding it. The popularity of Chinese takeaways is a case in point, as is the enthusiasm with which the wok has been adopted as a vital cooking utensil in most kitchens. Japanese sushi has passed into our collective gastronomic consciousness, and in the large cities we are familiar with Korean and Vietnamese restaurants.

China, with its population of more than a billion, its vast landmass and as many provinces and languages as Europe, is awesome. It is also a country with the oldest records of sophisticated cooking – noodles were invented there thousands of years ago. Chinese cooks have been first to master all the world's known cooking techniques, often combining several of them to make a single dish. They use steaming, roasting, deep-frying, baking, grilling, poaching, stewing and braising – everything except microwaving. And, of course, stir-frying in a wok; cooking morsels of food cut into small pieces, that provides the most economic use of fuel ever conceived. It also provides the freshest, tastiest and healthiest results.

Lavish banquets in China

At the opposite extreme to economy, Chinese eating is also associated with lavish banquets, originally prepared for the emperors of historic dynasties. They represented the ultimate in conspicuous consumption. It has been the custom in China, as in Roman feasts, to serve the rarest and costliest delicacies. These will include shark's fin soup (made from the connective muscle under a

shark's fin) and bird's nest soup, made from the gelatinous substance (semi-digested seaweed) that sea swallows spit out to coat their nests, high on dangerous cliffs. The Chinese have a recipe for almost every living thing, be it the reproductive organs of the virgin sturgeon or barely chewable lumps of sea slug.

There is no single Chinese style of cooking but many, although the aromatic use of ginger, garlic and spring onions is a feature common to all of its cuisines. They are also marked by the use of soy sauce and fermented soya beans. In the north, where the capital Beijing sits, the Chinese grow wheat, most of which is made into noodles. In the centre and west, which includes the province of Sichuan, the food is hot, spicy and aromatic. To the east, radiating from Shanghai, rice is the predominant base, and the cooking has an emphasis on sweet-and-sour flavours (using *shaoxing* wine and ginger). To the south, Canton is famous for its seafood and the skill of its cooks in preparing market-fresh goods, especially steamed delicacies.

The range of spices used in China is not great, but it is significant. Chinese five-spice powder sums it up: a potent and fragrant combination including star anise, Sichuan peppercorns, fennel, cloves and cinnamon or cassia bark.

Chillies, dried citrus peel (from tangerines and oranges) and dried mushrooms add extra flavour dimensions; sesame oil is used as an aromatic to finish off a dish; and rice wine, aged vinegars, oyster sauce, sweet and savoury *hoisin* sauce (made from soya beans, vinegar, sugar and spices) and yellow bean sauce are among other flavour enhancers used in cooking or at the table. And so is MSG (monosodium glutamate), the white powder used as freely as salt by many cooks, heightening the flavour of vegetables (although now frowned upon by health authorities – it can cause sweating, fever and headaches if eaten in excess).

If China's contribution to the world's gastronomic repertoire is overwhelming, Japan's food is largely mystifying to the West. While schoolchildren in the southeast of England now pack sushi in their lunch-boxes (sold in supermarkets), Japanese cooking remains a closed book to many, although now some ingredients can be found in healthfood stores and large supermarkets.

For example, the numerous kinds of seaweed, which the Japanese refer to as sea vegetables: kelp, *kombu*, *dulse*, *wakami* and delicious *nori* (the lacy brown seaweed the Welsh know as *laver*) which is cooked, dried and flattened into paper-thin sheets and used for wrapping sushi, or crumbled over food or incorporated into savoury, crunchy rice snacks. Other ingredients are equally unfamiliar, such as *dashi*, a stock made with seaweed, and *katsuobushi*, a block of dried tuna, which is grated into stock to make a savoury fish soup.

A little girl enjoys the street food in Beijing, China.

The soya bean is an essential foodstuff in Japan. Eaten as tofu, a white, cake-like, moist, young cheese, it is important to the vegetarian Buddhist community. So are other soya bean products, not only the famous Kikkoman soy sauce, but savoury, salty *miso*, made from fermented soya beans, sometimes with added wheat or rice. Soy milk is yet another by-product of this adaptable bean.

Japanese vegetables can be unfamiliar, too, such as *daikon*, a giant white radish, which is as hot as a raw turnip. It can be up to a metre long and is usually peeled and shredded into a fine string and dipped into soy sauce as a garnish for most dishes. It is often accompanied by tear-inducing blobs of green *wasabi*, Japan's native horseradish.

In Japanese cooking you may also encounter burdock, bamboo shoots, chrysanthemum leaves, gingko nuts, lotus root (showing a decorative pattern when sliced across) and many kinds of mushroom besides shiitake, as well as gourds and yams.

Japanese spices, herbs and other flavourings can be unusual to Westerners, such as *perilla* (*shiso*), an aromatic member of the mint family used like a decorative parsley leaf; and pickled plum (*umeboshi*), which is not a plum but a sour apricot pickled in salt. Other important flavourings include rice vinegars and wines, and sesame oil with its nutty perfume. The most common spice mixture is *gomasio* (salt and sesame seed mixture, to sprinkle on rice). But *shichimi-togarashi*, Japanese seven-spice powder, is the most complex; it usually includes chilli, *sansho* (see page 41), poppy seeds, mustard seeds, rape seeds and *yuzu* (dried citrus peel). It's often sprinkled over bowls of noodles to spice them up.

Japanese restaurants

Japanese restaurants in Western capitals give some sense of the rituals of this country's eating customs, but you need to travel to Tokyo to feel the full cultural impact. Japanese restaurant cooking is divided into some 30 categories; many of them are soup and noodle bars (choose between *udon*, the fat white noodles, or *soba*, delicious buckwheat noodles).

There are numerous sushi bars and teppanyaki restaurants, where the chef shows off at a stainless steel top in front of diners. In tempura bars they deep-fry morsels of food dipped in batter and serve them straight from the pan. Then there are grilled eel bars, sashimi bars (selling sliced raw fish), hot-pot bars such as *sukiyaki* and *shabu-shabu* where you dip razor-thin slices of meat into the hot-pot, and *oden* bars with vegetarian tofu, and even seaweed hot-pot bars.

This is the people's food but, little known to the West, Japan has its own *haute cuisine*: *kaiseki*. Ostensibly the menu offers 13 courses, but each one includes up to five miniature items, so a

A Vietnamese spice seller, Saigon.

meal may run to over 50 little dishes. Emphasis is placed on contrast in colour, flavour and texture. The aesthetics of presentation are given the highest priority; every dish served on a different plate, each saucer and bowl contrasting in design, shape, colour and texture and using various types of ceramic, glass and wood, including lacquered pine. A top restaurant changes every item of crockery four times a year to accommodate seasonal designs including spring cherry blossom or autumnal leaves.

Korea produces food which the Japanese admire. They go to Korean restaurants much as the West love Chinese and Indian food. The cooking is less formal than Japanese, and the tastes strong and assertive: hot with chilli and spring onion, salty with soy and salted dried fish (dried cuttlefish is chewed as a snack), and nutty with sesame seeds and sesame oil.

Rice and noodles are the staples along with barley and beans. The Koreans adore chargrilled meats (*bulgogi*), lightly cooked or steamed vegetables, crunchy salads and roots and leaves from the wild, from bamboo shoots to ginseng rootlets, which are cooked as a restorative.

Chilli paste is always to hand (*kochujang* – a mixture of soya bean paste and chilli powder), either bottled or homemade, ready to apply to the cooking pot or on the table as a dipping sauce.

The most famous Korean preparation, eaten at most meals, is their powerful *kim chee*, pickled Chinese cabbage. It is salted, then layered with chilli and ginger, and left to mature in Ali Baba ceramic pots, ready to be used throughout the year.

Vietnamese food is based on noodles and rice, like that of its neighbours, China and Thailand, but the flavours are loud and clear. The Vietnamese love crunchy spicy salads, sometimes with nuts, and near-raw vegetables. A rich, savoury soup (called *pho*) is eaten at any time of the day, sold on the streets by hawkers, and it is sure to be dosed with *nuoc mam* (the fermented fish sauce that verges on being an addiction in Vietnam). It will also be charged with heavy helpings of chopped garlic, spring onion and fresh ginger and, above all, chilli, freshly chopped, dried, or in the form of a dense sauce at the table.

Like the Thais, the Vietnamese love the perfume of fresh herbs, lemongrass, mints and basil. It is enchanting cooking and Westerners encountering Vietnamese restaurants never cease to be thrilled at the skill of the cooks, the magnificent presentations and the passion for perfection.

noodles with togarashi (JAPAN)

A poached egg floats like the moon in this popular noodle soup dish, which is known literally as 'looking-like-the-moon noodle' and is flavoured with the traditional Japanese seven-spice powder *shichimi-togarashi*. Bonito is dried tuna, available at Japanese and specialist shops. Kelp and *nori* are Japanese seaweeds that are sold dried, and are available in large supermarkets.

SERVES 4

1 litre water
Piece of kelp, about 10cm square, wiped and cut into a fringe
15g dried bonito shavings
125ml light soy sauce
2 tablespoons sweet rice wine (or sweet sherry)
150g spinach, washed
Salt
275g thick wheat-flour noodles (or other noodles)
4 eggs
1 sheet *nori*, about 10cm square
Seven-spice powder (see page 44), to garnish

Place the water and kelp in a large saucepan and bring to the boil. Just before it boils, remove the kelp and discard.

Add the bonito shavings and simmer for about 3 minutes. Add the soy sauce and rice wine or sweet sherry, bring to the boil again, then remove from the heat. Strain through a fine sieve (preferably lined with muslin) and keep the liquor warm in a saucepan over a low heat.

Cook the spinach in a large saucepan of boiling salted water for about 3 minutes. Drain, and rinse several times in cold water, then drain again. Squeeze gently to remove as much moisture as possible, and form into a roll. Cut into 4 slices (they will form nests for the eggs) and set aside.

Bring more water to the boil in a large saucepan and cook the noodles for about 5 minutes, until tender. Drain, then spoon the noodles into four large bowls with lids. Bring the soup to the boil again and pour it over the noodles. Place a spinach slice in each bowl. Break an egg carefully into each bowl, cover with the lids and leave the eggs to poach lightly in the soup.

Cut the sheet of *nori* into four strips and heat in a dry frying pan until crisp.

Sprinkle each bowl of soup with seven-spice powder, garnish with the *nori* strips and serve while still very hot.

hot-and-sour soup (CHINA)

This is quick to make and full of flavour and nutritional value. To make it hotter, as they do in the Sichuan province, heat and grind 1 teaspoon of Sichuan pepper, and stir it into the cornflour paste before adding to the soup.

SERVES 4

25g Chinese dried mushrooms, such as wood ear
50g lean pork (or beef), shredded
900ml beef or other stock
1 tablespoon dark soy sauce
1 teaspoon chilli oil (or Tabasco sauce)
3 tablespoons Chinese vinegar (or cider vinegar)
2 teaspoons sugar
Freshly ground white pepper
1 tablespoon cornflour, dissolved in 2 tablespoons cold water
50g prawns, cooked and peeled
1 egg, beaten
2 teaspoons sesame oil
2 spring onions, finely chopped, to garnish

Soak the dried mushrooms in just enough hot water to cover for 30 minutes. Drain, discarding any loose stems but reserving the liquid. Chop the mushrooms finely.

Bring a saucepan of water to the boil and add the pork or beef. Cook for a minute until a scum forms. Pour the water and pork or beef into a sieve and rinse with cold water.

Heat the beef or other stock and add the mushrooms, soy sauce, chilli oil (or Tabasco sauce), vinegar and sugar. Season with freshly ground white pepper and simmer for a few minutes. Stir in the cornflour paste, which adds texture to the soup. Add the pork or beef and prawns, and then pour in the beaten egg slowly, stirring steadily. As the egg sets, add the sesame oil.

Sprinkle with the spring onions and serve at once.

sesame spinach (JAPAN)

Sesame seeds are often used to season Japanese food. They are usually toasted and crushed. Sometimes they are mixed with salt to make the seasoning *gomasio*.

SERVES 4

450g spinach, washed
2 tablespoons sesame seeds
2 tablespoons soy sauce

Cut the spinach leaves crossways into 2.5cm strips. Place in a saucepan with a little boiling unsalted water. Cook for about 3 minutes and drain well.

Dry-roast the sesame seeds in a frying pan over a high heat, tossing them to prevent burning. Pound in a mortar, add a little of the soy sauce and pound once more.

Pour the dressing over the spinach with the rest of the soy sauce. Mix well and serve cold in small bowls.

cold noodles with sauces
(TAIWAN)

This spicy combination of tastes is typical street food in Taiwan. The noodles are served with the sauces poured around, and each person mixes the noodles and dressings together on their plate before eating.

SERVES 4

450g Chinese noodles
1 teaspoon Sichuan peppercorns
8cm ginger, finely chopped
12 cloves garlic, coarsely chopped
1 teaspoons salt
5 tablespoons water
4 teaspoons hot pepper flakes in oil (see page 45)
4 tablespoons finely chopped spring onions
4 tablespoons sesame paste (*tahina*)
8 tablespoons light soy sauce
2 teaspoons sugar

Put the noodles in a saucepan, cover with boiling water and boil rapidly for about 5 minutes, until tender but not soft. Drain, and rinse under cold water.

Heat a small frying pan, add the Sichuan peppercorns and dry-roast over a low heat for 2–3 minutes, shaking the pan to prevent burning. Leave to cool, then grind to a powder in a spice or coffee grinder or use a pestle and mortar.

In a mortar, pound the ginger, garlic and salt together to make a paste. Add the water and mix again.

Divide the noodles between four plates. On each, place a spoonful of the hot pepper flakes, ground roast peppercorns, ginger and garlic mixture, spring onions and sesame paste. Top each serving with 2 tablespoons soy sauce and sprinkle with ½ teaspoon sugar.

crispy duck (CHINA)

This is one of the classics of Chinese cooking and is less labour-intensive than the famous roasted Peking duck. The bird is seasoned with fragrant spices, such as star anise, steamed to tenderness, and finally deep-fried in a wok to crisp it up. It isn't complicated if you do it in stages.

SERVES 4–6 AS AN APPETISER

1 duck, about 2kg
1 teaspoon salt
2 teaspoons five-spice powder (see page 44)
5cm ginger, finely grated
3 cloves garlic, grated
5 spring onions, white parts only, finely chopped
1 tablespoon dark soy sauce
1 tablespoon Chinese wine (or medium-dry sherry)
1 tablespoon liquid malt (or honey)
1 litre corn, sunflower or groundnut oil, for deep-frying

Wash the duck, inside and out, and pat dry using kitchen paper. Rub with the salt and the five-spice powder, inside and out. Put the ginger, garlic and spring onions inside the bird. Cover with clingfilm or foil and leave to absorb the flavours for at least a couple of hours.

Mix the soy sauce, Chinese wine (or medium-dry sherry) and liquid malt (or honey). Rub into the duck, cover the bird again and put in the fridge to absorb the flavours overnight.

Using a steamer or a covered wok with a grid on the base, cook the duck for 1 hour until tender. Leave it to cool (you can keep it in the fridge until you are ready to complete the last stage).

In a deep-fryer or large pan, heat the corn, sunflower or groundnut oil to 180°C/356°F – check with a thermometer. When it starts to give off faint blue smoke, immerse the duck and fry for 15 minutes (the temperature of the oil drops quickly, but this doesn't matter). Turn it carefully in the oil to cook both sides. Remove, place on kitchen paper, and reheat the oil to 180°C/356°F. Immerse the duck again for a minute or two, turning once, to get crispy, golden skin.

Remove and drain on kitchen paper, and set aside for 5 minutes.

Serve cut into slices, or shred the meat, removing it from the bones with two forks. Serve with steamed Chinese pancakes (see below), rolled around strips of spring onion, cucumber matchsticks and plum sauce.

chinese pancakes

MAKES ABOUT 24

450g plain flour, plus extra for dusting
1 teaspoon sugar
350ml boiling water
Sesame oil, for brushing

Sift the flour into a mixing bowl and stir in the sugar. Pour in the boiling water, little by little, stirring with a wooden spoon to make a stiff dough. Knead on a floured board until smooth and elastic. Cover with a cloth and leave to rest for 30 minutes.

Divide the dough into two pieces, knead until smooth and roll into long cylinders. Cut across the cylinders to make 12 discs from each. Roll each into a small ball and then flatten into circles with a rolling pin.

Brush each circle with sesame oil, press them together in pairs, and roll out on a floured board to 15cm across.

Heat a non-stick pan to medium and cook each pancake for about 2 minutes on each side, until they start to puff up slightly. They are cooked when little brown spots start to appear on the surface.

Remove and peel the two pancakes apart. Brush with more sesame oil and, if not using immediately, fold in half and pile in a stack, covered in clingfilm, to store in the fridge.

To reheat, place in batches in a steamer for 3 or 4 minutes and serve hot.

chicken noodle soup (VIETNAM)

This popular dish is a meal in itself. It includes the essential *nuoc mam* – a brown savoury sauce made with fermented, salted anchovies and used to season many Vietnamese dishes.

SERVES 4

1.5 litres chicken stock
4 star anise
5cm stick of cinnamon or piece of cassia bark
20 coriander seeds
5cm ginger, grated
2 tablespoons *nuoc mam* or 3 tablespoons *nam pla*
  (fish sauces)
1 teaspoon brown sugar
½ teaspoon salt
Freshly ground black pepper
Sunflower or groundnut oil, for frying
4 large shallots, thinly sliced
450g rice noodles
125g chicken breast, lightly poached and finely sliced
6–8 spring onions, white parts only, finely sliced
1 small onion, sliced into thin rings
Handful of bean sprouts, plunged into boiling water,
  then drained
1 fresh red chilli, chopped very finely
Juice of 1 lime
4 stems of fresh coriander, chopped
***Hoisin* sauce and chilli sauce, to serve**

Heat the stock together with the star anise, cinnamon or cassia bark, coriander seeds and ginger. Cook gently for about 20 minutes, then add the *nuoc mam* or *nam pla* sauce, sugar, salt and some pepper. Strain the stock to remove the spices and keep hot.

Put some sunflower or groundnut oil in a frying pan, heat through and add the shallots. Gently fry for about 10 minutes until they are beginning to brown. Remove and set aside.

Cook the noodles in boiling water for a minute or two until just done. Drain and place in four warmed large soup bowls with the shallots, chicken, spring onions, onion rings, bean sprouts and chilli on top. Divide the hot broth between the four bowls. Splash with lime juice and sprinkle with coriander leaves.

Serve with *hoisin* sauce and chilli sauce in their bottles or in little dishes for people to help themselves.

squid with chilli and black beans (CHINA)

Records of Chinese cuisine reach back some 7000 years, embracing famous imperial dynasties. At the highest level, it is complex, extravagant and labour-intensive, but even everyday food is remarkable for its freshness and balance of flavours, colours and textures. This colourful, zingy stir-fry recipe is simple and quick, combining barely cooked squares of white squid with crunchy green peppers, the salty seasoning of black (soy) beans and the kick of hot, scarlet chillies.

SERVES 4

750g prepared squid, including tentacles (ask your
  fishmonger to prepare)
Sunflower or groundnut oil, for frying
2–3 spring onions, white parts only, chopped
2 cloves garlic, finely chopped
5cm ginger, finely shredded
2–4 fresh red and green chillies (to taste, with seeds and
  membranes removed, if required), finely chopped
1 onion, sliced
1 green pepper, deseeded and cut into 2.5cm pieces
1 tablespoon dry salted black (soy) beans, rinsed and chopped
½ teaspoon five-spice powder (see page 44)
1 level tablespoon cornflour
100ml vegetable or other stock
Freshly ground black pepper
1 teaspoon sesame oil (optional)

Cut the squid into 4cm pieces and lightly score the flesh. Throw into boiling water to blanch and remove as soon as the water boils up again. Plunge into cold water, then drain and set aside.

In a wok or large pan heat a tablespoon of the sunflower or groundnut oil on a high heat and, when hot, throw in the spring onions and cook for about 30 seconds until they sizzle. Add the garlic, ginger and chillies, and cook for about 15 seconds until they sizzle too. Don't let them burn.

Next add the onion and green pepper and cook for 1 minute, stirring all the time. Toss in the black beans, stir around, and add the prepared squid, cooking until it's heated through, no more. Season to taste with the five-spice powder.

Sprinkle with the cornflour, stir in well, and add the stock. As soon as the sauce thickens, within a minute, the dish is ready to serve. Season with a few turns of freshly ground black pepper and the sesame oil, if using.

Serve with noodles or plain boiled rice.

spicy soy-baked mackerel (CHINA)

The spices counteract the oiliness of the fish in this delicious recipe.

SERVES 4

4 mackerel, gutted
Juice of 10cm ginger (grated and squeezed)
1 teaspoon five-spice powder (see page 44)
Juice of ½ lemon
1 teaspoon salt
Bunch of spring onions, trimmed

FOR THE SAUCE
4 cloves garlic, chopped
2 tablespoons sunflower or groundnut oil
3 fresh red chillies, finely chopped
1 tablespoon Chinese black (soy) beans, rinsed and chopped
   (or 2 tablespoons dark soy sauce)
2 tablespoons Chinese dry white wine (or medium-dry sherry)
300ml fish or vegetable stock
1 tablespoon *hoisin* sauce

With a sharp knife, make three deep cuts at an angle on both sides of the fish. Rub ginger juice and five-spice powder into the slits. Rub the insides of the fish with the lemon juice and salt. Leave to marinate for 1 hour.

Preheat the oven to 190°C/375°F/gas 5.

Meanwhile, make the sauce. In a wok or large pan and over a high heat, fry the garlic for 30 seconds in the sunflower or groundnut oil until it starts to brown. Toss in the chillies and cook for about 15 seconds before adding the black beans, if using. Stir and cook for a further 15 seconds.

Add the Chinese wine or sherry and cook for two or three minutes until it sizzles and starts to evaporate. Add the stock, and if not using soy beans, the dark soy sauce. Turn down the heat to low and simmer gently for about 10 minutes, stirring in the *hoisin* sauce at the end.

Scatter the spring onions in a shallow oven dish, place the mackerel on top and then dribble the hot sauce over. Bake for 15 minutes on one side, then turn over the fish, making sure it is well basted. Serve in the sauce with plain boiled rice.

soy-braised duck (CHINA)

This sweet-and-sour marinade permeates the duck with its fragrant flavourings. The marinade can be frozen and reused to braise either duck or chicken. Star anise is frequently used in Chinese braised pork and duck dishes.

SERVES 4

1 duck, about 1.5kg, quartered
300ml groundnut or sunflower oil
1 litre chicken stock or water
1 litre dark soy sauce
275ml light soy sauce
400ml rice wine (or 200ml dry sherry mixed with 200ml
   chicken stock)
100g sugar
3 star anise
3 sticks of cinnamon
Coriander leaves, to garnish

Pat the duck quarters dry with kitchen paper.

Heat the groundnut or sunflower oil in a wok until just smoking, then add two pieces of the duck, skin-side down. Reduce the heat and fry over a low heat for about 15–20 minutes, until the skin is brown. Baste the duck in the oil but do not turn the pieces over. Remove and drain on kitchen paper. Repeat with the rest of the duck.

Place the chicken stock or water, dark and light soy sauces, rice wine or sherry mixed with chicken stock, sugar, star anise and cinnamon in a saucepan and bring to the boil. Add the duck, cover, reduce the heat and simmer for about 1 hour until the duck is tender.

Remove the surface fat from the top of the pan to prevent fat adhering to the duck. Then, using a slotted spoon, remove the duck pieces. Leave to cool, then chop into smaller pieces. Arrange on a dish, sprinkle with the coriander and serve with noodles or rice.

sushi (JAPAN)

Wasabi is the Japanese equivalent of horseradish, hot, brown and slightly bitter. It is a counterpoint to the sweet and salty soy dips served with *sashimi* (sliced raw fresh fish) and sushi rice rolls. Wasabi can be bought in a powder in a tin to be mixed with water to make a mustard-like paste. It can also be bought ready-made in tubes. While sushi is often rolled using a bamboo mat, it can also be made by putting a small ball of cooked rice in the palm of the hand and, making an indentation with the thumb, pressing in the filling, then sealing the rice around it. It's essential that the fish is fresh, so explain to the fishmonger that you are eating it raw.

MAKES 24 ROLLS

125g each of salmon, turbot, scallops, squid and langoustine
250g Japanese short-grain rice
250ml water
4 tablespoons rice vinegar
1 tablespoon sugar
1 teaspoon salt
1 teaspoon wasabi powder, made into a paste with water,
    plus extra to serve
A few Japanese radishes (*daikon*), finely sliced
Packet of pickled Japanese ginger slices
25g sesame seeds, toasted (optional)
Soy sauce, for dipping

Soak the fish in iced water for 2 hours to produce a silky texture. Meanwhile, wash the rice in several changes of water until it runs clear. Leave in a sieve to drain for an hour. Put the rice and measured water in a pan with a close-fitting lid. Bring to the boil, lower the heat and cook for 15 minutes, until the water is absorbed, but do not lift the lid to check. Turn the heat up for 10 seconds, then remove the rice from the heat and leave to stand, still covered, for 15 minutes.

Meanwhile, heat the vinegar, sugar and salt together in a pan until the sugar has melted.

Turn the rice into a shallow bowl and, using a wooden spatula, stir in the vinegar mixture, fanning to cool it as you go. You can make the sushi as soon as the rice is cool or you can keep the mixture for several hours, if you cover it with a cloth. The rice will be sticky, so it's useful to have a bowl of vinegary water beside you to rinse your hands as you work.

Spread a 0.5cm layer of rice on to a 20cm square bamboo mat. Carefully arrange a selection of the fish and other ingredients in a line across the middle. Roll the mat away from you, making one or two turns to produce a cylinder shape. Squeeze gently to firm it up. Set aside for 5 minutes, and then unroll the mat. If you like, roll the sushi roll in sesame seeds to coat. Cut the rice roll across into six, revealing the colourful ingredients inside. Repeat three more times until all the ingredients are used.

Serve with more wasabi paste on top, and soy sauce for dipping.

sansho (JAPAN)

Japan has very few spices and *sansho*, the Japanese equivalent of pepper, is one of them. They are possibly the only people in the world who don't use peppercorns (*Piper nigrum*).

Sansho is not related to pepper but is the dried berry of the prickly ash and a close relation of the Sichuan peppercorn. It is sold ready-ground in specialist stores and is used mostly to season rich, fatty foods like eel and grilled meat.

chilli-roast spare ribs (VIETNAM)

Chilli and lemongrass characterise this traditional barbecue cut, with a tickle of bottled fish sauce to intensify the savoury flavour.

SERVES 4

2 racks of belly pork ribs, with 12 ribs on each
About 250ml water

FOR THE MARINADE
4 fresh red chillies, finely chopped
2 stalks of lemongrass, bulb end only, finely sliced
2 cloves garlic, chopped
2 tablespoons rice wine (or medium sherry)
1 tablespoon soy sauce
1 tablespoon fish sauce (nuoc mam or nam pla)
1 teaspoon five-spice powder (see page 44)

First make the marinade. Using a pestle and mortar, crush the chillies, lemongrass and garlic, before adding the other ingredients. Stir well. Smother the racks of ribs with the marinade and leave for at least 4 hours or overnight in the fridge.

Preheat the oven to 200°C/400°F/gas 6. Place the ribs on the top shelf with a drip pan underneath. Roast for 45 minutes, brushing with the marinade several times. To check that the meat is cooked, insert a skewer between the bones.

Boil the water and pour it into the drip tray. Scrape up the juices and stir well to make a sticky barbecue sauce. Strain through a sieve, so the texture of the sauce is smooth.

Cut each rack of ribs in half to provide a serving of six ribs per person. Pour over the barbecue sauce and serve with plain boiled rice.

soy-braised beef with turnips (CHINA)

Slow-braising an inexpensive cut of beef with spices makes a rich and warming winter dish.

SERVES 4

1.5kg shin of beef
3 tablespoons groundnut or sunflower oil
2 onions, finely sliced
1 teaspoon five-spice powder (see page 44)
5cm ginger, peeled and thinly sliced
3 star anise
1 litre water
4 tablespoons dark soy sauce
2 teaspoons caster sugar
5 tablespoons Chinese Shaoxing wine (or medium sherry)
450g turnips, cut diagonally into 3cm pieces
2 tablespoons chopped coriander leaves

Blanch the shin of beef in boiling water for 10 minutes. Rinse in a colander under cold water to remove any scum. Pat dry using kitchen paper and cut into 2.5cm cubes.

Heat the groundnut or sunflower oil in a wok and stir-fry the pieces of meat until they change colour. Remove the meat using a slotted spoon and reserve. In the same pan, stir-fry the onions for about 7 minutes until soft. Stir in the five-spice powder, ginger and star anise, and heat through.

Add the measured water, soy sauce, sugar and wine or sherry, return the beef, and bring to the boil. Cover with a lid and simmer for 1½ hours. Check that the liquid doesn't boil dry. Preheat the oven to 200°C/400°F/gas 6.

Add the turnips to the pan, topping up the water level if it has evaporated, and transfer to a casserole dish. Cover and cook in the preheated oven for 1½–2 hours until the beef is juicy and tender. Check once or twice to make sure the liquid doesn't boil dry.

Sprinkle with the coriander and serve with plain boiled rice.

stir-fried spicy rice (CHINA)

Rice is eaten two or three times a day by over half the people in the world. In most of the Far East, a meal isn't considered a meal unless it includes rice, and there are many thousands of ways of preparing it. Stir-fried rice is best when you use rice that has been cooked the day before and left overnight in the fridge.

SERVES 4

500g cooked rice, cooled and left overnight in the fridge
2 tablespoons sunflower or groundnut oil
2 spring onions, white and green parts chopped separately
2 cloves garlic, chopped
2cm ginger, finely sliced
2 teaspoons cumin seeds
1 fresh red chilli, chopped
100g smoked bacon, cut into 1cm cubes
2 tablespoons frozen peas
1 carrot, cut into matchsticks
1 teaspoon salt
Freshly ground black pepper
2 tablespoons soy sauce
Coriander leaves, chopped, to garnish

Loosen the lumps in the rice with a wooden spoon. Heat a wok or frying pan until very hot, then add the sunflower or groundnut oil. Add the white parts of the spring onions and fry until they sizzle, then add the garlic, ginger and cumin seeds. Cook briefly for about 20 seconds, and add the chilli.

Add the bacon and stir together for about 1 minute until the flavours mingle. Add the peas and carrots and then the rice. Stir-fry for about 5 minutes until everything is well mixed and steaming hot.

Season with the salt, black pepper and soy sauce. Sprinkle with the coriander and the chopped green parts of the spring onions to garnish.

seven-spice powder (JAPAN)

This table condiment is known as *shichimi-togarashi*. *Shichimi* means seven-spice and *togarashi* is dried red chilli. In Japan it is sprinkled on to rice and soupy noodle dishes and it can be bought ready-prepared in most Japanese stores. Sometimes mustard seeds, rape seeds and *perilla* (Japanese mint) are also added, although the Japanese still call it seven-spice mixture regardless of the number of ingredients.

1 tablespoon white sesame seeds, lightly roasted
1 tablespoon *nori* (dried seaweed), crumbled
1 teaspoon dried tangerine peel, chopped
1 teaspoon dried red chillies, chopped
1 teaspoon *sansho* (see page 41) or sichuan peppercorns
½ teaspoon black peppercorns
½ teaspoon poppy seeds, lightly roasted

Grind all the spices together and store in an airtight jar.

five-spice powder (CHINA)

Although called five-spice because of the symbolic power of the number five, this finely ground, golden powder often has more than five ingredients. It usually includes cinnamon or cassia, cloves, star anise, fennel seed, or aniseed, Sichuan peppercorns, liquorice and, at times, ground ginger. It is used in marinades, and in Vietnam and southern China it is used to season meat for roasting. You can buy it ready-made in specialist stores, or make your own.

MAKES 1 JAR

2 star anise
10cm stick of cinnamon (or 1 tablespoon ground cinnamon)
1 teaspoon Sichuan peppercorns
1 teaspoon black peppercorns

Heat the ingredients in a dry pan for about 30 seconds until they start to release an appetising aroma. Grind using a spice or coffee grinder or use a pestle and mortar. Transfer to an airtight jar until ready to use.

gomasio (JAPAN)

This is a table seasoning used to sprinkle over boiled rice. You need twice the quantity of sesame seeds as salt.

Black sesame seeds
Sea salt

Roast the sesame seeds lightly in a hot oven for a few minutes or heat in a dry pan until they start to colour. Grind the seeds with the salt in a spice or coffee grinder or use a pestle and mortar. Keep in an airtight jar until required.

kim chee (KOREA)

This salted, chilli-hot pickled cabbage is the main condiment in Korea, served at the table with nearly every meal. Most families make it at home and store it in earthenware jars buried in the ground. It is very hot and pungent, and strangely addictive. It is made with Chinese cabbage leaves – reserve the thick white stems for use in a stir-fry.

MAKES 1 OR 2 JARS

1 Chinese cabbage, leaves only
150g salt
2 teaspoons chilli powder or cayenne pepper
8 spring onions, white parts only, chopped
10cm ginger, grated
2–4 small fresh red chillies, finely chopped
4 cloves garlic, grated

Cut the cabbage leaves into large squares. Place the leaves in layers in a large mixing bowl and sprinkle liberally with the salt and chilli powder or cayenne pepper. Place a plate on top and put a weight on it to compress the leaves. Leave to mature for a week while the salt draws the juices from the leaves.

Wash the leaves in a colander to rinse out the salt, and squeeze dry. Chop the leaves finely and mix with the spring onions, ginger, chillies and garlic. Press into a suitable container, weighted with a plate, cover with clingfilm (to prevent its odour from spreading) and store in the fridge for a week for the flavours to mature. Transfer to airtight jars, and store in the fridge until needed.

Serve small portions, as a hot pickle, with any kind of meat, chicken or fish.

hot pepper flakes in oil
(CHINA AND TAIWAN)

This is a fierce chilli oil you can buy or make at home. Known as *lajiao you*, it is added as a condiment to many Chinese and Taiwanese dishes. Stir well before use.

MAKES 1 JAR

3 tablespoons groundnut or sunflower oil
50g dried red chilli flakes (or dried red chillies, finely chopped)
½ teaspoon salt

Heat the groundnut or sunflower oil until very hot and smoking, then remove from the heat. Leave to cool for about 5 seconds, then add the chilli flakes or chopped chillies. The oil will foam up. When it subsides, add the salt. Mix well and store in a sealed jar.

One of the most significant influences on world cuisine today is the cooking of Thailand. The desire to explore something new and different dictates fashion, and momentum continually swings to and fro, from French to Italian, from Chinese to Indian, from Mexican to Middle Eastern. But the cooking of Thailand and Southeast Asia in general is something special. It is not only individual dishes (like red and green curries and *laksa* soups) but the whole philosophy of spicing which catches the imagination of new wave cooks in the world's top food capitals such as London, Sydney and New York.

London, which has enjoyed Indian and Chinese restaurants from the beginning of the nineteenth century, opened its doors to other Asian cuisines in the 1970s; Indonesian food was a cautious hit, spicy and hot like Indian food, but sweeter and more mysterious (our first taste of the dried shrimp paste, *blachan*, and fish sauces).

The first Thai restaurants, in the early 1980s, were a revelation, with similarly hot, sweet-sour tastes, but pulled together with sophistication; a balance of colour, texture and taste, even bitter notes, with an introduction to unfamiliar ingredients such as lemongrass and kaffir lime leaves.

The first books on Thai cooking by Vatcharin Bhumichitr, owner of several London restaurants, went some way to explaining its wonderful complexities. Holiday makers returning from Bangkok described the thrills of the street markets where every other stall is selling treats and delicacies.

The cheapest are dishes of noodles (*pad thai*), both wide and flat, and thin and transparent, with extra beef, pork, chicken or prawns to order. Red and green curries are everywhere, as are lovely spicy soups (*tom yam*). But at higher levels of gastronomy it has gradually emerged that Thailand (formerly the Kingdom of Siam) is heir to one of the great classic cuisines of the world, created by the cooks at the royal palace. We are lucky that the Australian scholar-cook from Sydney, David Thompson, has made a record of this. He made it his life's work to learn Thai and study their cooking at the feet of former palace cooks, enabling him to produce a complete history of food in this unique country.

The Indonesian experience

Thailand is an influential part of Southeast Asia, but is dwarfed in size by Indonesia, with the fourth largest population in the world (200 million) after China, India and the USA. It is an archipelago of some 1700 islands, the largest of which are Sumatra and Java.

Local cooking has developed largely under the influence of the Chinese, which explains much of its ingenuity and wide range of skills. Indonesian cooks easily convert modest piles of rice or noodles into a feast using morsels of pork, duck, chicken, fish, crab, shellfish and vegetables, with eggs and crunchy peanuts and dramatic spice pastes, often combined with savoury *terasi* (or *blachan*) which is dried shrimp paste.

Skewered pork, beef or chicken with a hot peanut sauce (*satay*) is an Indonesian speciality which has spread around the world; *gado gado* (crispy steamed vegetables in a spicy peanut sauce) is another.

Malaysian cuisine combines these different elements, a mixture of Malay, Chinese and Indian styles of cooking. Rice is the basis and, with coconut milk, provides the mild canvas for a bewildering range of fierce, hot curries and spicy stir-fries.

The curious gourmet, salivating over the prospect of enjoying these cuisines first-hand but without the required budget, could compromise with a short break in Singapore which will deliver most of them to your palate in a matter of days; for this small island state is a microcosm of the cooking of Southeast Asia and its restaurants provide an anthology of the tastes of all Asia.

Singapore is, in its own right, one of the spice capitals of the world, along with London and New York. Although it doesn't grow spices commercially, you can see a whole range of exotic spices growing in local parks: a reminder of the peppercorns, nutmeg, cinnamon and cassia which first drew adventurers to these parts.

When Singapore was established by Sir Stamford Raffles on behalf of the East India Company as a trading station in 1819, it became Britain's valuable jewel in the East, a key link in the British Empire's trading route to Hong Kong, via Gibraltar, Malta and Suez, Aden and Colombo. It had been an implacable island of swamp and rainforest (of which a segment remains, a few acres in the heart of the lovely botanical gardens). Today it is a prosperous island of more than three million people, an international crossroads of business and culture, a mini-New York with many dozens of high-rise banks and businesses.

Wealthy Singapore is rich in restaurants, too, an ideal place to sample an anthology of the best of Southeast Asian cuisines, including Chinese and Indian. These communities are represented by their own markets, where you can eat at hundreds of cooking stalls, each one offering its own speciality, such as Chinese chicken soup or Indian curried kebab.

In Singapore it is possible to eat out every day of the year and have something different. It offers a compendium of the spicing of dozens of cuisines, including Thai, Vietnamese, Indonesian, Burmese and Japanese. Bizarrely it can even be boldly innovative, offering an Asian-style Italian risotto (served at the world-famous Raffles Hotel).

Nonya cooking

But Singapore also has its own unique, very spicy, native cooking style, known as *Nonya*. This evolved from the Chinese workers originally recruited to service the colony by Raffles at the East India Company. Forbidden to bring Chinese women with them, they married Malaysian wives. *Nonya* cooking is a fusion of local flavours and Chinese cooking techniques.

Malaysian women naturally cooked with the tropical ingredients they knew so well, fish pastes (*blachan*), perfumed grasses and leaves (lemongrass and pandanus) and fiery fresh chillies; and the Chinese introduced improved techniques, such as the use of the wok, and provided their own essential ingredients, especially soy sauce, ginger, garlic and spring onions. The resultant cooking is much bolder and more exaggerated than the subtle cuisine of mainland China.

I had a chance to sample it, when I met cookery teacher Violet Oon, who lives a long way out of the skyscraper city. She literally steps outside her back door to gather a handful of lemongrass, and picks some kaffir lime leaves from the citrus tree. She throws fresh chillies into a sizzling hot wok

A woman sorting red and yellow chilli peppers, Bali, Indonesia.

and we are soon choking on the fierce fumes. Into the pan go chopped pieces of chicken, lemongrass, kaffir lime leaves, lime juice and about half a bottle of soy sauce. The flavours are more intense than you can imagine. Never has plain rice had a more dramatic companion.

If one dish has to sum up the island and the spirit of *Nonya*, it would be Singapore Chilli Crab, served with a sweet tomato sauce, so hot it will have you mopping your dripping brow and wiping off the sauce which inevitably drips on to your front.

Southeast Asia may have few of what in the West are rated as luxury ingredients. But, thanks to its spicing, it lacks nothing for passion and flavour. Every meal is theatre and every dish is a performance.

spicy vegetable soup (INDONESIA)

This thin vegetable soup has dramatic sweet, sour and spicy notes. Soothing coconut milk moderates the hot chilli.

SERVES 4

300ml boiling water
4 tablespoons desiccated coconut
1 tablespoon sunflower or groundnut oil
1 onion, thinly sliced
1 clove garlic, crushed
2.5cm ginger, peeled and grated
2 green chillies, finely chopped
1 teaspoon turmeric powder
1.2 litres stock
2 teaspoons brown sugar
2 carrots, thinly sliced
2 sticks of celery, thinly sliced
1 leek, thinly sliced
Handful of green beans, chopped
Salt or soy sauce, to taste
Juice of 1 lemon

Pour the boiling water over the desiccated coconut and steep for 15 minutes to make coconut milk. Strain to remove any fibres.

Heat the sunflower or groundnut oil in a pan and add the onion. Cook for 2 or 3 minutes until soft. Stir in the garlic, ginger, chillies and turmeric. Heat through to make a sticky paste, stirring to prevent burning.

Add the stock and coconut milk and heat through, then add the sugar, carrots, celery, leek and green beans. Simmer gently for 30 minutes. Add salt and soy sauce to taste. Just before serving, stir in the lemon juice.

laksa soup (SINGAPORE)

In Singapore all the eastern culinary cultures merge – the skills of the Chinese cook and up-front Indian heat meeting the native flavours of pungent shrimp paste, ginger and lemongrass. *Laksa* is the everyday soup with as many recipes as cooks, but contains a fairly consistent mantra of spicing. Adapt the ingredients to your taste, varying the seafood, adding finely chopped Asian vegetables such as bean sprouts or sliced *bok choi*, or pea-sized Thai aubergines. The workshy can substitute the *laksa* paste with one of the many good Asian spice pastes now on the market, such as Charmaine Solomon's.

SERVES 4

1 crab, about 500g
250g uncooked tiger prawns
250g mussels, scrubbed
2 tablespoons sunflower oil
1 stalk of lemongrass, sliced diagonally into 2cm pieces
3 kaffir lime leaves
2cm ginger, thinly sliced
2 tablespoons chopped coriander leaves
400ml coconut milk
600ml water
Salt
Juice of ½ lime
350g rice noodles
Parsley, mint, basil or coriander leaves to garnish

FOR THE *LAKSA* PASTE
100g shallots
3 cloves garlic
8 candlenuts (or macadamia nuts or blanched almonds)
1 stalk of lemongrass, cut into thin rounds
1 tablespoon sunflower oil
3 fresh or dried red chillies
½ teaspoon shrimp paste (*blachan*) or
    1 tablespoon fish sauce (*nam pla*)
1 tablespoon turmeric powder
1 teaspoon ground cumin
1 tablespoon jaggery (palm sugar), or demerara sugar

Crack open the crab and reserve the meat. Put the shells to one side. Shell the prawns, remove the black veins and reserve the heads and shells for stock. Cook the mussels in a covered saucepan with a glassful of water until they open, reserving both the mussels, still in their shells, and the cooking liquor. Fry the crab and prawn shells in

the sunflower oil briefly, then add the lemongrass, kaffir lime leaves, ginger and coriander. Stir in the mussel liquor. Cook until almost evaporated. Add half of the coconut milk and all the water. Simmer for 15 minutes, then strain to remove all shells and the spices.

Meanwhile, make the laksa paste. Using a pestle and mortar or a food processor, blend the shallots, garlic and nuts. Add the lemongrass and stir well. Fry the mixture in the sunflower oil until you begin to smell the aroma of the ingredients. Stir in the chillies.

Wrap the shrimp paste (if using) in foil, and heat over the hob for a few seconds to release its flavour, then crumble it into the

pan. Add the turmeric, cumin, fish sauce (if using) and sugar. Heat through. Add the shellfish stock and simmer for 10 minutes. Add the rest of the coconut milk. Finally, add the crab, prawns and mussels and simmer on the lowest heat for a further 5 minutes. Check and adjust the seasoning, adding salt if necessary. Remove from the heat and add the lime juice.

In a separate pan, boil the noodles according to the instructions on the packet. Divide between four bowls and pour the shellfish laksa on top. Garnish with your choice of fresh herbs.

grilled chilli prawns (INDONESIA)

Fish is always on the menu in Indonesia, a land made up of thousands of islands extending across an area larger than Europe. There are fish and seafood from the sea and also freshwater fish that are farmed in the flooded rice-fields. Here, prawns are spiced up with lime and chilli.

SERVES 4 AS AN APPETISER

12–16 uncooked king prawns
½ teaspoon shrimp paste (*blachan*; optional)
1 tablespoon olive oil
2 tablespoons lime juice
3 cloves garlic, crushed
½ teaspoon chilli powder
1 teaspoon brown sugar

Pinch the heads from the prawns. Remove the shells from the underside but leave the shells on the backs and tails. Cut lengthways into each prawn so that it opens out flat.

If using, grill the shrimp paste (wrapped in foil) for a few seconds on each side, and crush using a pestle and mortar. Mix the olive oil with the lime juice, garlic, prepared shrimp paste (if using), chilli powder and sugar.

Add the prawns, coat them in the mixture and leave to marinate for 30 minutes or more, turning from time to time.

Cook under a very hot grill for about 7 minutes, turning and brushing with the marinade occasionally.

Serve as an appetiser or with plain boiled rice as a main course dish.

country chicken soup

(SOUTHEAST ASIA)

Different versions of this light, tasty soup are served throughout Thailand, Vietnam and Malaysia.

SERVES 6–8

1 egg white
3 teaspoons cornflour
½ chicken or 2–3 chicken breasts, skinned, boned and cut into strips
2 stalks of lemongrass, cut into 2cm slices
1 litre chicken stock
10 small red chillies, roughly chopped
5cm galangal, finely sliced
750ml coconut milk
1 teaspoon jaggery (palm sugar) or brown sugar
Pinch of salt
2 tablespoons fish sauce (*nam pla*)
175ml groundnut oil
Juice of 1 lime or lemon
Freshly ground black pepper
2 tablespoons chopped coriander leaves

Mix the egg white and cornflour together to make a paste and stir in the chicken pieces to coat well. Chill in the fridge for up to an hour.

Bruise the lemongrass slightly using the flat of a knife to release the flavours. Put the chicken stock in a saucepan with the chillies, galangal and lemongrass and cook gently for about 10 minutes. Then add the coconut milk, jaggery or brown sugar, salt and fish sauce, and continue cooking gently for another 20 minutes.

Heat the groundnut oil in a wok and stir-fry the chicken pieces for 5–10 minutes until cooked.

Serve the chicken pieces in the soup, and season with the lime or lemon juice and freshly ground black pepper, and sprinkle over the coriander.

tom yam kung (THAILAND)

This characteristic Thai soup (*tom* means soup, *yam* means spicy) contains a complete set of flavours: pungent garlic and shallots, tingling hot chilli, sour lime juice, sweet palm sugar, salty fish sauce (*nam pla*), fragrant lemongrass and bitter kaffir lime leaves.

SERVES 4

1 tablespoon groundnut oil
4 shallots, chopped
3 cloves garlic, chopped
1 fresh red chilli, finely chopped
1 teaspoon salt
1 litre fish, chicken or vegetable stock
1 stalk of lemongrass, skinned and chopped into 5cm lengths
4 kaffir lime leaves
1 tablespoon fish sauce (*nam pla*)
1 tablespoon jaggery (palm sugar) or demerara sugar
500g uncooked prawns, peeled and deveined (use the crushed shells to enrich the stock, straining before use)
Juice of ½ lime or lemon
2 tablespoons chopped coriander leaves, to garnish
2 spring onions, chopped, to garnish

Heat the groundnut oil in a frying pan and then fry the shallots, garlic and chilli over a gentle heat for 2 or 3 minutes until they start to brown. Using a pestle and mortar, grind to a paste with the salt.

Heat the stock and add the paste, lemongrass, kaffir lime leaves, fish sauce and jaggery or demerara sugar. Simmer for 5 minutes. Check the seasoning and add a little more salt, sugar or fish sauce, to taste.

Add the prawns and heat through gently for a few minutes until they are coloured. Remove from the heat, stir in the lime or lemon juice and serve garnished with the coriander and spring onions.

chicken satay (INDONESIA)

In Indonesia, meat is scarce but chickens roam freely around village gardens and graze along roadsides. This recipe includes two sauces with contrasting flavours to accompany the chicken satay.

SERVES 4

3 shallots, crushed
2 cloves garlic, crushed
1 teaspoon ground ginger
Pinch of chilli powder or freshly ground black pepper
Salt
2 tablespoons dark soy sauce
1 tablespoon lime or lemon juice
1kg chicken, boned and cut into bite-sized pieces

FOR THE CHILLI-FLAVOURED SAUCE (*BUMBU KECAP*)
2 green chillies, deseeded and chopped
1 clove garlic, crushed
2 tablespoons dark soy sauce
2 teaspoons lime or lemon juice
1 tablespoon boiling water

FOR THE PEANUT SAUCE (*BUMBU KACANG*)
125g shelled peanuts, with skins on
2 tablespoons groundnut oil
2 shallots, finely sliced
2 cloves garlic, chopped
½ teaspoon shrimp paste (*blachan*)
½ teaspoon ground ginger
½ teaspoon ground coriander
½ teaspoon chilli powder
450ml water
1 teaspoon brown sugar
Juice of ½ lemon

Put the shallots and garlic in a large bowl and add the ginger, chilli powder or freshly ground black pepper and ½ teaspoon salt. Stir in the soy sauce and lime or lemon juice. Add the chicken pieces to the bowl and coat them well with the mixture. Cover and leave for at least 1 hour to marinate.

To make the chilli-flavoured sauce, mix all the ingredients together in a small bowl and leave for at least 1 hour.

To make the peanut sauce, fry the peanuts in 1 tablespoon of the groundnut oil for 4–5 minutes, until browned. Leave to

cool, then grind to a powder using a pestle and mortar or a spice or coffee grinder.

Pound the shallots with the garlic and shrimp paste using a pestle and mortar or in a food processor until they make a smooth paste. Stir in the ginger, coriander, chilli powder and salt to taste.

Heat the remaining oil in a saucepan, add the shallot paste and fry for a few seconds. Add the water and, when it comes to the boil, add the ground peanuts and sugar. Keep boiling and stirring until the sauce is quite thick. Add more salt if necessary. Just before serving, add the lemon juice.

When the chicken is well marinated, thread on to skewers, allowing six or seven pieces per skewer. Put on a rack and grill over charcoal or under a hot grill for 6 or 8 minutes, turning often.

Serve hot on the skewers with the sauces alongside in bowls for dipping.

soy-spiced chicken (SINGAPORE)

In the 1800s, when Singapore was an international trading post, the British engaged workers from mainland China, but did not let them bring their wives. They inter-married with Malaysian women and their cooking was a fusion of Chinese techniques (using a wok) and local ingredients, such as chilli, lemongrass, lime, jaggery (palm sugar) and *blachan*, the dried fish paste of Indonesia and Malaysia. The women were known as *Nonya* – the name given to this style of cooking. This dish is known as *ayam tempra*

SERVES 4–6

1kg chicken, boned and cut into bite-sized pieces
6 tablespoons dark soy sauce
100ml groundnut or sunflower oil
6 onions, thinly sliced
10 fresh red chillies, sliced diagonally
5 tablespoons jaggery (palm sugar) or brown sugar
100ml water
½ teaspoon salt
Juice of 2 limes or 1 lemon

Wash the chicken pieces and pat dry using kitchen paper. Marinate in 2 tablespoons of the soy sauce for 15 minutes.

Place a wok over a high heat and, when it gets hot, add the groundnut or sunflower oil. When the oil is very hot and starts to smoke, add the onions and stir-fry for about 30 seconds – the onions should still be slightly crisp. Add the chillies and stir-fry for about 30 seconds. Beware – the fumes are very strong and you might need to open a window. Remove about a quarter of the mixture and set aside to use as a garnish.

Add the chicken and stir-fry for about 2 minutes. Add the jaggery or brown sugar, water, remaining soy sauce and salt. Cook for about 30 minutes until the chicken is tender but not breaking apart.

When the sauce is thick, turn off the heat and add the lime or lemon juice – don't let it boil. Stir well. Spoon into a shallow bowl and garnish with the reserved fried onions and chillies.

Serve with plain boiled rice.

pork with soy sauce (MALAYSIA)

This dish, popular among the Chinese who settled in Malaysia, is in the style of *Nonya* cooking. It combines heavy spicing with Chinese ingredients, like pork, which the predominantly Muslim Malays do not eat.

SERVES 4

2½ tablespoons light soy sauce
2½ tablespoons dark soy sauce
1 tablespoon five-spice powder (see page 44)
350g pork leg or shoulder, cut into 3cm pieces
2 tablespoons vegetable oil
3 cloves garlic, crushed
6 black peppercorns, crushed
1 stick of cinnamon
6 cloves
1 star anise
300ml water
½ teaspoon sugar
100g white bean curd (tofu), diced
4 hard-boiled eggs, halved

Mix 2 teaspoons of the light soy sauce with 2 teaspoons of the dark soy sauce and add the five-spice powder. Stir the pork pieces in this marinade until well coated, then set aside for 1 hour.

Heat the vegetable oil in a large saucepan. Add the garlic, peppercorns, cinnamon, cloves and star anise, and stir-fry over a medium heat for about 5 minutes (until they give off their fragrance).

Drain the pork from the marinade. Increase the heat and add the pork to the pan, stirring quickly for a minute or two, until it is browned all over. Stir in the rest of the dark and light soy sauces, the water and the sugar, and bring to the boil. Lower the heat and cook gently for about 30 minutes or until the meat is tender and the sauce is reduced to a thick gravy. It shouldn't dry out – add a little boiling water, if necessary. Add the bean curd and eggs and cook for 5 minutes more.

Remove the star anise and cinnamon stick, and serve with plain boiled rice.

chilli crab (SINGAPORE)

This is one of the most renowned dishes of the Far East – the ultimate in finger food. It is best enjoyed in one of the waterside restaurants at the UMDC Seafood Centre on the East Coast road, half an hour out of the city, the lights of ocean-going freighters reflecting like stars in the tropical night. A faint breeze offers some cooling relief from the oppressive humidity, ever present in this equatorial island, but this hot dish is designed to provoke Nature's own cooling system. You'll need numerous paper napkins to mop your brow – and wipe the sticky juices from your fingers, for there is no other way to eat this delicacy.

The Chinese are not purists when it comes to using bottled sauces, and tomato ketchup is a favourite in the kitchen. They would use live crabs for this dish.

SERVES 2

1 large crab or 2 medium crabs, about 1kg
2 tablespoons groundnut or sunflower oil
3 cloves garlic, chopped
3 fresh red chillies, thinly sliced
1 teaspoon black (soy) beans, chopped
   (or 1 teaspoon soy sauce)
3 spring onions, roughly chopped, to garnish
3 tablespoons chopped coriander leaves, to garnish

FOR THE SAUCE
1 level tablespoon cornflour
2 tablespoons soy sauce
5 tablespoons tomato ketchup
1 teaspoon jaggery (palm sugar) or brown sugar
200ml water
Juice of ½ lime (or 1 tablespoon rice or wine vinegar)
Pinch of salt
Freshly ground black pepper

Break off the crab claws and legs and crack them with a mallet or hammer. Cut the crab in two with a cleaver. Remove the spongy, yellowish-grey 'dead men's fingers'. Chop the crab into several smaller pieces for ease of handling.

To make the sauce, dissolve the cornflour in the soy sauce and mix with the other sauce ingredients except the lime juice (or vinegar) and seasoning. Heat through, stirring until it's a slightly viscous consistency. Add a little more water if necessary. Keep warm.

In a wok, heat the groundnut or sunflower oil until very hot. Fry the garlic for 15 seconds and add the red chillies. Mind the fumes. Throw in the soy beans (if using). Toss in the crab pieces and stir well. If using a live crab, cook for a few minutes until the shell turns pink.

Pour the sauce over the crab, cover with a lid and cook for 7 minutes. Taste for seasoning, adding salt and freshly ground black pepper (and, if you haven't used black soy beans, a tablespoon of soy sauce).

Remove from the heat and stir in the lime juice (or vinegar). Garnish with the spring onions and coriander and, using your fingers (but a fork will help), eat very hot. Have bread to mop up the juices, if you like.

Make sure you have a bowl of water, with a slice of lemon in it, to rinse your fingers, and plenty of paper napkins.

Fresh crab is one of the world's great gourmet tastes, as they well know in Southeast Asia.

fillet of beef marinated
in rendang (BALI, INDONESIA)

Indonesia has the third largest population in the world after
China and India; it is primarily a Muslim country, but the
exception is Bali, with four million deeply religious Hindu
souls. Food plays a big part in their devotions and every meal
is prefaced with an offering to the gods of rice wrapped in
banana leaf.

Indonesia was the first target of the spice explorers and
every spice and herb the Balinese cook might need grows
abundantly. Pounded together, they are used to make
rendang, a spice paste used for flavouring meat. This
sophisticated and elegant dish from the Four Seasons Resort
in Sayan uses fillet steak, which cooks in minutes, rather than
the traditional buffalo, which requires hours.

4 fillet steaks, 150–200g each
Salt and freshly ground black pepper
1 tablespoon coriander seeds, dry-roasted and ground
***Rendang* spice paste (see page 63)**

Rub the steaks with plenty of salt and freshly ground black pepper
and rub over the ground coriander. Leave to stand for 15 minutes.
Smear both sides of the meat with *rendang* paste.

Heat the grill to maximum or use a griddle pan heated to high.
Cook the steaks until done, about 2 minutes each side for rare, or
4 minutes each side for medium to well-done.

Serve with green salad leaves, dressed with olive oil and the
juice of half a lime or lemon, and plain boiled rice.

karadok salad with peanut dressing (JAVA, INDONESIA)

This dish underlines the Indonesian liking for raw vegetables served with a rich peanut sauce. *Sambal ulek* (crushed red chillies with salt) can be bought in specialist stores. Eat this salad on its own or served with meat and rice.

SERVES 4

125g sweet potato, cut into matchsticks
Salt
125g green beans, cut into 1.5cm lengths
125g bean sprouts
125g white cabbage, shredded
4 small aubergines, quartered
½ cucumber, peeled and sliced
2 tablespoons chopped fresh mint, plus extra to garnish

FOR THE DRESSING
125g shelled peanuts with skins on
1 tablespoon groundnut oil
½ teaspoon shrimp paste (*blachan*)
1 clove garlic
1 teaspoon *sambal ulek*
300ml boiling water
1 teaspoon jaggery (palm sugar) or brown sugar
Juice of ½ lime

Place the sweet potato in a bowl and add 1 teaspoon salt. Pour cold water over to cover and set aside.

To make the dressing, heat a heavy-based pan and dry-fry the peanuts for about 5 minutes, tossing frequently to prevent burning, until browned all over. Pound using a pestle and mortar and transfer to a saucepan.

Heat the groundnut oil in another pan and fry the shrimp paste for about a minute, turning once. Remove from the heat and, using a pestle and mortar, pound with the garlic, *sambal ulek* and a little salt. Add the mixture to the peanuts.

Add the boiling water, jaggery or palm sugar and lime juice. Cook over a medium heat for about 2 minutes, stirring constantly. Remove from the heat and leave to cool.

Arrange the green beans, bean sprouts, cabbage, aubergines, cucumber and mint in a bowl or on a plate. Drain the sweet potato matchsticks and add these. Pour the peanut dressing over the top and garnish with extra mint.

savoury spiced pork (MALAYSIA)

This is another Malaysian spicy recipe with roots in *Nonya* cooking (see page 47). Many of the *Nonya* dishes are started with a savoury paste called *rempeh*. This contains candlenuts, which grow locally, but you can substitute peanuts, macadamia or other nuts; It also includes pandanus, another local flavouring – or you can use a splash of vanilla essence instead.

SERVES 4

½ teaspoon *rempeh* paste (see page 63)
750g pork belly, cut into bite-sized pieces
250ml coconut milk or reconstituted coconut milk powder
2 tablespoons vegetable oil
1 teaspoon salt
4 teaspoons sugar
1 stalk of lemongrass, crushed
3 kaffir lime leaves (or grated rind of 1 lime)

Heat the *rempeh* paste in a wok or large saucepan, and add the rest of the ingredients. Simmer, stirring, for about 5–10 minutes until the meat is cooked and the sauce reduced. If the sauce reduces too quickly, add a little water.

Remove the lemongrass and lime leaves and serve with plain boiled rice.

red and green curries (THAILAND)

The most renowned Thai dishes around the world are their fragrant, richly scented red and green curries, the colours defined in part by the use of red or green chillies. Every family has its own preferred recipe. Essentially the curry pastes are made patiently, every ingredient pounded, usually the drier ones first, the fresh ones last, until each is a pulp, and a little water is added, if necessary, to moisten it. An alternative is to use a blender, making small batches at a time – a food processor doesn't work so well. To start the cooking, you must fry the mixture in a little oil to temper it, reducing the raw flavour of the spices. For milder curries, coconut milk is used during cooking to moderate the heat and balance the flavours.

green curried beef with noodles

SERVES 4

250g rump steak (or topside)
1 level tablespoon cornflour
1 tablespoon soy sauce
1 egg white, beaten
1 spring onion, white part only, finely chopped
350g fresh egg noodles (or dried)
2 carrots, cut into matchsticks
2 stick of celery, outside fibres removed with a potato peeler, cut into thin diagonal slices
4 tablespoons groundnut or sunflower oil
1 clove garlic, chopped
2cm ginger, cut into matchsticks
1 tablespoon green curry paste (see page 62)
100ml beef stock (or chicken or vegetable stock)
1 teaspoon sesame oil
1 tablespoon soy sauce

Cut the beef against the grain into very thin slices (it helps if you freeze the beef for 30 minutes in the freezer first). Mix together the cornflour, soy sauce, egg white and spring onion. Stir in the beef and set aside for 30 minutes.

Plunge the egg noodles into boiling water and, when it comes to the boil again, cook for 3 minutes. Drain in a colander and then plunge into a bowl of cold water to arrest the cooking process. Drain again and leave to stand.

Blanch the carrots and celery in boiling water for 2 minutes, then drain and reserve.

In a wok, heat the groundnut or sunflower oil until very hot. Drain the meat slices in a sieve and fry the pieces in the wok on one side for 1 minute, without stirring, then stir-fry the pieces for 1 minute more. Remove to drain on kitchen paper and reserve.

Pour off the oil, leaving 1 tablespoon only, and fry the garlic and ginger for 30 seconds until they give off an aroma. Add the green curry paste and stir-fry until it sizzles. Add the celery and carrots and stir-fry until hot. Pour in the stock. When it comes to the boil, add the noodles, stirring until heated through. Stir in the beef, and cook until very hot. Sprinkle with the sesame oil and soy sauce. Serve at once.

red chicken curry with noodles

SERVES 4

300g chicken breast, skinned
1 teaspoon cornflour
2 tablespoons soy sauce
1 egg white
250g transparent rice noodles (rice vermicelli)
1 tablespoon groundnut or sunflower oil
1 clove garlic, chopped
1 tablespoon red curry paste (see page 62)
100ml chicken stock

Cut the chicken into thin slices. Mix together the cornflour, 1 tablespoon of the soy sauce and the egg white. Stir in the chicken and leave to stand for 1 hour.

Plunge the rice noodles into boiling water and when the water returns to boiling point, drain in a colander and plunge into cold water to arrest the cooking process.

Heat the groundnut or sunflower oil in a wok and fry the garlic for a minute or two until it starts to change colour. Add the red curry paste and stir-fry until it sizzles. Stir-fry the chicken pieces for 2 or 3 minutes until cooked. Add the stock and bring to the boil. Quickly stir in the rice noodles. Splash with the remaining soy sauce to serve.

acar campur vegetable salad
(INDONESIA)

In Indonesia, where vegetables are eaten in abundance, they are always laced with generous quantities of herbs and spices – for both their flavour and medicinal qualities. The vegetables are crunchy and sweet and sour to the taste.

SERVES 4

6 cashew nuts
1 shallot, chopped
2 cloves garlic, peeled
2 tablespoons groundnut oil
½ teaspoon turmeric powder
½ teaspoon ground ginger
1 fresh red or green chilli, deseeded and cut into 4
10 pickling onions, peeled
4 tablespoons rice vinegar (or white wine vinegar)
1 teaspoon salt
225g carrots, cut into 3cm chunks
225g cauliflower florets
225g green beans, cut into 3cm pieces
1 red pepper, cut in to strips
1 green pepper, cut in to strips
300ml water
1 cucumber, peeled and cut into 3cm chunks
2 teaspoons brown sugar
1 teaspoon French mustard

Crush the nuts, shallot and garlic together to form a paste. Heat the groundnut oil in a wok and fry the paste for 1 minute.

Add the turmeric, ginger, chilli and onions and stir well. Then add the vinegar and salt. Cover and cook for about 3 minutes.

Stir in the carrots, cauliflower, green beans and peppers. Add the water, cover again and continue cooking for another 8 minutes. Add the cucumber, sugar and mustard. Cover and cook for a further 2 minutes. Remove the lid and stir constantly to cook the vegetables for a further 3 minutes.

Serve hot or cold with rice.

tropical salad with palm sugar sauce (MALAYSIA)

Many fruits and crispy vegetables are eaten with savoury spicy dips in Southeast Asia. This recipe from the Four Seasons Resort, Sayan, includes sour tamarind, salty shrimp paste (*blachan*) and chopped hot chillies. It is known locally as *rujak*. For the fruits listed below you can substitute others that have a crisp bite and good colour or texture contrast, such as avocado cubes.

SERVES 4

150g ripe papaya, cut into bite-sized pieces
150g pineapple, cut into small wedges
1 unripe green mango, sliced
1 firm apple, sliced

FOR THE PALM SUGAR SAUCE
½ teaspoon shrimp paste (*blachan*)
100g jaggery (palm sugar) or brown sugar
200ml water
50g dried tamarind fruit, soaked for 30 minutes in a
    little boiling water, stones removed (or 2 teaspoons
    tamarind paste)
4 fresh red or green bird's-eye chillies, finely chopped
Generous pinch of salt

To prepare the sauce, wrap the dried shrimp paste in foil and toast it for about 2 minutes in a dry frying pan. Remove and crumble with the back of a spoon.

Boil the jaggery or brown sugar in the water until dissolved to make a syrup. Lower the heat and stir in the crumbled shrimp paste, tamarind fruit pulp or paste, chillies and salt. When well mixed, turn off the heat and leave to cool, then chill in the fridge.

Just before serving, mix the fruits in a bowl, and stir in the palm sugar sauce.

slow soy-stewed pork with mushrooms (MALAYSIA)

This is a Chinese dish converted by Malaysian Chinese cooks (*Nonya*) to embrace local spicing – it is much hotter and more savoury than the Chinese original.

SERVES 4

20 mixed dried mushrooms, wood-ear, porcini and shiitake
3 tablespoons sunflower or groundnut oil
5 shallots, chopped
10 cloves garlic, chopped
5 green chillies, roughly chopped
1 tablespoon salted black (soy) beans, chopped and ground
1 tablespoon ground coriander seed
500g pork shoulder, cut into 3cm cubes
2 tablespoons dark soy sauce
750ml water
1 tablespoon caster sugar
2 cloves
5cm stick of cinnamon, broken in half
2 star anise, ground
Salt and freshly ground black pepper

Soak the dried mushrooms in hot water for 1 hour. Drain, discard the stalks and squeeze out any excess liquid. Reserve the liquid for other uses, such as stock.

Heat a wok and add the sunflower or groundnut oil. When hot, add the shallots and stir-fry briefly. Add the garlic and the chillies. Turn down the heat and simmer for 5 minutes. Then stir in the black (soy) beans and mix briefly before adding the ground coriander.

Add the pork and stir-fry for about 5 minutes until the meat starts to colour. Now stir in the mushrooms and simmer for 5 minutes more.

Add the dark soy sauce and stir-fry for a few minutes. Then add the water, sugar, cloves, cinnamon stick and star anise. After it boils, lower the heat and simmer gently for about 1½ hours until the pork is tender. The sauce should be thick but should not dry out, so add a little boiling water, if necessary.

Season to taste with salt and freshly ground black pepper before serving with plain boiled rice.

green curry paste (THAILAND)

1 teaspoon coriander seeds
½ teaspoon cumin seeds
3 cloves garlic
6 small shallots (Thai red, preferably)
½ teaspoon shrimp paste (*blachan*)
1 teaspoon white peppercorns
2 stalks of lemongrass, bulb end only, finely chopped
2cm ginger, shredded
Shredded rind of ½ kaffir lime (or lime or lemon)
2 kaffir lime leaves, stems removed, finely chopped
6 leaves of fragrant Thai basil (or other), chopped
6 stems of coriander, including roots, chopped
Pinch of grated nutmeg
Generous pinch of salt

Heat the coriander seeds and cumin seeds in a dry pan until they release their aroma. Grind in a spice or coffee grinder, or use a pestle and mortar.

In the same pan, dry-roast the garlic and shallots for a few minutes until they start to brown. Remove and chop. Using the same pan, dry-roast the shrimp paste for a minute or two, wrapped in a small piece of foil (to reduce burning and the pungent smell).

Pound everything using a pestle and mortar or a blender, adding all the ingredients gradually, until you have a rough purée. If using a blender, you may need to add a little water as the mixture is so dense the blades may not turn.

The paste is ready to use at once. Any left over may be stored in an airtight jar in the fridge and used within 2 weeks. You can stir in some vegetable oil to give the paste a longer shelf life, but try to use within a month for maximum freshness and flavour.

red curry paste (THAILAND)

20 dried red bird's-eye chillies (or 8 fresh red chillies), seeds and membranes removed and chopped
1 teaspoon cumin seeds
2 teaspoons coriander seeds
½ teaspoon shrimp paste (*blachan*) or 1 teaspoon fish sauce (*nam pla*)
4 shallots
2 cloves garlic
12 white peppercorns
2 cloves, crushed
Pinch of grated nutmeg
5cm ginger, grated
1 teaspoon grated fresh galangal (if available) or 1 teaspoon dried galangal, soaked in water, squeezed dry and chopped
1 teaspoon salt
2 stalks of lemongrass, bulb end only, finely chopped
2 kaffir lime leaves, stems removed, finely chopped
Grated rind of ½ kaffir lime (or lime or lemon),
2 stems of coriander, including roots, chopped
5 leaves of fragrant Thai basil (or other), chopped

Soak the dried chillies (if using) in hot water for 30 minutes, squeeze out the excess liquid and chop finely.

Heat the cumin and coriander seeds in a dry pan until they release their aroma. Grind in a spice or coffee grinder, or use a pestle and mortar.

Wrap the shrimp paste (if using) in foil and heat in the same pan for 1–2 minutes to develop the flavour. Remove. In the same pan, heat the shallots and garlic until they begin to brown and caramelise.

Using a pestle and mortar, crush the white peppercorns, cloves, nutmeg, shrimp paste, shallots and garlic. Add the ginger, galangal chillies (dried or fresh) and salt, and continue pounding to a pulp. Then add the lemongrass, kaffir lime leaves, lime or lemon rind, coriander leaves and roots, and basil, and continue to pound. If using a hand blender, you may need to add some water to prevent sticking. If you are using fish sauce instead of the shrimp paste, add it now.

The paste is ready to use. Store any left over in an airtight jar in the fridge and use within 2 weeks. You can stir in some vegetable oil to give the paste a longer shelf life, but try to use within a month for maximum freshness and flavour.

rendang spice paste

(BALI, INDONESIA)

2 tablespoons vegetable oil
4 fresh red or green bird's-eye chillies, finely chopped
1cm galangal, sliced
1cm ginger, sliced
2 shallots, sliced
1 clove garlic, sliced
1 stalk of lemongrass, bulb end only, thinly sliced
2 candlenuts (or 6 macadamia nuts or blanched almonds), chopped
1 teaspoon coriander seeds, dry-roasted and ground
1 teaspoon cumin seeds, dry-roasted and ground
1 kaffir lime leaf, stem removed, shredded
4 large fresh red chillies, sliced thinly on the diagonal
100ml water

Heat the vegetable oil in a small pan and add the bird's-eye chillies, galangal, ginger, shallots, garlic, lemongrass and nuts. Stir-fry over a low heat for 4–5 minutes. Add the coriander and cumin seeds and the kaffir lime leaf. Stir-fry for 1 minute, then remove from the heat.

Pound using a pestle and mortar or process using a hand blender, until smooth. Return to the pan and add the sliced large red chillies. Add the water and bring to the boil.

Cook the spice mixture over a low heat for about 10 minutes, stirring often, until it thickens. Add a little more water if the mixture threatens to stick.

The paste is ready to use. Store any left over in an airtight jar in the fridge and use within 2 weeks. You can stir in some vegetable oil to give the paste a longer shelf life, but try to use within a month for maximum freshness and flavour.

rempeh paste (MALAYSIA)

5 candlenuts (or 100g peanuts), skinned
3 fresh green chillies, chopped
5 dried red or green bird's-eye chillies, crumbled
½ teaspoon shrimp paste (*blachan*)
1 tablespoon ground coriander
2 pandanus leaves or essence (or several drops of real vanilla essence)
150g shallots or spring onions, white parts only, chopped

Combine all the ingredients in the order given in a food processor. Whizz until well combined.

The paste is ready to use. Store any left over in an airtight jar in the fridge and use within 2 weeks. You can stir in some vegetable oil to give the paste a longer shelf life, but try to use within a month for maximum freshness and flavour.

Fresh chillies, lemongrass, ginger – essential ingredients in Southeast Asian cooking – in the central market at Kompong Cham Tom, Cambodia.

After enjoying a multi-course feast in Istanbul, a French food critic was asked if there was anything else he would like. 'Yes,' said the Frenchman, 'I'd like a glass of water without aubergine.'

Turkey, heir to the Ottoman empire's tradition of fine cuisine, is renowned for the intricacy of its numerous stuffed vegetables (*dolmas*). These feature in the many *mezze* of the area, including dips such as taramasalata (smoked cod's roe), hummus (chickpea and garlic dip), tsatsiki (yoghurt and garlic dip) and tabbouleh (cracked wheat salad).

Turkish cooks consider it a labour of love to spend hours gouging out vegetables, such as courgettes, carrots and potatoes, to fill with sweet and savoury stuffings, nuts, raisins, spices and herbs. And Turks are masters of the aubergine, a mild vegetable that absorbs other flavours put to it. The most renowned of such dishes is *imam bayildi*, which means 'fainting imam'. They cannot decide if the holy man swooned at the silky texture and delicious taste or (imams being notably thrifty folk) fainted in shock at the cost of the copious amounts of fine olive oil used in its preparation. There are many versions of this dish but, basically, the aubergine is stuffed with fried chopped onion, green peppers, tomatoes, raisins and nuts, seasoned with parsley, cinnamon and allspice, breadcrumbed, then drizzled with more virgin olive oil and baked. Eaten cold it is a magical dish.

Mezze galore

Dolmades (stuffed vine leaves) are another patiently prepared *mezze*, as are stuffed baby squid, but none is quite so intricate (or so delicious) as rice-stuffed mussels. Each live mussel must

Sackfuls of richly coloured pulses, be and spices for sale i Istanbul, Turkey.

be prised open by hand to be stuffed with a seasoned mixture of part-cooked rice, chopped fried onion, dried fruit and tomato, before being clamped shut to be cooked in a shallow bath of stock. It is a counsel of perfection to use a fine thread to tie each mussel shut, cutting it off after cooking. Perfection is not too much to expect from a Turkish cook.

Back to aubergines. Some Western cookery books, describing how to make *baba ghanoush*, the garlicky, spiced aubergine dip, suggest the easy way to do it is by cooking the aubergine first (grilling, baking, boiling or steaming it), before removing the flesh and whizzing it in a blender with oil and garlic. It may be easier but it's certainly not tastier. To see a Turkish chef make it is a revelation, with each step designed to maximise texture, colour and flavour.

The chef will grill the aubergines until the skin is charred and black (preferably in the glowing ashes of a wood fire). This both cooks the inside flesh until soft and also transmits a smoky, bitter taste, which fuses with the aubergine's own naturally bitter flavour. Taking the stem of the aubergine between finger and thumb (a Turkish chef has fingers as impervious to heat as asbestos) and using a sharp knife, he strips off the flaky, black skin in a few downward movements. When the green flesh is clean, he cuts it away from the stem so that it falls with a plop into a ready-prepared bowl beneath, in which he has crushed a clove of garlic with sea salt, dissolving it in lemon juice.

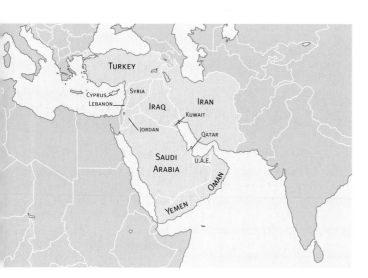

He takes a chef's whisk in one hand and a bottle of golden olive oil in the other and proceeds to whisk the spluttering hot mass to a purée, dribbling in oil to make it smooth and glossy. All the flavours come together: the sweetness of the oil, sour lemon, bitter aubergine, salt and the hot bite of the garlic combining with the aubergine's naturally astringent taste. The Turkish way of making this dish shows an exact appreciation of heightening all the flavours. The Western way is bland and loses them. Even the texture of the Western dip is dull; the uniform purée made in a blender having nothing to commend it compared to the silky threads left by the whisk.

Turkey, of all the countries of the Near East, comes closest to Europe, and its history goes some way to explaining its complexity. Istanbul was a Greek city first, known as Byzantion, and a major spice trading post and part of the great Byzantine empire, until Rome's first Christian emperor, Constantine, colonised it in 306AD, naming it Constantinopolis. So it remained until 1453, the year of the Ottoman invasion.

The Ottomans

The Ottomans, lovers of art and culture – and of fine eating – established the fabulous Topkapi Palace under Sultan Suleyman the Magnificent. The palace, with its elaborately decorated quarters for the harem, was serviced by a staff of over 1000. The cooks would, on occasion, prepare banquets for 10,000 people. Records show that they were masters of grilling (a kebab of

minced lamb skewered on a sword has an especially Turkish ring about it) and making rich rice dishes with spiced meat cooked in stock (*pilaffs*). They also made pies, sweet pastries (such as *bakhlava*), jams and sweets. At the palace, among the many specialist cooks, there were six making different kinds of *halva* (the sesame paste sweet made with sugar and flavourings).

Istanbul, a city of 5000 mosques, continues to take the visitor's breath away, and a visit to the Egyptian spice market tells you all you need to know of the exalted place food has in this society. You will find spices, especially, although they also sell every sort of cheese, yoghurt, baked goods, olives, oils, perfumed rose water, herbs and roots and barks for medicines.

This area, embracing Babylon and Assyria (now Iran, Iraq and Syria), is regarded as the cradle of civilisation (they created the first schools, among many other achievements), and the cooking of these countries resonates through the centuries. They were among the first to know and trade in spice: the Phoenicians who inhabited the coastal area, which is now Lebanon, were intrepid sailors who followed the Mediterranean coastline to the Atlantic (they founded the Spanish port of Cadiz) and further north to Cornwall and northern Europe. Saffron was the most expensive spice they traded, which was then grown in parts of Turkey, Persia and India.

The Persian empire dates back some 2500 years and was responsible for introducing, from China and the east, oranges, lemons, aubergines, rice and sugar. The cooking of Iran marries meat with sour fruits, apricots, grapes and even rhubarb.

For political reasons much of the Near East is out of bounds to the average traveller, although the food is mouth-watering. In many capital cities Lebanese restaurants have established themselves cooking to the highest standards; the Four Seasons Hotel in Cairo, for example, employs Lebanese cooks to raise the level of sophistication.

Nestling in the crossroads between the Mediterranean, Africa and India, the Near East provides a wealth of eating experiences. Market stalls overflow with ripe fruits: pomegranates blush like teenagers, dates plump up with sweetness and melons glow. Vegetables entice with a rainbow of colours, and the cornucopia of nuts is fresh, crisp and crunchy. A babble of voices rises and swells and, from each doorway, the unmistakable, heady perfume of spices and herbs lingers in the air and along the alleyways.

The secret is balance. With so many riches to hand, it can be tempting to include too many in each dish. It is what you leave out that counts. Years of tasting and testing, chopping and mixing have made master chefs of almost every housewife. And weaving together the simple, fresh, perfect ingredients, are the magical spices and herbs.

es and dried
s spill out on to
street at a spice
in Hama, Syria.

lentil and rice soup (YEMEN)

Lentils flavoured with spices are enjoyed throughout the Middle East and in many parts of Asia. Here, cooked to a mush, they are transformed into a warming, nourishing winter soup.

SERVES 4

225g red lentils
2 tablespoons vegetable oil
1 onion, chopped
1 clove garlic, crushed
1 litre chicken stock
Salt and freshly ground black pepper
Juice of ½ lemon
½ teaspoon ground coriander
½ teaspoon ground cumin
1 small dried red chilli, chopped
3 tablespoons long-grain rice or pasta shells (optional)

Rinse the lentils in water, drain and spread out on a plate to check there are no pieces of grit or stones.

Heat the vegetable oil in a saucepan and fry the onion until it starts to brown. Add the garlic and fry for a few more minutes. Stir in the lentils, then add the stock. Season with salt and pepper to taste and add the lemon juice, coriander, cumin and chilli.

Bring to the boil, lower the heat and cook on the lowest heat for about 40 minutes.

For a thicker dish, add the rice or pasta shells and extra boiling water, if the soup seems to be too thick. Continue cooking gently for another 20 minutes or so until the rice or pasta shells are cooked.

stuffed chard leaves (TURKEY)

In the Middle East vine leaves are stuffed with all sorts of different fillings. They also use chard, a robust leaf similar to spinach. You could use cabbage leaves if chard is not available. This tasty, spicy vegetable dish is lovely for lunch.

SERVES 4

450g chard leaves, stalks removed
4 cloves garlic, sliced
150ml olive oil
150ml water
1 teaspoon sugar
Juice of 1 lemon

FOR THE FILLING
225g long-grain rice
3 tomatoes, peeled and chopped
1 large onion, finely chopped
2 tablespoons finely chopped parsley
4 tablespoon chopped fresh mint
Pinch of ground cinnamon
Pinch of ground allspice
Salt and freshly ground black pepper

Blanch the chard leaves in boiling water for 1 minute, then drain.

To make the filling, wash the rice well, then mix it with the tomatoes, onion, parsley and mint. Add the cinnamon and allspice and season with salt and freshly ground black pepper.

Place a teaspoon of filling at the bottom end of each leaf. Fold the leaf up over the mixture, then roll it like a cigar. Repeat until all the filling is used.

Put any remaining or torn leaves in the bottom of a saucepan to act as a lining. Lay the stuffed leaves on top and tuck the slices of garlic between them.

Mix the olive oil, water, sugar and lemon juice together and pour over the leaves. Place a small plate on top of the leaves to stop them falling open.

Cover the saucepan with a lid and cook on the lowest heat for about 2 hours, adding water from time to time to prevent them from sticking. Leave to cool in the saucepan, and serve cold.

stuffed courgettes (TURKEY)

Stuffed vegetables are served almost everywhere in the Near East and each family has their own favourite version. The stuffing can be used for other vegetables too.

SERVES 4

12 courgettes
2 tomatoes, thinly sliced
300ml water
2 tablespoons tomato purée
Juice of 1½ lemons
2 cloves garlic
Salt
1 teaspoon dried mint or 2 teaspoons chopped fresh mint

FOR THE FILLING
75g long-grain rice
225g lean minced lamb (or beef)
1 tomato, peeled and chopped
2 tablespoons finely chopped parsley
½ teaspoon ground cinnamon
½ teaspoon ground allspice
Salt and freshly ground black pepper

Cut the stems off the courgettes and, using an apple corer, make a hole at the stem end of each courgette. Scoop out all the pulp but make sure the other end stays closed.

To make the filling, wash the rice and drain it, then put it in a mixing bowl with the lamb or beef, chopped tomato, parsley, cinnamon and allspice, and season with salt and freshly ground black pepper. Mix well together. Half-fill the courgettes, leaving space for the rice to expand as it cooks.

Layer the bottom of a saucepan with the tomato slices. Place the courgettes side by side in the saucepan in as many layers as you need.

Heat the water in a small saucepan with the tomato purée and most of the lemon juice (reserve a tablespoon for later). Bring to the boil, then cook gently for about 2 minutes.

Pour this sauce over the courgettes, cover the saucepan and cook on the lowest heat for about 1 hour, adding more water if necessary to prevent sticking.

Crush the garlic with ½ teaspoon salt, the mint and reserved lemon juice. Add to the courgettes and continue cooking for a further 5 minutes.

stuffed aubergines (TURKEY)

This dish is called 'fainting imam' (*imam bayildi*) in Turkey because, the story goes the imam swooned when it was first placed before him, enchanted by its aroma and succulence. This dish can also be made as an appetiser for eight people (see variation below).

SERVES 4

4 medium aubergines
Salt and freshly ground black pepper
4 tablespoons olive oil
2 onions, finely sliced
2 green peppers, deseeded and finely sliced
4 cloves garlic, finely chopped
3 medium tomatoes, peeled, deseeded and chopped
50g sultanas
3 tablespoons finely chopped parsley, plus extra to garnish
1 teaspoon ground allspice
¼ pint water
Juice of 1 lemon

Make a deep slit lengthways down each aubergine, stopping short of the top and base, and place in very salty water for 30 minutes.

Heat 2 tablespoons of the olive oil in a heavy frying pan and gently fry the onions, green peppers and garlic for about 15 minutes until soft. Add the tomatoes, sultanas, 2 tablespoons of the chopped parsley and the allspice, and season with salt and freshly ground black pepper. Transfer to a bowl and leave to cool.

Preheat the oven to 160°C/325°F/gas 3.

Drain the aubergines and squeeze out any excess moisture with your hands. Dry on kitchen paper. Add the remaining olive oil to the frying pan and fry the aubergines, turning from time to time very gently to avoid altering their shape, until they are soft. Remove the pan from the heat and stuff each aubergine with as much filling as possible. Press the remaining filling on top.

Transfer the stuffed aubergines to a baking dish, add the water and lemon juice and bake in the preheated oven for 45 minutes. Leave to cool, then chill in the fridge and serve garnished with the remaining parsley.

Variation

Cut the aubergines in half, after soaking (as main recipe). Scoop out the flesh and chop it, then fry it in olive oil before blending with the other ingredients. Fill the aubergine halves, drizzle with oil and bake in a hot oven for 30 minutes.

tabbouleh (LEBANON)

A refreshing summer salad with grains of cracked wheat impregnated with the flavour of fresh parsley. For added richness, you can leave the bulgur or cracked wheat to soak overnight in fresh tomato juice.

SERVES 4

150g bulgur or cracked wheat
Salt
150ml lukewarm water
6 spring onions, finely chopped
3 tablespoons olive oil
1 tablespoon sumac or juice of ½ lemon
½ green pepper, deseeded and chopped
Bunch of parsley, finely chopped
4 or 5 sprigs of mint, leaves finely chopped
450g ripe tomatoes, peeled and chopped
Lemon wedges, to garnish

Place the bulgur or cracked wheat in a bowl and sprinkle with 1 teaspoon salt. Add the water, cover and leave for 15 minutes.

Using a wooden spoon, mix in the spring onions. Then add the olive oil, sumac or lemon juice, green pepper, parsley, mint and tomatoes. Place in the fridge for at least 30 minutes. Test for flavour and add more salt if necessary.

jewelled rice (IRAN AND TURKEY)

This luxurious dish known as 'the king of Persian dishes'
turns simple rice into a bejewelled dish fit for kings. *Pilav* is
prized throughout Turkey, the Middle East and northwest
India, a legacy of the great Mogul cooking traditions. It
comes in various forms and numerous spellings, transliterated
from Arabic and including Turkish *pilav* and central Asian
plov, Albanian *palaw*, Indian *pillau* and Iranian *polow*
(pronounced 'polo').

The essence of the dish is the same: layers of rice
interspersed with spicy ingredients, cooked meat or
occasionally fish or vegetables. Acidic fruit, such as quince,
sour cherries, mulberries, barberries and pomegranate seeds,
add jewel-like colour and variety. Use your imagination to
introduce 'jewels' of your choice to this recipe.

The savoury crust that forms at the bottom of the dish is
much prized, and known in Iran as *tah dig*. The *pilav* method
described here is basically Turkish with added decorative
touches from Iran.

SERVES 4

300g basmati rice
20 strands of saffron (or 2 teaspoons turmeric powder)
1½ tablespoons brown sugar
4 tablespoons boiling water
25g currants
25g dried barberries (from Iranian stores) or sultanas
75g butter, plus extra for frying
75ml sunflower oil
1 small red onion, finely sliced
2 teaspoons salt
450g carrots, diced
½ red pepper, deseeded, peeled and diced
600ml chicken or veal stock (or water)
25g almonds, finely sliced
25g pistachio nuts, finely sliced

FOR THE SPICE MIXTURE
1 teaspoon cumin seeds
1 teaspoon coriander seeds
Cardamom seeds, scraped from 5 pods
10 black peppercorns
Pinch of grated nutmeg

Wash the rice in several changes of water until the water runs clean. This removes the starch and helps prevent the grains from sticking together. Place in a saucepan with three times its volume of water and leave to soak for at least an hour. Drain.

To make the spice mixture, heat the spices for a few minutes in a dry frying pan until they release their aromas. Grind using a spice or coffee grinder or use a pestle and mortar.

Heat the saffron strands (not the turmeric powder, if using) in a dry pan without burning, then, using a pestle and mortar, crush with ½ teaspoon of the sugar. Dissolve in the boiling water. Leave for 30 minutes to develop the full colour and aroma.

Gently fry the currants and barberries or sultanas in a little of the butter for 1 minute. Drain and set aside.

In a large casserole, melt the remaining butter and add the sunflower oil. Fry the onion until it starts to brown.

Add the spice mixture and salt, and cook for a few minutes gently, without burning. Sprinkle with the remaining sugar and, when dissolved, stir in the rice until well coated in the spiced butter and oil. Stir in the currants, barberries, carrots and red pepper, coating them well in the spice mixture.

Pour in the stock or water and bring to the boil. Cook rapidly, uncovered, for 5 minutes until all the stock is absorbed. Cover with

a folded cloth and weighted lid and cook on the lowest heat for a further 10 minutes. Remove from the heat and leave to cook in its own steam for a further 15 minutes.

Lift out a ladleful of the rice and blend with the saffron liquid or stir in the turmeric powder, if using. Reserve. Heat a little extra butter and brown the almonds and pistachio nuts.

To serve, fork over the rest of the rice and transfer it to a large serving dish. Sprinkle the saffron- (or turmeric-) coloured rice on top. Garnish with the nuts.

minced lamb kebab (TURKEY)

This dish, known as a *kofta* kebab, can be a more delicious dish than a *shish* kebab and is more digestible, because it's minced. It is also tastier because of the spicing, often with cinnamon, cumin and coriander together. There is no need to cut away the fat from the lamb for this recipe – it makes the meat juicier and moister. The meat needs to be ground very finely to adhere to the skewers – authentic flat kebab skewers are almost essential.

SERVES 4

750g lamb, off the bone, including fat
1 onion, grated
1 tablespoon chopped parsley
2 teaspoons ground cinnamon
2 teaspoons ground coriander
1 teaspoon ground cumin
¼ teaspoon chilli powder
Salt and freshly ground black pepper
Olive oil, for brushing

Grind the lamb twice through a mincer or use a food mixer with sharp blades (or ask your butcher to do it for you). Mix with the onion, parsley, cinnamon, coriander, cumin, chilli powder, salt and freshly ground black pepper, then work into a thick paste with your hands.

Roll the mixture into balls, and press on to flat skewers, flattening them into sausage shapes.

Brush with olive oil and cook over a barbecue or under a grill for up to 5 minutes on each side, until browned all over but still juicy inside.

Serve with tomatoes and green salad, and hot pitta bread or Arabic flatbread.

prawns in tamarind sauce (IRAN)

Along the coast of East Africa and right up the Persian Gulf cooking has been influenced by trading nations, the Portuguese, Dutch and English swapping goods and cultures with the Arabs and Africans – and above all the Indians, who brought their cargoes of precious spices from Cochin in Kerala, south India. Indian tamarind feeds the Iranian love of sour flavours in this peppery, Indian-style curry.

SERVES 4

100g dried tamarind fruit (or 1 tablespoon tamarind paste)
200ml boiling water (if using dried tamarind)
4 tablespoons olive oil
2 onions, finely sliced
2 cloves garlic, chopped
1–2 heaped teaspoons good curry powder or paste
3 tomatoes, peeled, deseeded and finely chopped
   (or 2 tablespoons tomato purée, diluted with water)
Salt and freshly ground black pepper
6 stems of coriander (or parsley), chopped
8 uncooked large prawns, peeled

If using dried tamarind fruit, soak them in the boiling water for 30 minutes. When cool, rub the fruit through a sieve to remove the stones and coarse pulp. Reserve the liquid.

Heat 2 tablespoons of the olive oil in a frying pan and fry the onions and garlic for about 3 minutes until they start to colour. Stir in the curry powder or paste and cook for a few minutes to cook out the raw flavour.

Add the chopped tomatoes (or diluted tomato purée) together with the tamarind fruit liquid, if using, or the tamarind paste. Heat through, then cover and simmer for 20–30 minutes until the onions are soft. If necessary, cook rapidly without the lid, to drive off excess liquid and leave a rich sauce.

Taste, and season generously with salt and freshly ground black pepper, and add the chopped coriander or parsley.

Heat the remaining oil and fry the peeled prawns on each side until they change colour, which will take a couple of minutes. Transfer them to the thick sauce and heat through gently, until the prawns are well coated.

Serve with plain boiled rice.

mussels stuffed with spicy rice (TURKEY)

This is a classic *mezze* dish that is also sold as street food. It is probably the finest mussel dish in the world, and well worth the trouble it takes to prepare.

SERVES 4 AS AN APPETISER

4 tablespoons olive oil, plus extra for brushing
2 onions, finely chopped
150g long-grain rice
1 tablespoon pine nuts
1 tablespoon currants
1 teaspoon ground allspice
Pinch of ground cinnamon
Pinch of chilli powder
2 teaspoons caster sugar
400ml water
Salt and freshly ground black pepper
24 large mussels
Lemon slices, to garnish

Heat the olive oil in a heavy saucepan, add the onions and cook gently for about 10 minutes until they change colour. Stir in the rice and pine nuts and cook, stirring, over a gentle heat for a few minutes until the rice is well coated.

Stir in the currants, allspice, cinnamon, chilli powder and sugar, and add half the water. Season with salt and freshly ground black pepper. Cover with a lid and continue cooking for about 10 minutes until the water is absorbed. The rice will be nearly cooked. Remove from the heat and leave to cool.

Rinse and scrub the mussels, removing the beards and discarding any which are broken or already open. Using a cloth to hold each mussel, slide a sharp kitchen knife between the two shells to prise them apart – this is not as difficult as it sounds if you press the mussels between thumb and finger to loosen them.

Stuff a teaspoon of the rice filling into each mussel and close them. It's fiddly but you can either tie them shut with fine string or use small elastic bands.

Crowd the stuffed mussels together in a saucepan, cover with the remaining water, bring to the boil, cover with the lid, lower the heat and simmer for 15 minutes. Remove from the pan and leave to cool.

Brush with extra olive oil before serving with the slices of lemon.

lamb and red bean stew (IRAN)

Many of the rich, flavoursome stews of Iran, called *khoresht*, are flavoured with sour fruit, such as apricots, bilberries and unripe grapes, thickened with sweetened fried onions, and balanced with fresh or dried herbs, such as the bitter fenugreek leaf. Dried limes or lime powder, available from specialist stores, will give the dish a true Iranian character. You need to prepare the beans a day in advance.

SERVES 4

150g dried red kidney beans, soaked overnight
3 tablespoons olive oil
2 onions, sliced
4 leeks, white parts only, chopped
500g lamb, off the bone, cut into 6cm pieces
150g parsley, chopped
100g coriander leaves, chopped
25g dill, chopped, or 1 teaspoon aniseed
25g fresh fenugreek leaves (or 2 tablespoons dried)
3 dried limes, pierced with a skewer (or 2 tablespoons dried lime powder)
Juice of 1 lemon
Salt

Boil the kidney beans in unsalted water very fast for 10 minutes, then drain and rinse. Cover with fresh water, bring to the boil and cook for 30 minutes. Drain.

Heat 2 tablespoons of the olive oil in a large frying pan, and fry the onions and leeks for about 5 minutes until soft. Add the lamb and cook for a further 2 or 3 minutes until well browned.

Meanwhile, heat the remaining oil in another pan and fry the parsley, coriander, dill and fenugreek for about 5 minutes over a low heat to release their flavour.

Add the herbs to the lamb mixture. Add the kidney beans and enough water to cover. Cook on the lowest heat, covered, for 1 hour.

Add the dried limes or dried lime powder and cook gently for another 45 minutes until the beans are tender. Add lemon juice and salt to taste.

Serve with plain boiled rice.

saffron chicken (IRAN)

Saffron is grown in Iran, and has a slightly more smoky style than the saffron grown in Spain. It is used in many dishes, giving both aroma and colour.

SERVES 4

2 tablespoons olive oil
1 onion, sliced
Salt and freshly ground black pepper
100ml chicken or vegetable stock
4 chicken breasts
3 teaspoons saffron water (see below)

Heat the olive oil in a frying pan and fry the onion for about 10 minutes until soft. Season with salt and freshly ground black pepper, and add the stock and chicken breasts. Cover and simmer for about 20 minutes until the chicken is tender.

Add the liquid saffron to the chicken liquid. Simmer for 10 minutes with the lid off, turning the breasts to cover evenly.

Serve hot with plain boiled rice.

saffron water (IRAN)

Saffron is so well used in Iran, it is often prepared as an infusion, and put by ready for use.

MAKES ABOUT 60ML

About 40 strands of saffron
½ teaspoon caster sugar
4 tablespoons boiling water

Dry-fry the strands of saffron in a frying pan over low a heat, watching so as not to burn them. Transfer to a mortar, add the sugar and crush with a pestle to a powder. Pour on the boiling water, mix in well, and leave to stand for an hour to infuse and release its full rich golden-orange colour and smoky aroma.

Transfer to a small airtight jar and store in the fridge. It will keep for a fortnight or so. Use to add colour and fragrance to rice dishes, or to white fish or chicken dishes.

carrot and orange conserve
(TURKEY AND THE MIDDLE EAST)

Many fruits in the Middle East are preserved in a dense, sticky, spiced sugar syrup, including apricots, quinces, green walnuts, pistachios, baby aubergines and melon peel, and this is similar; it's more of a sticky dessert than a jam. Eat it by the spoonful with a tisane or bitter coffee in the afternoon with little cakes.

MAKES ABOUT 3 JARS

2 oranges
750ml water
750g caster sugar
2kg carrots, sliced into rounds
1 tablespoon rose water
Cardamom seeds, scraped from 3 pods and ground
25g pistachio nuts
25g blanched almonds, thinly sliced

Peel the oranges thinly and cut the peel into fine matchsticks. Boil in 100ml of the water, then strain. Repeat this operation three times to reduce any bitterness. Drain and set aside. Squeeze the oranges and collect the juice.

Place the sugar in a saucepan, add the remaining water and bring to the boil. Turn down the heat and cook gently for 5 minutes until syrupy.

Add the orange-peel matchsticks and carrots and boil rapidly for about 10 minutes until the carrots are tender and the sauce is beginning to thicken. Add the rose water, orange juice, ground cardamom and nuts and continue boiling until the conserve reaches 110°C/230° F (or test on a saucer that has been chilled in the freezer – the conserve should wrinkle when you push it with your thumb).

Remove from the heat, leave to cool for 10 minutes, pour into sterilised jars and seal.

aubergine conserve with cardamom (LEBANON)

This is an unusual and surprising conserve – utterly delicious in both colour and texture. Associated with savoury dishes, aubergines have the characteristic of being able to soak up flavours like a sponge. This works best with very small aubergines, not much larger than your thumb, which are often available at Greek Cypriot and specialist stores.

MAKES 3 JARS

1kg baby aubergines, topped and tailed
500g preserving sugar
500ml water
2 cardamom pods
5 cloves
5cm stick of cinnamon
1 tablespoon rose water

Make two sharp cuts in each baby aubergine to let the water penetrate and put them in a saucepan. Cover with boiling water and cook gently for 15 minutes. When cool enough to handle, gently squeeze excess moisture out of the aubergines.

Place the sugar in another saucepan, pour on the measured water, bring to the boil and cook until the sugar dissolves.

Put the aubergines in the sugar syrup with the cardamom pods, cloves and cinnamon. Boil gently for about 1 hour, until the syrup thickens. Remove from the heat and add the rose water. Discard the cinnamon stick, cloves and cardamom pods. Leave to cool slightly, then spoon into warm, sterilised jars and seal.

pine nut ice cream (TURKEY)

Mastic, a resinous gum with a coniferous flavour, is used in some Turkish milky desserts, including ice cream, lending both a chewy texture and a keen, clean taste. The Turkish would use *salep*, a ground powder obtained from the root of an orchid, in preference to cornflour, but it is not yet widely available outside the Near East.

SERVES 4

1 tablespoon cornflour, dissolved in 1 tablespoon milk
1 gum mastic crystal, crushed with ¼ teaspoon caster sugar
500ml creamy milk
150g double cream
100g caster sugar
100g pine nuts (or pistachio nuts or almonds), finely chopped

Mix the dissolved cornflour with the crushed gum mastic and set aside. Put the milk, cream and sugar in a saucepan and bring to the boil, stirring continuously until the sugar is dissolved.

Remove from the heat, add the cornflour and mastic paste, and stir well until dissolved. Then return to a gentle heat, and continue to stir for 5–10 minutes until it thickens. Pour into a bowl through a sieve, and leave to cool. Add the chopped nuts and chill the mixture in the fridge.

When completely cold, churn in an ice cream machine or spread the mixture on a tray and put it in the freezer, breaking it up with a fork or whisking every hour or so (for up to 6 hours) to prevent large ice crystals forming. Transfer the ice cream to the fridge about 15 minutes before eating to allow it to soften slightly.

semolina pudding (SYRIA)

In Damascus they serve this cinnamon-flavoured milk and butter pudding for breakfast. If you like a really milky pudding, omit the water and use all milk instead.

SERVES 4

100g butter
150g semolina
350ml milk
250ml water
175g caster sugar
Ground cinnamon, for sprinkling
Chopped almonds (optional)

Put the butter in a large saucepan and melt it over a medium heat. Add the semolina, turn down the heat and cook, stirring, for about 5 minutes.

In a separate saucepan, heat the milk and water, add the sugar, bring to the boil and cook until the sugar is dissolved.

Stir this liquid into the semolina and keep stirring, until it cooks and thickens to a cream. Remove from the heat and leave to stand for 15 minutes.

Sprinkle generously with cinnamon and decorate with chopped almonds, if using.

turkish delight (TURKEY)

Gum mastic is the secret of the mysterious glutinous texture and keen refreshing notes of this jellified Turkish confection, known in Turkey as *lokum*. It will keep well for several weeks.

MAKES ABOUT 24 SQUARES

500g caster sugar
650ml water
75g cornflour
4 teaspoons gum mastic crystals, crushed with the same
    volume of caster sugar
500ml rose water
Few drops of red or pink food colouring
Butter, for greasing
Icing sugar, sifted, for dusting

Make a sugar syrup by boiling the sugar and water in a saucepan, and stir until the sugar is dissolved.

In a cup, dissolve the cornflour with an equal volume of cold water and stir to make a paste. Stir in the gum mastic and sugar mixture, the rose water and colouring.

Gradually add 3–4 spoonfuls of the sugar syrup to the cup, mix well, then return everything to the pan. Bring to the boil again, then lower the heat and stir continuously for about 10 minutes until the mixture thickens. Test the mixture is ready by dropping a teaspoonful into a cup of cold water – it should form a ball.

Line a small baking tray with buttered greaseproof paper and pour the mixture in. Leave to cool.

Turn out on to a tray sprinkled with sifted icing sugar. Cut into 24 squares and toss in a bowl with more sifted icing sugar.

Store in an airtight tin, dusting with more sifted icing sugar.

zhug (YEMEN)

This is a kind of green chilli pesto; a fiery paste to spread on pitta and similar breads.

MAKES 1 JAR

5 mild green chillies
1 fresh hot red chilli
3 cloves garlic, crushed
6 stems of parsley, leaves chopped
6 stems of coriander, leaves chopped
1 tablespoon cumin seeds, lightly roasted in a dry pan
**   and ground**
12 black peppercorns, ground
Cardamom seeds, scraped from 12 pods and ground
Up to 4 tablespoons olive or sunflower oil
Salt

Split the chillies and remove the membrane and seeds. Chop finely.

Put all the ingredients, except the olive or sunflower oil and salt, in a food mixer and blend well. Add the oil, a dribble at a time, to make a thick paste. Season to taste with salt.

Use at once or store in a glass jar in the fridge. It will keep for some weeks if you add a film of oil on top, replacing it each time you use the paste.

za'atar (JORDAN)

This fragrant spice mix has an appetising scent of wild thyme and is a used throughout the Middle East. The sumac gives it acidity and the sesame seeds lend it nutty sweetness. It is often sprinkled on flatbreads before baking, sometimes on a dough covered with halloumi cheese, producing a pizza-like result, known as *mankoushi*.

MAKES 1 JAR

½ tablespoon sesame seeds
2 tablespoons dried thyme, crumbled
1 tablespoon crushed sumac
½ teaspoon salt

In a dry frying pan, heat the sesame seeds until they start to brown and release their nutty perfume. Remove from the heat. Mix with the thyme, sumac and salt, and use at once or store in an airtight jar.

sweet advieh (IRAN)

This *advieh* mix is sweet and fragrant and, like an Indian *garam masala*, is sprinkled over food at the last moment. Rose petals are available from Middle Eastern stores.

MAKES 1 JAR

30 strands of saffron
100g unrefined brown sugar
Pinch of dried rose petals, crushed
100g pistachio nuts, shelled and ground
50g ground coriander
25g cinnamon, from a stick, freshly ground
10 cardamom pods, shelled and ground

To develop the saffron colour and flavour, dry-fry the saffron strands in a frying pan on a low heat, being careful not to burn them. Crush in a mortar with a ¼ teaspoon of the sugar, using a pestle. Then combine all the ingredients, including the remaining sugar, and store in an airtight jar, preferably in the fridge.

savoury advieh (IRAN)

This spice mixture has roots in Persian medicine. Traditionally it is prepared in the home, but commercial mixes are sold, some fragrant and perfumed, others savoury and strong. This is a strong blend, ideal for using in a mutton stew, for example, to moderate the fatty flavour.

MAKES 2 JARS

20 black peppercorns, crushed
50g cumin seeds, ground
50g coriander seeds, ground
50g turmeric powder
25g cinnamon, from a stick, freshly ground
10 cardamom pods, shelled and ground
3 cloves, ground

Combine all the ingredients and either use at once or store in airtight jars.

mixed pickles (IRAN AND TURKEY)

Pickled vegetables are found in every country in the Middle East; pickling is a convenient method of preserving foods that would otherwise be wasted in the glut of harvest time.

Many kinds of vinegar are used – not only grape and wine vinegar, but cider vinegar and date vinegar – usually in a pickling mixture of half-vinegar and half-water. Water-retaining vegetables are often salted to extract excess liquid, and others soaked in brine. Sometimes all the ingredients are cooked in a vinegar mixture for 5 minutes and allowed to cool before being bottled.

MAKES ABOUT 2 LITRES

1 large cauliflower, cut into florets and sliced into
    2 or 3 pieces
3 red or green peppers, cored and cut into 2.5cm pieces
250g carrots, cut into 2.5cm pieces
250g celery, tough membranes removed with a potato peeler,
    cut into 2.5cm lengths
4 small cucumbers, sliced in 4 lengthways and halved
100g green beans, topped and tailed and cut into 3 pieces
4 cloves garlic, halved
3 sprigs of dill
750ml water
300ml white wine vinegar or cider vinegar
50g salt
2 tablespoons coriander seeds
2 tablespoons nigella seeds
1 teaspoon dried mint

Arrange the vegetables and garlic in sterilised preserving jars, interleaving with sprigs of dill.

In a saucepan, boil the water, vinegar and salt with the coriander and nigella seeds and dried mint. Turn down the heat and simmer for 5 minutes. Pour over the vegetables in the jars. Seal firmly and keep in a cool place for 6 weeks to mature.

The cuisines of Africa are immensely diverse, unsurprisingly so since it embraces 53 countries in all. The cooking is largely shaped by geographical perspectives: it is a land facing three oceans – looking west across the Atlantic to the Americas; east across the Indian Ocean to the Far East; and north to the Mediterranean and old Europe and the Near East. But modern Africa, as history has unfolded, has developed its dramatically different cultures, which reflect history rather than geography and terrain.

Its location in the world has contributed to Africa being at the hub of the world spice trade for many thousands of years, as amply recorded in the Bible. Cairo was a marketplace for the caravans which brought spices from the east across India and Persia, serving the Mediterranean merchants, who took them first to Greece and then Rome, later dealing through the great spice ports of Venice and Genoa.

North Africa is unique. Having been locked into the world of ancient Greece and Rome, it was overrun in the eighth century AD and became part of the new world of Islam, an Arab empire stretching across Tunisia, Algeria and Morocco, and into Spain.

The invaders introduced the fine cooking skills which originated in Persia. The cooking of the Mahgreb, as it's known, is subtle, spicy and sophisticated, marked by the use of sugar, honey, dates, almonds, fresh herbs like mint, dried fruit and warming spices. Some of its dishes are world classics, such as meat, chicken or vegetable couscous stews with their numbingly hot *harissa* sauces, and *tagines*, which are slow-simmered casseroles of tender meat with rich spices. Equally delicious are the savoury pastries such as fried *borek* (which might have a raw egg in it), or *b'stilla*, pancake layers with spiced pigeon and sprinkled with icing sugar. A roll-call of piquant salads of mixed cooked and uncooked vegetables, plus tomatoes, olives, herbs, oil and lemon juice, complement the heartier dishes. Their spice mixtures are as complex as any in the world, such as *chermoula*, rubbed into fish before grilling, or *ras-el-hanout*, which may contain dozens of different spices.

The coastal regions

Despite its vast size and geographical spread, Africa as a whole has never been an important source of world spices. Much of Africa is covered by barren landmasses of desert that support no foodstuffs, or fairly impenetrable, dense equatorial rainforest which separate the main segments of the continent. The exception is the west coast. Here European seafarers discovered perfumed, peppery 'grains of paradise' (*melegueta* pepper; also called 'Guinea grains') which were used as a cheap substitute for expensive pepper in Rome and later to flavour drinks such as hippocras in medieval Britain. The use of grains of paradise lingers on in Scandinavia as a flavouring for the spirit Aquavit.

Off the east coast, Zanzibar (now part of Tanzania) became one of the world's great spice islands, when it was part of the Oman sultanate, which extended along the east coast of Africa. Zanzibar became a base for expeditions to the Congo to plunder ivory and slaves for trade. The Oman rulers also employed slaves

An African boy makin bread the traditional way, Sinai, Egypt.

in the swathes of clove plantations they planted on the island, in order to wrestle the profitable clove monopoly from the Dutch East Indies. It is still a major producer of cloves, and all the tropical spices grow here including nutmeg, ginger and cardamom, contributing to an exotic island cuisine.

The one spice every African country has in common is the chilli pepper, inexorably linked to the slave trade. Along its coast, Ghana has some 20 forts, which held the slaves as they were captured. Over three million souls were delivered to the Americas (to Brazil, the Caribbean and Louisiana to service the sugar plantations). They took from Africa the cheap and nourishing staples of their homeland, which flourish in a similar climate: the sweet potato, yam, cassava, okra and beans. But then, through the so-called Columbian Exchange (of foodstuffs), turkey, chocolate, vanilla, tomatoes, maize and chillies were introduced. Soon, in Africa, searingly hot injections of chilli began to lift the modest diet of soupy stews of skinny chicken, fish and vegetables, and to season the heavy helpings of cornmeal dumplings or *fou fou* (fermented cassava porridge) and *foutou* (mashed plantain).

South Africa

South Africa, by contrast, is a gastronomic curiosity, an anthology of food cultures. The simple native fare of grain, such as *sorghum*, small birds and even insects, was soon overlaid by a succession of colonisers including the English, Dutch and French, with their solid, but hardly exotic, cooking.

Then, in the nineteenth century, needing cheap labour, the government hired workers from Sri Lanka, India and Malaysia. They were known rudely as Cape Coloured at first, then as Cape Malays and more recently as Cape Muslims. It is they who introduced the brightest colours into a truly rainbow cuisine, which includes uniquely South African dishes, such as *bobotie* (a sweet meat loaf with an egg topping) and *sosaties* (spicy kebabs), curried vegetables and hot *sambal* relishes and chutneys.

Cape Malays monopolise Cape Town's street food, running all the little stalls. Order your food and, behind a curtain, someone rustles up a piping-hot paratha with a potato or vegetable stuffing, keenly spiced. They are fantastic.

Durban, on the east of South Africa, is Little India – with wonderful Indian food. And India is also an influence farther to the north, where it fuses with Arabic cuisine – the crossroads being the island of Zanzibar, which also bears the stamp of British and Portuguese colonists. In fact, the last of the Oman Arabs were summarily driven out as recently as the early 1960s. In this corner of Africa there are the ancient cuisines of the Sudan and Ethiopia

– home to the murderously hot *berberi* chilli sauce, which will burn your tongue and probably make you cry.

Lastly, is Egypt, a feast of history, with the Pharaohs, the great pyramids, the Sphinx, the temples of Luxor and the Valley of the Kings. Cairo houses the Museum of Antiquities with Tutankhamun's golden tomb, surely one of the richest archaeological treats in the world. Here in Cairo, on a cruise boat on the Nile, you can join Egyptian families taking Sunday lunch and, close to the cradle of civilisation, you can eat a traditional soupy bean dish, *foules mesdames*, while contemplating the thought that you are part of an unbroken 5000-year-old tradition.

A Spice seller, Khan El Khalili Bazaar in Cairo.

six salads from morocco

Morocco has a vast repertoire of salads, using both raw and cooked ingredients (and sometimes a combination) and usually containing tasty fresh herbs and spices. Quite often up to a dozen such salads will be served as appetisers in small bowls at the beginning of a meal.

lemon salad

This makes a piquant, refreshing appetiser. Olives are salty, so the salad may not need added salt; taste to check.

SERVES 4–6

4 lemons
12 black olives, stoned
12 green olives, stoned
½ wine glass extra virgin olive oil
1 teaspoon ground cumin
½ teaspoon chilli powder
1 tablespoon finely chopped parsley, to garnish

Peel the lemons and chop the flesh. Mix with the rest of the ingredients.

Garnish with the chopped parsley to serve.

spicy carrot salad

So simple, yet so delicious and unexpected.

SERVES 4

500g carrots, scraped
2 tablespoons olive oil
Juice of 1 lemon
½ teaspoon chilli powder or cayenne pepper
1 teaspoon ground cinnamon
1 teaspoon sugar
1 clove garlic, chopped and crushed with 1 teaspoon salt
½ teaspoon ground ginger
Chopped parsley, to garnish

Cover the whole carrots with water, bring to the boil and cook for about 20 minutes until soft. Leave them in the cooking liquid for 1 hour. Strain and, when cool enough to handle, cut the carrots into slices or chunks – any size you like.

Return to the pan, cover with the rest of the ingredients except the parsley, and heat for a few minutes to blend the flavours. Leave to cool.

Serve garnished with the chopped parsley.

orange and olive salad

Salty, sweet, sour and bitter, this is a perfectly balanced and refreshing salad. It is common in Morocco, which is home to the wonderful rich olives and sweet oranges often used.

SERVES 4–6

6–8 oranges
At least 20 purple or violet olives (such as Greek kalamata), stoned
Juice of ½ lemon
Generous pinch of ground cumin
Pinch of chilli powder
1 teaspoon caster sugar
Pinch of salt

Cut the peel and pith from the oranges. Cut away the segments using a serrated knife, reserving the juice. Leave the segments whole or chop them smaller, as preferred.

In a bowl, mix the olives with the orange segments and juice, and add the lemon juice, cumin, chilli powder, sugar and salt.

Serve chilled.

beetroot salad

This is a colourful and tasty salad that can be a meal in itself.

SERVES 4–6

1kg uncooked beetroot
500g ripe tomatoes, peeled, deseeded and diced
1 red onion (or ½ Spanish onion), finely chopped
1 tablespoon chopped flat-leaf parsley
Juice of 1 lemon
4 tablespoons extra virgin olive oil
½ teaspoon ground cumin
Salt and freshly ground black pepper
1 teaspoon sugar
Pinch of chilli powder (optional)
500g new potatoes, boiled, peeled and sliced or cubed
Black olives, stoned, to garnish

Wash, but do not peel the beetroot. Cook them in boiling water until tender; this will take about 30 minutes depending on size. Remove the skins and dice.

In a bowl, mix together all the ingredients, apart from the potatoes and olives.

Arrange the potatoes around the edge of a large serving dish, and heap the salad into the middle. Garnish with black olives.

carrot and orange salad

You can add orange flower water for extra aroma.

SERVES 4–6

2 oranges
500g carrots, grated
Juice of ½ lemon
1 teaspoon ground cinnamon
1 tablespoon caster sugar

Cut the peel and pith from the oranges. Cut away the segments using a serrated knife, reserving the juice. Toss with the carrots, orange and lemon juice, cinnamon and sugar.

Chill before serving.

Cinnamon, shown here in its various forms, is a great ingredient for spicing up salads.

grilled green pepper and tomato salad

One of the most common Moroccan salads, this is made with cooked vegetables served cold. There are variations in which the peppers and tomatoes may be grilled, roasted or even fried.

SERVES 4–6

4 green peppers
8 large ripe tomatoes
4 spring onions, chopped
2 tablespoons olive oil
Juice of 1 lemon
Generous pinch of ground cumin
Salt and freshly ground black pepper
1 tablespoon chopped flat-leaf parsley
Black olives, to garnish

Preheat the oven to 200°C/400°F/gas 6. Roast the peppers and tomatoes for 30 minutes or until tender. Skin the tomatoes and remove the seeds. To loosen the skins on the peppers, put them in a plastic bag and tie it. After 5 minutes, you can remove the skins easily with a knife. (Alternatively, cook the peppers over a gas flame, turning until the skins are blackened, then remove the skins.) Cut the peppers and tomatoes into small cubes.

Mix the peppers, tomatoes and spring onions with the olive oil, lemon juice and cumin and season with salt and freshly ground black pepper. Sprinkle with the parsley and garnish with olives.

crispy fried puffed patties
(SOUTH AFRICA)

These delicious, spicy, deep-fried balls, known as *dhaltjies*, are ideal served as an appetiser. They are an inheritance of the Indians who settled in South Africa.

MAKES ABOUT 24 PATTIES

175g gram (chickpea) flour, sifted
75g plain flour
150ml water
1 teaspoon baking powder
½ teaspoon cayenne pepper
1 teaspoon turmeric powder
1cm ginger, grated
1 teaspoon ground cumin
1 teaspoon *garam masala* (see page 31)
2 eggs, beaten
3 stems of coriander, chopped
Large pinch of salt
1 litre corn oil, for deep-frying

Whisk the gram flour with the plain flour and water and add the baking powder, cayenne pepper, turmeric, ginger, cumin, *garam masala* and eggs. Stir in the chopped coriander and salt.

In a deep fryer, heat the corn oil to 180°C/356°F (check with a thermometer), or until it starts to give off faint blue smoke, and deep-fry spoonfuls of the batter, about six at a time. Remove with a slotted spoon when they turn golden and float to the top.

Drain on kitchen paper and serve while still hot.

sosatie lamb kebabs

(SOUTH AFRICA)

Sosatie is the traditional kebab of South Africa, originating in Malaysia. Apricot jam is the basis of the sweet sauce poured over the lamb and apricot kebabs. Prepare the lamb a day in advance.

SERVES 4

1kg leg of lamb, off the bone
2 onions, finely sliced
2 cloves garlic, chopped
2cm ginger, grated
2 bay leaves, crumbled
4 cloves
1 tablespoon *garam masala* (see page 31)
1 teaspoon turmeric powder
2 tablespoons dark soft brown sugar
300ml malt vinegar
Large pinch of salt
16 dried apricot halves, soaked in hot water for 1 hour
1 teaspoon cornflour
4 tablespoons water
2 tablespoons apricot jam

Cut the lamb into 2.5cm chunks and place in a bowl with the onions, garlic, ginger, bay leaves, cloves, *garam masala* and turmeric.

Dissolve the sugar in the vinegar, add the salt, and stir into the meat mixture. Cover with clingfilm and leave in the fridge overnight.

Skewer the lamb pieces and dried apricots alternately on to eight wooden skewers (soaked previously in water so they don't scorch) and cook under a hot grill for 10–15 minutes until sizzling, turning over to cook both sides.

Dissolve the cornflour in 2 tablespoons of the water. Melt the apricot jam in a pan with the remaining 2 tablespoons water and stir in the dissolved cornflour. Mix well and heat gently, stirring, until thickened, then pour over the kebabs.

Serve with plain boiled rice.

sweet potato stew with peanuts (GHANA)

Ghana has a wealth of produce and, although some of the basics are very starchy, the flavours are always intense and usually quite hot.

SERVES 4–6

3 tablespoons sunflower or groundnut oil
2 onions, finely sliced
2 cloves garlic, chopped
5cm ginger, grated
750g sweet potatoes, cut into cubes
½ white cabbage, cut into 2.5cm pieces
1–2 teaspoons chilli powder, to taste
1 tablespoon paprika, plus extra to garnish
1 teaspoon salt
4 tomatoes, peeled, deseeded and chopped
1 tablespoon tomato purée
350ml chicken (or other) stock
200g peanuts (or ½ jar of crunchy peanut butter)
Cubed pineapple, to garnish
Sliced bananas, to garnish
Coriander leaves, to garnish

Heat the sunflower or groundnut oil, and gently fry the onion for 10–15 minutes until golden. Stir in the garlic and ginger, and cook for another minute.

Add the sweet potatoes, cabbage, chilli powder, paprika and salt, and stir-fry for a minute to blend the flavours. Add the tomatoes, tomato purée and chicken or other stock. Simmer for about 20 minutes until the sweet potatoes are soft.

In a frying pan, roast the peanuts (if using) without oil, until the skins loosen. While they are still hot, use a cloth to rub off the skins. Reduce the nuts to coarse grains by processing in a blender (or use a pestle and mortar). Stir the ground peanuts (or peanut butter, if using) into the stew and simmer for a further 2 or 3 minutes. Taste, and add more salt, if necessary. Garnish with the pineapple and bananas and sprinkle over some coriander and paprika.

chicken tagine (MOROCCO)

This dish combining chicken with the sour smoothness of preserved lemons, olives and a cornucopia of spices is a delicious North African classic. For the best flavour, marinate the chicken the day before.

SERVES 4

1 chicken, quartered
2 onions, chopped
2 tablespoons chopped flat-leaf parsley
2 tablespoons chopped coriander leaves
1 stick of cinnamon
2 preserved lemons, cut into quarters or strips
250g green or purple olives, rinsed and stoned
Juice of ½ lemon

FOR THE MARINADE
2 cloves garlic, finely chopped
Pinch of saffron strands
½ teaspoon ground ginger
½ teaspoon ground cumin
½ teaspoon paprika
½ teaspoon salt
¼ teaspoon freshly ground white or black pepper
4 tablespoons sunflower or olive oil

Prepare the marinade by combining in a bowl the garlic, saffron, ginger, cumin, paprika, salt, freshly ground white or black pepper and the sunflower or olive oil. Spread over the chicken and leave, covered, in the fridge for several hours or overnight.

Place the chicken and the marinade in a large saucepan. Add the onions, parsley, coriander and cinnamon stick and half-cover with water. Bring to the boil, cover and simmer for about 30 minutes, frequently turning the chicken pieces in the liquid. Add more water if it starts to reduce. Cook for a further 20 minutes, partly covered, until the chicken is tender and almost falls from the bone.

Add the preserved lemons and the olives and continue cooking for a further 10 minutes to combine the flavours.

Transfer the chicken pieces, lemon and olives to a serving dish and cover to keep warm.

Discard the cinnamon stick and reduce the sauce to about 250ml by rapid boiling, uncovered, for several minutes. Add the lemon juice and season to taste with more salt and freshly ground white or black pepper.

Pour the sauce over the chicken and serve immediately.

bredie lamb stew (SOUTH AFRICA)

This is the South African version of a North African *tagine* (see left) – a slow-simmered stew of meat and vegetables. Lamb is usually the meat of choice but you can use beef. Cook the first stage one day, leave to cool, and continue cooking the next day. This version contains pumpkin or butternut squash, but you can use cabbage, cauliflower, peas, beans, spinach, lentils or tomatoes instead for variety, as they do in South Africa.

SERVES 4

3 tablespoons sunflower or groundnut oil
3 onions, sliced
1kg leg of lamb, off the bone, cut into 3cm pieces
2 dried chillies, chopped
Large pinch of salt
1 tablespoon brown sugar
100ml water
1kg pumpkin or butternut squash, cut into 2.5cm squares
2.5cm ginger, grated
1 tablespoon *garam masala* (see page 31)

In a large pan, heat the sunflower or groundnut oil and cook the onions for about 10 minutes over a medium heat until soft. Raise the heat, add the lamb, and cook for about 15 minutes until it changes colour.

Add the chillies, salt and brown sugar, stirring to mix all the flavours. Add the water, bring to the boil, cover with a lid and simmer for about 1 hour, adding a little boiling water as the liquid evaporates.

When the meat is tender, remove from the heat. Leave to cool and rest overnight in the fridge.

Add the pumpkin or butternut squash and ginger to the precooked lamb mixture, simmer for 1 hour until the pumpkin or squash is tender, adding a little boiling water if it starts to dry out. Finish by stirring in the *garam masala*.

fattoush mixed salad (EGYPT)

In ancient Egypt the Pharaohs became rich beyond imagining, controlling the world's spice trade, their country being a half-way house for the caravans arriving from the East and the maritime traders of the Mediterranean. Although Egypt is geographically part of North Africa, its Arab food culture looks towards near neighbour Lebanon – the source of the best chefs in modern Cairo. Expect to find masses of mint, not only in tea, but also as a flavouring in fresh salads.

SERVES 4

1 large cucumber, peeled and diced
4 tomatoes, cut into large cubes
8 leaves of crisp lettuce, torn into pieces
1 green pepper, deseeded and diced
Juice of 1 lemon
4 tablespoons extra virgin olive oil

FOR THE GARNISH
2 stems of mint, leaves roughly chopped
2 stems of parsley, leaves roughly chopped
2 slices of white bread, fried crisp in olive oil and cut into squares
1 teaspoon ground sumac

Mix the cucumber, tomatoes, lettuce, green pepper, lemon juice and olive oil together in a large bowl and garnish with the mint, parsley, fried bread and sumac.

seven-vegetable couscous

(MOROCCO)

North African food is some of the spiciest you can eat, usually due to the addition of a fiery, hot chilli paste called *harissa*. This Moroccan dish is a richly flavoured stew with many herbs and spices, but fortunately the *harissa* sauce is served on the side, so you can modify the degree of heat to suit yourself. This version, based on a recipe from Fez, includes the contrasting shades of red peppers, red tomatoes, yellow squash and orange carrots, but you can exchange these for vegetables of your choice. For added flavour and convenience, you can cook the first part the night before.

SERVES 4

25g butter
1 tablespoon olive oil
1 chicken, cut into 8 pieces
4 large onions, quartered
8 carrots, quartered
2 green chillies, pierced, not sliced
Bunch of coriander, chopped
1 Stick of cinnamon (or 2 pieces of cassia bark)
½ teaspoon turmeric powder
Salt and freshly ground pepper
Pinch of saffron strands
1.5 litres water (or chicken stock)
250g chickpeas, cooked (or canned, drained)
2 turnips, quartered
1 red pepper, cored and cut into 8 pieces
4 tomatoes, peeled, deseeded and quartered
3 courgettes, cut into 3cm pieces
200g Hubbard squash (or pumpkin), cut into 3cm pieces
425g couscous, cooked according to packet instructions, to serve

FOR THE *HARISSA* SAUCE
1 teaspoon *harissa* paste (see page 98)
Juice of ½ lemon
1 tablespoon olive oil
Coriander or parsley leaves, chopped, to garnish

In a heavy iron pan, melt the butter with the olive oil, and cook the chicken pieces for about 5 minutes until browned.

Add half of the onions and carrots, and the chillies, coriander, cinnamon or cassia bark and turmeric and season well with salt and freshly ground black pepper. Place the saffron in a small cup, add a little boiling water and press with the back of a spoon to release the flavours, then add to the pan. Cover and cook over a low heat for ten minutes.

Add the measured water (or chicken stock), bring to the boil, then lower the heat and simmer for 1 hour. (This can be done the night before you want to serve the dish.)

Skim off the fat and reheat. Add the chickpeas and remaining vegetables, according to the time they take to cook, with the rest of the onions and carrots first and the courgettes and squash or pumpkin last.

Meanwhile, make the *harissa* sauce. Place the *harissa* paste, lemon juice and olive oil in a small pan. Add 4–6 tablespoons of the liquid from the casserole. Heat through, then transfer to a bowl and sprinkle with coriander or parsley leaves to serve.

Pour some of the stew on to a mound of the cooked couscous, and the remainder into a casserole dish. Offer the *harissa* sauce separately.

bokoboko beef porridge

(ZANZIBAR)

This is a very tasty, useful recipe from Zanzibar, where African and Indian cooking cultures meet. It is a nourishing savoury porridge eaten at home and in restaurants. You can buy whole wheat from healthfood shops and large supermarkets.

SERVES 4–6

1kg whole wheat
100g *ghee* (see page 14) or clarified butter
1kg minced beef
Cardamom seeds, scraped from 5 pods and ground
2 x 5cm sticks of cinnamon, broken

Grind the wheat in a spice or coffee grinder, cover with boiling water and leave for 30 minutes.

Heat the ghee or clarified butter and cook the beef for about 5 minutes until it changes colour. Stir in the cardamom seeds and cinnamon sticks and cook for a few minutes more.

Transfer to a large saucepan and stir in the wheat and water. Cook on top of the stove on a low heat for 2–3 hours, adding boiling water if necessary to prevent it from drying out.

falafal (EGYPT)

These spicy deep-fried patties, which have also become the street food of Israel, originate in Egypt. They are traditionally stuffed into pitta bread with a chopped salad and tahina (sesame seed paste). In Egypt they are made with large broad beans, but you can use chickpeas as they do in Israel, Lebanon, Syria and Jordan.

SERVES 4

450g dried broad beans (or chickpeas), soaked for 24 hours
1 onion, grated
6 spring onions, finely chopped
2 cloves garlic, crushed
2 teaspoons ground cumin
2 teaspoons ground coriander
Bunch of coriander leaves or parsley, chopped
Pinch of cayenne or chilli powder
Salt and freshly ground black pepper
Groundnut oil, for frying
Sesame seeds, to garnish (optional)

Drain the soaked beans (or chickpeas), which should by now be very tender. Put them in a blender (or use a pestle and mortar) and grind to a paste.

Add the onions, spring onions, garlic, cumin, ground coriander, chopped coriander or parsley, cayenne or chilli powder, salt and black pepper, mixing them well. Leave to rest for at least 30 minutes.

Shape spoonfuls of the mixture into small balls or patties, about 2.5cm across. Heat the groundnut oil to very hot and fry the balls in batches, a few at a time.

Drain on kitchen paper and roll in sesame seeds to garnish, if desired. Serve with a side salad and pitta bread.

bobotie meat loaf (SOUTH AFRICA)

This is the national meat loaf of South Africa, consisting of minced beef enriched with sweet onions, curry spices and apricot jam, baked with an egg custard on top – quite delicious.

SERVES 8

1 tablespoon sunflower or groundnut oil
2 onions, finely sliced
1 clove garlic, chopped
1kg minced beef
2 tablespoons curry powder
1 teaspoon *garam masala* (see page 31)
3 slices of dry bread, broken into crumbs
25ml malt vinegar
2 eggs, beaten
15g raisins
3 tablespoons apricot jam
Large pinch of salt
Butter, for greasing

FOR THE TOPPING
2 eggs
300ml milk
20 blanched almonds, sliced

Preheat the oven to 180°C/350°F/gas 4.

Heat the sunflower or groundnut oil in a frying pan and stir-fry the onions and garlic for about 3 minutes or until the onion starts to soften. Add the minced beef. Cook for about 3 minutes until it changes colour. Stir in the curry powder and *garam masala*.

Add the breadcrumbs, vinegar, beaten eggs, raisins, apricot jam and salt. Simmer for 30 minutes.

Lightly grease a loaf tin about 8cm in depth, spoon in the mixture and bake in the preheated oven for 30 minutes.

To make the topping, beat the eggs and milk together, and pour over the top of the meat loaf, dotting with the almonds. Bake for another 20 minutes until the top puffs up and turns golden.

Serve in slices, while still hot.

ful mesdames (EGYPT)

This soupy dish of dried broad beans was originally cooked overnight and served at breakfast to farm workers. Just a small portion makes a filling start to the day, or you can have it as a lunchtime dish. Prepare the beans a day in advance.

SERVES 4

450g dried broad beans, soaked overnight
Salt and freshly ground black pepper
Olive oil
2 lemons, quartered (or preserved lemons)
1 teaspoon cumin seeds, dry-roasted and ground
2 teaspoons coriander seeds, dry-roasted and ground
Finely chopped parsley
2 cloves garlic, chopped
Bunch of spring onions, chopped

Drain the soaked beans and cover with fresh water in a saucepan. Bring to the boil, cover with a lid, and cook gently for at least 2 hours until tender. Season to taste.

Spoon the beans into bowls while still hot. Set out the other ingredients on little dishes and leave everyone to help themselves. Serve with pitta bread.

salt fish curry (TANZANIA)

All round the world, fish is salted to preserve it. The Portuguese spice traders (Portugal is the home of the famous salted fish dish *bacalhau*) brought the tradition to Tanzania.

SERVES 4

500g salt cod, soaked for 3 hours in water to remove salt
2 tablespoons sunflower or groundnut oil
1 onion, finely sliced
2 cloves garlic, chopped
2 potatoes, diced
1 green pepper, deseeded and chopped
1 tomato, peeled, deseeded and chopped
1 tablespoon ground coriander
2 teaspoons ground cardamom seeds
1 teaspoon turmeric powder
½ teaspoon chilli powder

Drain the salt cod, place it in a saucepan, cover with fresh water and simmer for 15 minutes. Drain. Remove the skin and bones, and break up the fish.

Heat the sunflower or groundnut oil and then add all the ingredients except the fish. Cook for 10 minutes.

Finally, add the cooked salt cod and simmer for a further 5 minutes until the potatoes are cooked.

Serve with plain boiled rice.

spicy lamb stew (ETHIOPIA)

The thick, spicy stews of this ancient land are known as *wots* – this one is called *yebeg wot*. The essential seasoning is the fiery chilli mixture known as *berberi* (pronounced 'bari-bari'). Sometimes hard-boiled eggs are added at the end of the cooking to make the stew go further.

SERVES 4–6

2 tablespoons groundnut or sunflower oil
2 onions, finely chopped
50ml *berberi* red pepper paste (see page 96)
50ml clarified spiced butter (see page 99)
2.5cm ginger, grated
1 clove garlic, chopped
6 large tomatoes, peeled and chopped
Salt and freshly ground black pepper
1kg leg of lamb, off the bone, cut into 3cm pieces

In a heavy cooking pot, heat the groundnut or sunflower oil and fry the onions until soft. Add the red pepper paste and continue cooking for a few minutes. Then add the clarified spiced butter and cook for a further 10 minutes.

Stir in the ginger and garlic and cook gently for another 5 minutes. Add the tomatoes, season to taste with salt and freshly ground black pepper, and cook for 15 minutes.

Put the lamb into the mixture and simmer gently for 1 hour, stirring occasionally, until the meat is tender, adding a little water, if necessary. Serve with plain boiled rice.

A woman sells palm oil for cooking and other goods on the Congo River.

masala fish steaks cape malay
(SOUTH AFRICA)

The Muslim community in South Africa has adapted the spices
of India, Sri Lanka and Southeast Asia to partner local fish
with firm texture: you could use cod, haddock, salmon, mullet
or monkfish.

SERVES 4

4 fish steaks, about 250g each, skinned
Sunflower or groundnut oil, for frying

FOR THE MASALA PASTE
2 tablespoons sunflower or groundnut oil
2 teaspoons *garam masala* (see page 31)
2.5cm ginger, grated
1 green chilli, deseeded and finely chopped
1 clove garlic, crushed
Juice of 1 lime or lemon
Generous pinch of salt

Make the masala paste by mixing all the ingredients in a blender or
crushing with a pestle and mortar.

Use a knife to spread the paste on both sides of the fish and
leave to marinate for ½–1 hour.

Preheat the oven to 200°C/400°F/gas 6.

Heat a little sunflower or groundnut oil in a heavy-based ovenproof frying pan and fry the marinated fish for 1 minute on each
side. Transfer the frying pan to the oven and bake for 8 minutes.

Use oven gloves to remove the frying pan from the oven and
keep the handle covered with a cloth to avoid burning yourself.

Serve with plain boiled rice and Onion Sambal (see page 98).

milk tart (SOUTH AFRICA)

Milk tart is the classic dessert of South Africa, and is
sweetened with cinnamon and sharpened with dried
tangerine peel. You can make this easily by placing some finely
chopped tangerine peel in a very low oven for a few hours
until crisp. Any left over can be stored in an airtight jar.

SERVES 6–8

Butter, for greasing
350g homemade or frozen shortcrust pastry, thawed if frozen
Flour for dusting
4 eggs, beaten
4 tablespoons caster sugar
1 teaspoon vanilla essence
2 tablespoons plain flour
600ml milk
2 teaspoon ground cinnamon
1 tablespoon dried tangerine peel, crushed

Preheat the oven to 220°/425°F/gas 7.

Butter a tart tin 23cm in diameter and 3cm deep. Roll out the
pastry on a floured surface and use to line the tin. Cover the pastry
with foil and a layer of dried beans to keep its shape during baking.
Bake for 15 minutes. Remove from the oven and turn the oven
down to 200°C/400°F/gas 6.

Whisk together the eggs, sugar and vanilla essence.

Dissolve the flour in a little of the milk, then add the remaining
milk and heat in a pan, stirring until it thickens. Add the cinnamon
and tangerine peel.

Off the heat, whisk in the egg, sugar and vanilla essence
mixture, and stir until thick.

Remove the foil and dried beans from the pastry case and pour
in the egg and milk mixture. Return to the oven and bake for 20
minutes or a little longer, until golden. This is best eaten warm.

ras-el-hanout spice mixture
(MOROCCO)

This is one of the world's most complex spice mixtures. It sometimes contains literally dozens of ingredients – and it is used to flavour game and lamb dishes, and is sprinkled over rice and couscous. Common to all variations are cardamom, nutmeg, mace, cinnamon, allspice, peppercorns, ginger and cloves. Also often included are chilli, turmeric, galangal, cubebs, coriander, and grains of paradise (*melegueta* pepper), dried garlic, lavender blossom and saffron, not to mention unusual herbs and spices little known outside north Africa. This simple version conveys the essential character.

MAKES 1 VERY SMALL JAR

Cardamom seeds, scraped from 12 pods
1 teaspoon black peppercorns
2 cloves
1 stick of cinnamon, crumbled
1 nutmeg, grated
1 teaspoon ground mace
1 teaspoon ground allspice
1 teaspoon turmeric powder
1 tablespoon ground ginger
1 teaspoon chilli powder

Dry-roast the cardamom seeds, black peppercorns, cloves and cinnamon in a heavy pan until they give off their aromas. Grind in a spice or coffee grinder or use a pestle and mortar.

Mix with the remaining ingredients and store in an airtight jar.

Use as a flavouring in *tagines* and stews, or sprinkled on rice or couscous dishes.

berberi red pepper paste
(ETHIOPIA)

This spicy mixture, which is added to most Ethiopian stews, is also served at the table as a condiment. Sometimes more chilli is added, making it very fiery indeed. It can be stored in the fridge for months.

MAKES 1 JAR

1 tablespoon chilli powder
1 tablespoon paprika
1 teaspoon coriander seeds, dry-roasted and ground
1 teaspoon freshly ground black pepper
Pinch of grated nutmeg
4 cloves
Pinch of ground cinnamon
Pinch of ground allspice
1 teaspoon ground cardamom seeds
4 shallots, chopped
2 cloves garlic, chopped
1 tablespoon salt
250ml boiling water
Olive oil, to cover

Mix all the ingredients, except the olive oil, in a blender, adding the boiling water to make a paste.

Put in an airtight jar with a topping of olive oil to seal. Store in the fridge.

onion sambal (SOUTH AFRICA)

This fresh onion pickle is typical of Cape Malay cuisine.

SERVES 4–6

2 onions, thinly sliced
2 green chillies, seeds and membranes removed, finely chopped
1 clove garlic, finely chopped
1 tablespoon malt vinegar (or juice of 1 lemon or lime)
1 teaspoon sugar
Generous pinch of salt

Place the onions in a bowl and cover with boiling water. Leave for 30 minutes to remove the fierce, crude flavours. Drain, rinse with cold water, drain again and pat dry using kitchen paper.

Mix all the ingredients together, and serve as a relish or pickle.

cucumber sambal (SOUTH AFRICA)

In Cape Malay cooking, they use the term *sambal* for the spicy, pickled side dishes served with main courses. They can be made with onion, carrot, tomato, or even apple. This is a cucumber sambal.

SERVES 4–6

1 cucumber, peeled and thinly sliced
3 teaspoons salt
1 green chilli, finely chopped
1 clove garlic, finely chopped
1 teaspoon malt vinegar or wine vinegar
1 teaspoon caster sugar

In a dish, sprinkle the cucumber with the salt. Leave for 1 hour, then drain and rinse, patting dry with kitchen paper.

Mix the cucumber slices with the chilli, garlic, malt or wine vinegar and sugar before serving.

harissa paste (NORTHERN AFRICA)

You can buy this ready-made in tubes or tins but, using a blender, you can also quickly make a supply that will last for a few months. If you have whole spices, heat them in a frying pan (without fat) until they start to give off their aromas. Grind in a spice or coffee grinder or pound with a pestle and mortar.

MAKES 1 SMALL JAR

25g dried red chillies
1 clove garlic
1 teaspoon caraway seeds
½ teaspoon ground coriander
½ teaspoon ground cumin
½ teaspoon tomato purée
½ teaspoon salt
4 tablespoons olive oil

Put the chillies in a cup, cover with boiling water and leave to soak for 1 hour. Drain and chop finely. Put them in a blender with the garlic, caraway seeds, coriander, cumin, tomato purée, salt and 2 tablespoons of the olive oil, and whizz to a paste.

Transfer to a small jar. Cover with the remaining olive oil and store in the fridge.

The *harissa* paste will keep in the fridge for at least a couple of months, as long as you keep the surface covered with a little oil. It even improves with the keeping.

fiery spice mix
(NIGERIA AND GHANA)

In west Africa this fiery mix is used to enhance meat and vegetable stews.

MAKES 1 JAR

1 tablespoon dried red chillies, finely chopped
¼ habanero chilli, finely chopped
1 tablespoon ground grains of paradise (*melegueta* pepper)
10cm ginger, grated
1 teaspoon ground cubebs (if available)

Using a spice or coffee grinder or a pestle and mortar, grind all the ingredients to a fine powder. Store in an airtight jar.

clarified spiced butter (ETHIOPIA)

MAKES 1 JAR

100g unsalted butter
50ml water
1 small onion, chopped
1 clove garlic, chopped
2.5cm ginger, grated

Heat the butter and water in a saucepan until the butter melts.

Add the onion, garlic and ginger, and bring to the boil until it starts to foam. Leave to settle and cool, then strain.

Store in a covered, sterilised jar in the fridge. It will keep for several months.

pili pili sauce (NIGERIA AND GHANA)

In west Africa the generally bland food is electrified by an injection of hot spice, such as this *pili pili* sauce.

MAKES 1 LARGE JAR

4 ripe tomatoes, peeled, deseeded and chopped
½ habanero chilli, deseeded and finely chopped
½ onion, finely chopped
2 cloves garlic, finely chopped
1 tablespoon fresh horseradish, peeled and grated
2 tablespoons sunflower or groundnut oil

Using a hand blender, mix all the ingredients well. Put in an airtight jar and store in the fridge. Use as a relish to spice up cooked and uncooked dishes.

mango pickle (ZANZIBAR)

The influence of India on the east African coast is enormous. This very sour pickle enhances both meat and fish dishes.

SERVES 4–6

6 unripe mangoes, thinly sliced
1 onion, finely sliced
2 green peppers, deseeded and chopped
5cm ginger, grated
2 cloves garlic, chopped
2 teaspoons salt

Mix all the ingredients together. Put in a large airtight container and keep in the fridge for 2 weeks before using.

Spices heaped up into perfect cone shapes in a shop in Djerba, Tunisia.

A love of fiery, hot flavours is a common thread that runs through the cooking of the Caribbean and Latin America. You find it in the West Indies in jerk paste marinades and Jamaican pepperpot soups and in Brazil in fiery prawn dishes, especially in African-influenced Bahia in the north. Above all, you will find the hot flavours of chillies in Mexico, where nearly every dish has a peppery bite.

Latin America is a vast geographical area, including the humid Caribbean basin in the north, the equatorial rainforests of Brazil, Peru and Ecuador in the centre, the arid, blazing deserts of northern Chile and the cold plains of south Argentina's Patagonia with its frozen toes in the Antarctic. The Andes, a 3000 mile-long backbone of monumental mountains, divides the continent from west to east, creating contrasting climates on either side, its snows melting into rivers which water the vines of Argentina to the east and the fruit farms of Chile to the west.

The cooking in the West Indies has always been influenced by the spices available. Allspice is the pervasive flavour, where it's also known as *pimiento de Jamaica* (Jamaican pepper) because the Spanish thought they had discovered pepper. It is one of the ingredients in Angostura bitters, made on the island of Trinidad.

Westerners tend to think of the Caribbean as the source of fantastically hot and spicy food: the island of Grenada produces the world's best nutmeg and the climate encourages the growth of all the world's significant spices.

The explorers arrive

When Columbus set off in 1492 with the main aim of not so much discovering America as bringing back gold from these distant lands, he was given a shopping list of valuable spices, such as cinnamon and mastic. He found none of them, but he did stumble on allspice, which he thought, because of its shape, might be pepper (allspice grows in a kind of myrtle bush; peppercorns grow on a vine), and certainly it was a valuable flavour. The name all-spice (in English) summarises its many facets, the odours of nutmeg and cinnamon. Using these spices, the Spanish and French colonists developed a style of cooking often known as Creole – from Spanish *criolla* meaning 'mixture'.

Many forms of chilli feature in Caribbean cooking – combined with herbs and spices which grow outside the back-door – these include allspice and the ferociously hot bonnet peppers (equivalent to Mexican *habanero*), and others, which Spanish, Portuguese and British merchants introduced, such as ginger, cinnamon and nutmeg. All of these are combined in jerk paste, spread on to pork and other meats before grilling – hot and heavily scented.

Vanilla is an important Central American spice, originating in the rainforests of Mexico, and cocoa must also count as a flavouring here, since it is often the final ingredient added to a rich *mole* sauce (a mixture of 12 to 16 spices and dried herbs).

Annato seed is widely used, although more for its colour than its slightly acid flavour. The pulp is sometimes added to a sauce, and the ground seeds are used in Mexico as a rub before grilling fish. In Chile the seeds are heated in pork fat or oil and then strained to provide the cooking medium known as *color Chileno*. In the past, annato colouring was used in the UK dairy industry, lending orange and primrose hues to both cheese and butter.

But everywhere you go in Latin America, the predominant flavour is chilli. Nearly every meal is accompanied by bottles of chilli sauce or saucers of fresh green chillies and slices of sour limes, or, in Mexico, soupy sauces in bowls, purées of lime, chilli and avocado and puréed fried chilli beans. In the markets, especially in Mexico, you'll see up to 60 varieties of fresh and dried chillies and not all are hot. They vary on the Scovell heat scale from a gentle two or three for peppers used for stuffing, such as *ancho* and *mulato*, to a searing ten, such as *habanero* or Scotch bonnet.

But heat is not necessarily the only quality that Mexican cooks look for in a chilli; instead they seek subtlety and flavour more than heat. Many dried chillies, some of them smoked, such as *chipotle*, provide intensely tropical fruit notes. The cook must exercise great skill to tease the full range of flavours from them.

The 31 provinces of Mexico boast remarkably different styles of cooking. In the west, the coastal region of Guerrero specialises in fish and prawn dishes. Grilled snapper may be first smeared with a paste of four kinds of dried chillies, such as *ancho*, *pasilla*, *mulato* and *de arbol*, as well as a coating of annatto.

To the south of Mexico City, there is Oaxaca (pronounced 'wah-haca') with its predominantly intermarried Indian and Spanish population (known as *mestizo*). They boast the seven *moles* of Oaxaca, which they consider to be the country's most authentic, claiming the word comes from the native Nahuatl term for a mixture. The sauce, a slow-cooked mixture of herbs, spices, nuts and often dried fruit, is poured over plainly poached meat, poultry and fish.

Mexican *moles*

The king of Oaxacan *moles* is the *mole negro*, the key ingredient being a local black, round chilli called *chilhuacle*. Others are the brick-red *mole coloradito*, *mole rojo* (red with dried chillies) and *mole verde* (green with herbs and jalapeno chillies). *mole amarillo* (containing yellow chillies) is often used to stuff *empanadas* and corn-husk *tamales*. The sixth *mole* is known as *mancha manteles*, which translates as 'tablecloth stainer'. The seventh *mole* is *chichilo mole*, taking its name from a locally grown chilli, whose seeds are blackened over a flame, before combining with other seasonings.

The daily fare of the average Mexican is based on the many forms of *tortilla*, a flat brown pancake made with maize (corn) flour. Staples also include beans and rice, as they do in most other Latin American countries, served with a saucer of chopped chillies by the side or a chilli sauce. But the further south you go, the more the potato comes into its own, since the tuber originates in the *altiplano* of Peru, where it's been eaten for 2500 years. They love the potato, too, in Colombia – a land of dramatic contrasts, facing two oceans, the Atlantic and the Pacific, and divided by the Andes. In the coastal regions there are delicate fish stews made with coconut milk; in the Andes there are rich meat and chicken stews.

Chile boasts great seafood such as abalone and clams that turn pink when cooked, and *piures* (Californian squirt), a shellfish resembling a rook's nest, gathered many metres below sea level clinging to the rocks. Fish is the most expensive item in the elegant, iron-framed Central Market of Santiago (usually served with melted cheese in restaurants), but other satellite markets sell grain and dried beans, and market cooking stalls offer simple chilli-flavoured soups and stews of lamb and tripe.

To the east of Chile lies Argentina, a breathtakingly beautiful country with the richest grazing for beef cattle in the world: the *pampas*. Here the national cuisine is based on grilling and spit-roasting, and the meat is basted with hot chilli sauce.

The largest country in Latin America is Brazil, with a population of 200 million and a land mass similar in size to that of the USA. Its 500-year-old history, first as a colony of the Portuguese, accounts for the diversity of its cooking.

Two of its cities are among the largest in the world (after Mexico City and Calcutta): Sao Paolo with 16 million inhabitants and Rio de Janeiro with 12 million. The national dish, *feijoada*, is a multi-coloured stew of black beans with a dozen kinds of dried, salted and smoked meats, green *couve* (kale), white rice, golden toasted *farofa* meal (made from cassava root) and slices of orange, and flavoured with chillies.

Sao Paolo has a large Japanese population and boasts a thousand sushi bars and some of the best Italian restaurants outside Italy. In Rio there are fine seafood and meat restaurants, embracing the *gaucho* roasts of the south. But the most important style of cooking comes from the state of Bahia in the northeast. Here 90 per cent of the population is descended from the one million West African slaves Brazil accommodated to work the sugar plantations. Great dishes include *xinxim* (chicken and prawn stew), *casqwuinhos recheados* (spicy stuffed crab), *moqueca* (chilli-hot fish stew) and a deep-fried bean fritter called *acarje* which is dispensed at the roadside by grand ladies dressed like princesses in white ball gowns.

Brazilians love to snack on street foods, which are known as *salgadinhos* (little bites). These include fried and baked pastries such as *empanadas*, deep-fried balls called *bolinhos*, toasts (*torradhinos*) and innumerable sugary sweets (made with pumpkin and sweet potato) and desserts – the heritage of Portuguese nuns who taught the natives how to make the sugary egg puddings of their homeland, often flavoured with cinnamon.

In Brazil, as in most Latin American countries, although heat is not imposed on food, it is never far away; an optional dish of chopped chillies or a bottle of chilli sauce is to hand at every meal.

es of chillies,
ery variety, on
xican stall.

potatoes with cheese sauce
(MEXICO)

The humble potato is turned into a fiery dish with this rich cheese sauce spiced with chilli.

SERVES 4

Salt and freshly ground black pepper
Juice of ½ lemon
3 dried hot red chillies, deseeded and crumbled
1 onion, sliced into rings
8 potatoes, peeled
1 fresh green or red chilli, cut into thin strips
2 hard-boiled eggs, halved, to garnish
12 black olives, stoned, to garnish

FOR THE SAUCE
175g melting cheese such as mozzarella, roughly grated
225ml double cream
1 teaspoon turmeric powder
1 fresh green or red chilli, finely chopped
3 tablespoons olive oil

Mix the lemon juice and dried chillies in a bowl, and season with salt and freshly ground black pepper. Add the onion and leave to marinate. Boil the potatoes in lightly salted water for about 15 minutes or until cooked.

Make the sauce by combining all the ingredients except the olive oil in a blender. Heat the olive oil in a pan. Add the sauce ingredients and simmer for about 5 minutes until the sauce thickens.

Place the boiled potatoes in a warmed serving dish and pour over the sauce.

Drain the marinated onion rings and place on top of the potatoes, together with the chilli strips.

Serve garnished with the hard-boiled eggs and black olives.

black-eyed bean fritters
(BRAZIL)

These black-eyed bean fritters, known as *acaraje*, originated in Africa and were brought across by slaves in the sixteenth century. They are the cousins of Egyptian falafal. The addition of prawn paste and chilli makes them uniquely Brazilian and in Bahia, in the north, they are sold on the pavement as street snacks by women in colourful costumes. If you prefer, you can omit the dried prawns, which have a strong, pungent aroma.

MAKES 20 FRITTERS

450g dried black-eyed beans
50g dried prawns (optional)
2 tablespoons olive oil (if using dried prawns)
1 onion, chopped
¼ teaspoon cayenne pepper or chilli powder
Salt
***Dende* or corn oil, for deep-frying**

Slightly crush the black-eyed beans in a food processor to split the skins. Leave to soak in water for at least 4 hours or overnight.

Drain, then put the beans in a bowl of cold water and rub them vigorously between your hands to remove the skins. As the skins rise to the surface, skim them off and discard. Finally, cover the beans with very hot, but not boiling, water and leave to soak until cool enough for you to rub away any remaining skins. Drain.

If using, cover the dried prawns with water in a small saucepan and bring to the boil. Simmer for 1 minute. Drain, rinse with cold water, then dry on kitchen paper.

Fry the prawns in the olive oil for 1 or 2 minutes or until crisp. Chop roughly.

Add the prawns and onion to the black-eyed beans and purée in small batches in a blender or food processor to make a thick paste. Season with the cayenne or chilli powder and a little salt.

Pour about 8cm of the *dende* or corn oil into a deep pan and heat to 180°C/356°F – check with a thermometer.

Using a dessertspoon, scoop up spoonfuls of the paste and form into compact oval shapes, smoothing with your fingers. Deep-fry, in small batches of about five at a time, for about 4 minutes each, or until golden.

After frying each batch, wait for the temperature to return to 180°C/356°F before adding the next batch, and skim off any floating crumbs. Drain the fritters on kitchen paper and keep warm.

Serve whole or split open with Chilli Salsa (see page 115).

guacamole (MEXICO)

If many Mexican dishes test the culinary skills and patience of the cook, this avocado dip is simplicity itself. It is typically Mexican in the contrast of colour, texture and flavour, the sweet, smooth, green avocado, the acid freshness of tomato and lime juice and the keen bite of garlic, spring onion and chilli. Taste as you go along, adjusting the flavours to your preference. Eat it as a dip with *tacos*, *tortillas* or pitta bread, or serve as the centrepiece of a salad.

SERVES 4

2 ripe avocado pears
Juice of ½ lime (or lemon)
1 tablespoon olive oil
1 ripe tomato, peeled, deseeded and chopped
1 green chilli, deseeded and finely chopped

4 spring onions, white and green parts chopped separately
2 or 3 sprigs of coriander, finely chopped, reserving a few
   leaves to garnish
1 clove garlic
½ teaspoon sea salt
Scant ¼ teaspoon cayenne pepper or paprika, to garnish

Use a fork, not a blender, to mash the avocado flesh roughly with the lime juice and olive oil. Gently stir in the tomato, chilli, white parts of the spring onions and the chopped coriander. Crush the garlic in the sea salt with the back of a broad-bladed knife and stir into the mixture.

Return the mixture to the empty avocado shells or place in a bowl and cover with clingfilm to prevent browning.

Garnish with a sprinkling of cayenne pepper or paprika, the green parts of the spring onions and a few coriander leaves before serving.

grilled spiced snapper (MEXICO)

The *talla* is a grid used in outdoor barbecues, a feature of the popular beach restaurants on the Pacific west coast and in the countryside areas of Guerrero, north of Acapulco. You sit on outdoor benches at long wooden tables under palm roofs, looking across a lagoon where shrimpers are casting their nets. You choose your own freshly caught fish and they grill it to order. The most common chilli used here, fresh or dried, is called *de arbol*, from one of the taller, stragglier chilli bushes, producing thin red chillies, about 5cm long. You'll probably have a burning-hot red chilli soup first, while they quickly marinate your fish for 20 minutes before grilling. A feature of the marinade is the common Mexican spice *achiote*, which colours the fish and gives it a slightly sour taste.

SERVES 4

4 red snapper or firm fish such as bream, scales not removed

FOR THE MARINADE
Juice of 2 limes
1 tablespoon *achiote*

FOR THE SAUCE
8 dried *guajillo* chillies
4 dried *ancho* chillies (but substitute others as available, such as *pasilla* or *de arbol*)
500g tomatoes, peeled and deseeded
1 tablespoon white wine vinegar
250ml water
1 red onion, chopped
3 shallots, chopped
3 cloves garlic, chopped
1 teaspoon ground cumin
1 teaspoon dried oregano
1 teaspoon dried thyme
1 teaspoon dried marjoram
2 tablespoons sunflower oil
Salt and freshly ground black pepper
50g butter, melted

Using a sharp knife, cut the fish along the belly, opening the fish up and flattening it out, leaving the backbone intact. (A fishmonger can do this for you.)

Mix the marinade ingredients with 1 tablespoon salt in a blender and rub on to the exposed inner surfaces of the fish. Leave for 20 minutes while you make the sauce.

Put the dried chillies in a bowl and cover with boiling water. Leave to soak for 10 minutes. Drain and place in a blender with the tomatoes, white wine vinegar, measured water, onion, shallots, garlic, cumin, oregano, thyme and marjoram. Whizz to make a soupy paste.

Heat the sunflower oil in a heavy pan and add the spice mixture. When it comes to the boil, lower the heat and simmer slowly for 15 minutes or longer, until the sauce thickens. Season to taste and set aside to cool.

Grill the fish, scale-sides down, over an outdoor barbecue grill or on a domestic grill for around 10 minutes, basting with the hot sauce. Turn over, scale-sides up. Brush with the melted butter and grill for another 5–10 minutes.

Serve with rice and a green salad.

Beans in the pot (MEXICO)

Beans, known as *frijoles*, are eaten every day in Mexico. A large pan (*olla*) lasts for several days and this dish is known as *frijoles de olla*. Dried chilli and *epazote* are two essential seasonings. *Epazote* is a straggly, pungent herb with a mustard flavour like rocket and an aroma like creosote, which disappears in the cooking. Bay leaf is often suggested as a substitute, but a little English mustard is also effective.

This recipe makes about 2kg of cooked beans, enough for four, providing meals over several days. Halve the ingredients if this quantity is not required.

SERVES 4

450g dried beans (red kidney, pinto or black beans)
1 tablespoon bicarbonate of soda
1 onion, chopped
12 cloves garlic
2 sprigs *epazote*, fresh or dried or 3 bay leaves or
    1 tablespoon mustard
3 dried red chillies
6 litres water
Salt

Soak the beans overnight, covered with 2 litres water, adding the bicarbonate of soda, which softens the skins. Drain the beans in a colander and rinse well. Place in a pan, cover with 2 litres fresh water and boil for 10 minutes. Drain and rinse again, removing the scum that forms.

Return to the saucepan, cover once more with 2 litres water, and add the onion, garlic, *epazote* (or bay leaf or mustard) and chillies but not the salt – at this stage it would harden the skins.

Simmer for 1½–2 hours or until tender (test by pressing a bean between finger and thumb), adding more boiling water if necessary. Boiled in a pressure cooker they take less than 30 minutes.

When tender, scoop up 4 tablespoons of the beans and crush them to a paste with the back of a spoon. Return them to the pot to thicken the sauce. Finally, add salt to taste. Serve hot with plain boiled rice and soured cream or yoghurt.

bean purée (MEXICO)

Beans have a second life when puréed and served as *frijoles refritos* the next day. It means literally 'refried beans', but actually it is beans cooked with bacon fat and seasoning and mashed to make a purée.

SERVES 4

3 tablespoons lard or vegetable oil, plus extra as needed
250g cooked beans (see left)
Salt

Heat the lard or vegetable oil in a heavy frying pan. When hot, add several tablespoons of the cooked beans at a time, crushing them with the back of a wooden spoon, until they break up.

Season to taste with salt, adding more lard or vegetable oil as needed to make a smooth purée.

Cook the purée until it starts to crisp up. Serve at any meal as a vegetable accompaniment to fish or meat and rice.

prawn and chilli salsa (BRAZIL)

The typical orange colour and distinctive flavour of this north Brazilian dish, known as *moqueca*, comes from using the rich *dende* oil from the *dende* coconut. It's authentic but not essential. The hot-sour flavour comes from the essential salsa side dish and fiery *malagueta* chilli (not to be confused with *melegueta* pepper, or grains of paradise).

SERVES 4

100ml olive oil
2 large tomatoes, peeled, deseeded and sliced
1 large mild onion, thinly sliced
Salt and freshly ground black pepper
700g peeled prawns, uncooked
4 tablespoons *dende* oil (optional)

Heat the olive oil in a large pan, add the tomatoes and onion and simmer for about 20 minutes until they soften and release their juices. Season to taste with salt and freshly ground black pepper.

Add the prawns and simmer for a further 5 minutes, shaking the pan to make sure they are cooked evenly. Add the *dende* oil, if using, and stir.

Serve hot with plain white rice and a bowl each of Chilli Salsa (see page 115) and *Malagueta* chilli.

spiced steak (COLOMBIA)

Touching on two oceans, the Pacific and Atlantic, with icy mountain ranges and tropical forests, Colombia has extremes of climate and food sources. It also has a fusion cuisine combining native and Spanish traditions. This recipe marries European techniques with Caribbean spicing.

SERVES 4

2 tablespoons olive oil
900g flank steak, rolled and tied with string
1 onion, chopped
1 clove garlic, chopped
2 sticks of celery, chopped
4 small green chillies, split lengthways
1 teaspoon ground cumin
Salt and freshly ground black pepper
about ½ litre water
1 tablespoon cornflour
25g butter, melted
50g breadcrumbs

Heat the olive oil in a heavy casserole dish and brown the steak briefly, then remove and set aside. Add the onion and garlic to the casserole and cook gently for about 5 minutes until soft.

Return the steak to the casserole with the celery, chillies, cumin, 1 teaspoon salt and a little freshly ground black pepper. Cover with the water and simmer on top of the stove for 2 hours or until the steak is tender.

Remove the steak and untie. Drain and pat dry with kitchen paper. Use some of the liquid to make a sauce, thickening with the cornflour dissolved in 1 tablespoon water. Season to taste and press through a sieve.

Place the steak on a grill rack, coat with the butter and breadcrumbs and brown under a very hot grill until crispy.

Slice and serve with the sauce, potatoes and salad.

callaloo soup (JAMAICA)

This unique, gooey, succulent soup dates back to the time when slaves made use of foodstuffs not wanted by their owners, such as crabs from the beach, pigs' tails and the tropical root vegetable, eddoe. Serve the cracked claws of the crab in the soup to pick over with your fingers.

SERVES 4

2 medium crabs or 250g crab meat (or white fish fillet)
2 tablespoons sunflower oil or 25g butter
1 onion, finely chopped
125g salt pork or bacon, cut into 2cm pieces
4 spring onions, chopped
2 cloves garlic, chopped
¼ teaspoon Scotch bonnet chilli, chopped
3 cloves, ground
¼ teaspoon ground allspice
Pinch of dried thyme
425g callaloo leaves, roughly chopped
1.5 litres chicken stock
125g okra, sliced lengthways
Salt and freshly ground black pepper

Crack open the crabs and remove the flesh; crack the claws and reserve.

Heat the sunflower oil or butter in a frying pan and fry the onion until soft but not brown. Add the salt pork or bacon and cook until the fat starts to run.

Add the spring onions, garlic, chilli, cloves, allspice and thyme and cook a minute longer. Stir the callaloo leaves into the pan.

Transfer to a large saucepan, add the stock, bring to the boil and simmer for about 20 minutes, until the pork is tender. Add the okra and simmer for another 10 minutes. Finally, add the crab, including the cracked claws or the fish (if using), and cook for another 5 minutes or so.

Season to taste with salt and plenty of freshly ground black pepper and serve with plain boiled rice.

chilli-spiced chicken stew
(MEXICO)

This is a Mexican *mole* (pronounced 'mo-lay') – one of the seven famous *moles* of Oaxaca, the ancient *mestizo* city to the south of Mexico City. *Mole* comes from the Nuahatl word meaning a stew, and usually includes poached pork, chicken, turkey or fish covered with a rich, piquant sauce, with up to a dozen different herbs and spices. It is thickened with nuts or even pumpkin seeds (*pipian verde*) or in one version, bitter chocolate. Inevitably, the rich sauce drips on to your clothing, and indeed this *mole* is known as the 'tablecloth stainer' (*mancha manteles*). The addition of fruit to celebratory dishes is also common in Mexico.

SERVES 4

2 tablespoons sunflower oil
1.5kg chicken, cut into pieces and skin removed
500ml water
1 bay leaf
1 teaspoon salt

FOR THE *MOLE* SAUCE
10 dried Mexican chillies (preferably a combination of
    ***mulatto*, *pasilla* and *ancho* chillies)**
1 onion, chopped
1 tablespoon sunflower oil
2 cloves garlic, chopped
Pinch of dried oregano
Pinch of dried thyme
1 stick of cinnamon (or 2 teaspoons ground cinnamon)
2 cloves
250g canned Mexican tomatillos (or 3 large tomatoes,
    peeled)
8 almonds (or walnuts), blanched and skinned
Sprig of coriander (or parsley)
2 plantains (or 1 small sweet potato), cubed
1 pear, cubed
2 slices fresh pineapple, cubed
1 dessert apple, cored, peeled and cubed
25g butter

Heat the 2 tablespoons sunflower oil in a heavy casserole dish and fry the chicken pieces until they start to colour. Add the water, bay leaf and salt, and simmer for about 20 minutes until nearly tender. Remove the chicken pieces and reserve the cooking liquid for stock.

To make the *mole* sauce, heat an iron pan and dry-roast the chillies until they start to colour and give off their aromas. Put the chillies in a small bowl and cover with hot water. Leave to soak for 20 minutes, then drain.

In the same pan, gently fry the onion in 1 tablespoon sunflower oil until soft, then add the garlic, oregano, thyme, cinnamon and cloves. Stir in the tomatillos (or tomatoes) and simmer for 5 minutes.

Combine this mixture in a blender with the chillies, adding the almonds (or walnuts) and coriander (or parsley). Whizz to make a smooth paste. Add 300ml of the reserved chicken stock and simmer for 20 minutes, until the sauce reduces and thickens. Check the seasoning. Add the sauce to the chicken in the casserole dish and simmer for five minutes.

Finally, gently fry the plantains (or sweet potato) in the butter until soft, adding the pear, pineapple and apple towards the end. Add to the *mole* and continue cooking over a low heat for about 5 minutes until well blended.

spicy beef stew (GUATEMALA)

This is a typical midday meal throughout Central America, using cheaper cuts of meat.

SERVES 4

3 tablespoons groundnut or vegetable oil
1 onion, chopped
2 cloves garlic, chopped
1 *serrano* chilli, deseeded and chopped
2 green peppers, deseeded and chopped
1kg stewing beef, cut into cubes
150ml beef or chicken stock or water
250g canned Mexican tomatillos (or 3 tomatoes, peeled)
1 bay leaf
2 cloves
½ teaspoon dried oregano
1 dry *tortilla* (or 1 tablespoon cornmeal)
Salt

Heat the groundnut or vegetable oil in a heavy saucepan and fry the onion for about 10 minutes until soft. Add the garlic, *serrano* chilli and green peppers and fry for another 5 minutes until soft.

Add the beef and fry until brown, then add the stock, tomatillos (or tomatoes), bay leaf, cloves and oregano.

Crumble the tortilla (if using) and soak in water for a few moments or, using a little of the stock, mix the cornmeal to a paste. Add to the saucepan to thicken the stew and simmer for about 2 hours. Make sure it doesn't boil dry.

Season to taste and serve with plain boiled rice.

pepperpot (WEST INDIES)

Traditionally, the slaves of the Caribbean made the most of every last scrap of meat and bone to produce rich, flavoursome stews. You can use any inexpensive cut of meat for this dish.

SERVES 4

1.5kg stewing beef or leg of mutton, cut into 2.5cm cubes
2 tablespoons vegetable oil
2 teaspoons brown sugar
500ml beef or chicken stock
2 chillies (or as many as you can handle), chopped

FOR THE MARINADE
1 onion, grated
1 clove garlic, chopped
2 teaspoons ground allspice
1 teaspoon dried thyme
1 teaspoon ground coriander
Salt and freshly ground black pepper

Prepare the marinade by combining all the ingredients. Put the beef or mutton in a bowl and rub with the marinade spices. Leave several hours or overnight.

Heat the vegetable oil in a heavy saucepan until very hot, then sprinkle in the sugar. It will quickly caramelise. Stir in the marinated meat and cook until it starts to colour and stick to the pan. Turn it over and continue to brown.

Add the stock and the chillies, and bring to the boil, then lower the heat. Cover with a lid, and simmer on the lowest heat for 3 or 3 hours or until the meat is tender. If the liquid level drops, add a little warm water.

Serve with rice, sweet potatoes or yam and green vegetables.

stuffed chilli peppers (MEXICO)

The stuffing for this popular dish varies all over Mexico, depending on the ingredients available, ranging from last night's leftovers to exotic delicacies for festive occasions, but always the balance of spices sets the tone for the dish. The mincemeat filling or *picadillo* can also be used to fill rolled *tortillas*.

Poblano chilli peppers are large and mild like European green peppers but slightly hotter. If using European green peppers, use *serrano* chillies to spice up the stuffing mixture.

SERVES 4

4 large *poblano* chillies or 4 green peppers
Salt and freshly ground black pepper
1½ tablespoons flour
Lard or vegetable oil, for frying

FOR THE FILLING
2 tablespoons olive oil
1 onion, chopped
500g minced pork or beef
4 cloves garlic, chopped
2 *serrano* chillies, chopped (if using green peppers)
2 tablespoons raisins or sultanas
1 dried apricot, finely chopped
1 apple or pear, peeled and chopped (optional)
3 medium tomatoes, peeled, deseeded and chopped
25g blanched almonds, pine nuts or cashew nuts, sliced
Pinch of ground cinnamon
Pinch of ground cloves or allspice

FOR THE SAUCE
450g tomatoes, peeled, deseeded and chopped
½ medium onion
1 clove garlic
2 tablespoons olive oil
225ml stock

FOR THE BATTER
2 eggs
½ teaspoon salt

Char the *poblano* chillies or green peppers over an open flame. Place in a sealed plastic bag for 5 minutes and then rub off the blackened skin. Make a slit in the side of each pepper and scrape out the seeds and pith.

To make the filling, heat the olive oil in a frying pan and fry the onion until soft and yellow. Add the meat and garlic and cook for 10 minutes. Stir in the *serrano* chillies (if using green peppers). Finally, add the raisins or sultanas, apricot, apple or pear (if using), tomatoes, almonds, pine nuts or cashew nuts, cinnamon and cloves or allspice, and salt to taste. Cook uncovered on a low heat for 15 minutes.

To make the sauce, put the tomatoes, onion and garlic in a blender and whizz until smooth. Heat the olive oil in a frying pan, add this mixture, then the stock, and season with salt and freshly ground black pepper. Cook gently for about 15 minutes.

To make the batter, separate the eggs and beat the whites until stiff, then add the salt. Beat the egg yolks and fold them gently into the whites.

Stuff the peppers with the meat filling. Coat with the flour, and dip into the batter mixture.

Pour lard or vegetable oil into a deep frying pan to a depth of 2cm. Fry the stuffed peppers until golden. Remove and drain on kitchen paper.

Pour the hot tomato sauce and serve around the stuffed peppers and serve with plain rice or *tortillas*.

jerked pork (JAMAICA)

The world-famous dish of jerked pork originated in Jamaica. The word 'jerky' was borrowed from the Spanish, who claimed the island in the 1490s – in Spanish *charqui* is meat cured by drying, either in the sun or over smoke.

When the British seized the island in 1665, the Spanish fled to Cuba and the slaves into the mountains, where, known as Maroons (from the Spanish word *marrones*, meaning 'the brown ones'), they provided their own food, hunting down wild pig that they dried and smoked. They eventually became skilled hawkers, evolving delicious spice rubs to tenderise and season meat before cooking. All the spices grew to hand, including scorching-hot Scotch bonnet peppers, black pepper, allspice, cinnamon, ginger and thyme. Recipes vary from one family to another, but here is a typical version.

This dish needs to be prepared a day in advance. You can prepare chicken and fish in the same way.

SERVES 4

Jerk paste (see page 115)
4 pork chops

Rub the jerk paste well into the chops, then leave them on a plate in the fridge overnight.

Cook under a very hot grill for about 5 minutes on each side.

curried goat (JAMAICA)

Goats were introduced to the islands of the Caribbean by the Spaniards along with sheep and other animals, but while sheep never settled down to the rough terrain, goats flourished in the wild and were hunted like game. For full flavour, purists would use 2.5kg meat on the bone, roughly chopped, but it tends to leave splinters in the stew. The method of caramelising the meat with oil and sugar is characteristic of the West Indies. This recipe works also with lamb and mutton instead of goat.

SERVES 4–6

750g goat meat (or lamb or mutton), off the bone and cubed
Juice of 2 limes or 1 lemon
1 medium onion, grated
1 clove garlic, grated

2.5cm ginger, grated
1 teaspoon salt
25ml sunflower or vegetable oil
1 tablespoon caster sugar
4 teaspoons curry powder or 1 teaspoon each of ground allspice, cumin, coriander and chilli powder
500ml chicken or lamb stock
2 stems of fresh thyme or 1 teaspoon dried thyme
1 bay leaf

Put the meat into a bowl and rub with the lime or lemon juice, onion, garlic, ginger and salt. Leave for 2 hours.

In a heavy casserole, heat the sunflower or vegetable oil over a high heat and sprinkle with the sugar. As it starts to caramelise, immediately add the meat and cook for 3–5 minutes until golden brown.

Lower the heat and add the curry powder or spices, stirring well. Cover with a lid and leave to sweat over a low heat for a further 10 minutes.

Remove the lid and raise the heat. Stir in the stock. When it starts to bubble, turn down the heat, add the thyme and bay leaf, place the lid on again and simmer on the lowest heat for 2 hours. Every 30 minutes or so, check that it hasn't boiled dry, adding more warm water as necessary. The sauce should be quite thick.

Serve with plain rice, sweet potatoes and green vegetables.

mother-in-law's eyes (BRAZIL)

In this Brazilian dish, prunes are stuffed with coconut and a clove placed in each to represent the pupils of the eye. The effect is quite startling when you see rows of these 'eyes' displayed in a sweet shop. Cloves are best removed before eating as their flavour is intensely fierce.

MAKES ABOUT 30

200g caster sugar
100ml boiling water
250g fresh coconut, grated
2 egg yolks
750g prunes, stones removed
30 cloves
Icing sugar

Dissolve the sugar in the boiling water. Remove from the heat and stir in the grated coconut. Beat in the egg yolks, one at a time. Use

a heat diffuser or bain-marie to prevent burning and return to the heat, stirring until the mixture thickens.

Remove from the heat and leave to cool.

Open up each prune and spoon in the filling, smoothing over the surface to represent the eyeball.

Place the icing sugar in a bowl and coat each sweet in it. Insert a clove in the centre of each one to represent the pupil and place in paper cases to serve. Warn people not to eat the sometimes hidden cloves.

caramel custard (MEXICO)

This popular Mexican dessert, known as *flan*, came across the ocean from mainland Spain. The Mexican version uses ground almonds and is often served in one large dish rather than many small ones.

SERVES 4

175g caster sugar
900ml milk
1 vanilla pod or 1 teaspoon vanilla extract
2 eggs and 6 egg yolks
25g ground almonds
Pinch of salt

Place half the sugar in a small saucepan and, over a medium heat, stir until it turns deep brown, but do not let it burn. Stand a 1.5 litre mould in hot water to warm it.

Tip the caramel into the mould and turn the mould slowly so that the caramel coats the bottom and also comes half-way up the sides.

Preheat the oven to 160°C/325°F/gas 3.

Heat the milk in a small saucepan with the vanilla pod or extract for 5 minutes, then leave to cool. Remove the pod, if using.

Beat the eggs in a bowl with the egg yolks and the rest of the sugar. Slowly stir in the vanilla milk, almonds and a pinch of salt. Mix well and pour the mixture into the mould. Place the mould in a roasting tin half-filled with hot water.

Bake for 15 minutes. Turn down the heat to 120°C/250°F/gas ½ and cook for a further 40 minutes. The *flan* is ready when a knife inserted into the middle comes out clean. Leave the *flan* to cool, then turn it out carefully on to a plate.

Serve at room temperature.

milk sweet (BRAZIL)

Vanilla and cinnamon enrich this popular dessert that resembles condensed milk in taste and texture.

SERVES 4

3 litres milk
1kg caster sugar
1 vanilla pod
2 sticks of cinnamon

Bring the milk and sugar to a rapid boil, stirring with a wooden spoon until the sugar dissolves. Add the vanilla pod and cinnamon. Turn the heat down very low and simmer for about 1½ hours, stirring occasionally to prevent sticking.

As the mixture gradually thickens and reduces in volume, the sugar begins to brown and form lumps. Stir until smooth. Remove and discard the vanilla pod and cinnamon sticks. Take off the heat and leave to cool, then chill.

Serve chilled with fruit salad or ice cream. It will keep in the fridge for a week.

cinnamon dreams (BRAZIL)

These sweet desserts puff up when deep-fried. Rolled in a cinnamon mixture, they make a dream finish to a meal.

MAKES ABOUT 12

250ml milk
1 tablespoon granulated sugar
¼ teaspoon salt
150g fine tapioca flour
4 egg yolks
Vegetable oil, for deep-frying
2 tablespoons icing sugar
1 teaspoon ground cinnamon

Heat the milk in a non-stick saucepan. Add the sugar and salt, stirring to dissolve.

Bring to the boil and tip in the tapioca flour, stirring with a wooden spoon. Immediately remove from the heat and beat well until the mixture leaves the side of the pan, forming a hot ball of dough.

Beat in the egg yolks one at a time, mixing each one in thoroughly before adding the next.

Heat a pan of vegetable oil for deep-frying to about 180°C/356°F – check with a thermometer. Shape the balls of dough with a tablespoon and fry, a few at a time, until golden. Drain on kitchen paper.

Mix the icing sugar and cinnamon together and roll each cake in it. Eat hot.

coconut pudding (CUBA)

This is a wonderful way of combining basic natural ingredients – sugar and coconut – in a rich, sweet dessert. Use fresh coconut if you can. Cinnamon – one of the many spices brought to the Caribbean to break the monopoly of the Dutch East India Company – is a natural partner for coconut.

SERVES 4

350g caster sugar
150ml water
350g fresh coconut, grated
3 egg yolks, lightly beaten
1 teaspoon ground cinnamon
4 tablespoons dry sherry

Put the sugar and water in a small saucepan and stir over a low heat to dissolve the sugar. Turn up the temperature and boil hard until it reaches 104–107°C (just above the boiling point of water) on a sugar thermometer. If you don't have a thermometer, place some syrup on a spoon, then pull it to see if it forms a fine thread.

Stir in the coconut, egg yolks, cinnamon and sherry. Cook over a low heat, stirring constantly, until the syrup thickens.

Transfer to an ovenproof serving dish and place under a hot grill for a few minutes to brown the top.

Serve with cream or, even better, ice cream.

chilli salsa (BRAZIL)

A small saucer of this smooth, hot-and-sour salsa accompanies almost every main dish in Brazil.

SERVES 4

1 red onion (or any mild onion), chopped
1 large tomato, peeled, deseeded and diced
2 tablespoons red wine vinegar or juice of 1 lime
1 clove garlic, chopped
2 tablespoons olive oil or sunflower oil
1 tablespoon chopped coriander leaves or flat-leaf parsley
A few drops *malagueta* **chilli oil or other chilli sauce**
Salt and freshly ground black pepper

Mix all the ingredients together in a bowl. Adjust the seasonings to get a good balance of hot, salt, sour and smooth.

Chill for 1 hour to allow the flavours to blend before serving.

fresh chilli sauce (ARGENTINA)

Aji molido con aceite, as it's called (it means 'crushed chilli with olive oil') is a table seasoning freely used in Argentina, much as we use a bottle of chilli sauce. Diluted with white wine, it is also used to baste cuts of beef and lamb grilled over the *parilla* (barbecue grill).

Remember never to touch your eyes while handling chillies. Wear rubber gloves if it helps and always rinse your hands in cold water afterwards.

MAKES 1 JAR

25g small dried chillies
5 tablespoons olive oil
1 clove garlic, finely chopped
Generous pinch of salt
300ml beef stock or water

Split the chillies and shake out the seeds. Put the chillies in a bowl and cover with boiling water, leaving them to soak for 30 minutes. Drain through a sieve and discard the water.

Put the chillies in a food mixer with the olive oil, garlic and salt. Heat the beef stock (or water) and add the chillies. Process until smooth. Transfer to a lidded jar to store in the fridge. Cover the sauce with a thin layer of olive oil to make it airtight.

To use the sauce as a basting mixture for grilled meat, dilute several dessertspoons with a large glass of white wine and brush on to the meat several times while grilling fiercely.

jerk paste (JAMAICA)

This is the most universal spice used in the West Indies.

MAKES 2 JARS

12 spring onions, finely chopped
100g allspice berries, ground
50g black peppercorns, ground
½ tablespoon ground cinnamon
50g dried thyme, rubbed (or 100g fresh thyme, chopped)
50g ginger, grated
1 Scotch bonnet chilli, finely chopped
100g salt
4 tablespoons olive or sunflower oil

Pound the dry ingredients together using a pestle and mortar, and stir in the olive or sunflower oil. Alternatively, process all together in a blender. Seal in airtight jars and store in the fridge.

The cooking of northern Europe and North America is tied by climate, customs and culture. And while there is no lack of imported exotic spices, there is also a garden of tasty, home-grown ones, providing variety and character that have helped to shape indigenous cuisines.

For centuries the most established and useful home-grown spice on both sides of the Atlantic has been mustard seed, but dill and caraway seeds and juniper berries enliven Scandinavian and German cooking. Only a little to the south, large red pimentos flourish in both Hungary and Spain to provide the paprika and *pimenton* powder, which characterise their cuisines. Spain also boasts the most expensive spice in the world, the fiery-red stigmas of the purple-flowering autumn crocus that produce saffron. The saffron that grows on the high plains of La Mancha, southeast of Madrid, is considered the best in the world.

On the other side of the Atlantic ocean, only a few degrees to the south and on the same latitude as Marrakesh, the renowned Tabasco chilli grows in Louisiana, the constituent of one of the world's most prized table condiments.

It was the cooks of Rome who shaped the modern European usage of spices. Roman cooking is well documented in a famous cookery book credited to the first-century writer Apicius (who may have been not one, but several different authors). All meat and fish dishes were accompanied by spicy sauces containing fresh herbs such as mint, coriander, rue, savory, lovage, parsley, fennel and bay leaves, as well as ground pepper and ginger, cumin, coriander, nutmeg, cloves, mustard seeds and peppercorns, and usually combined with olive oil, vinegar, honey and liquamen (the Roman fish sauce like the Southeast Asian *nam pla*).

Spiceless France

The French were the natural heirs to Roman cooking and up to the fourteenth century their cooks were using a wide range of spices. An early cookery book, *Viander* by Guillaume Tirel, describes the use of cinnamon, cloves, ginger powder, black pepper and long pepper, cubebs, grains of paradise, nutmeg, mace and saffron together with, in savoury preparations, a great deal of sugar, almost as much as salt.

Then, according to food historian David Burton, a strange thing happened. In the mid-seventeenth century, in the cookery book which shaped modern French cooking, *Le Cuisinier Francais*, the celebrated chef La Varenne established a new cuisine. He made a complete break with the medieval past, declaring native herbs to be superior to (and healthier than) imported spices, which could be used to disguise second-

rate ingredients. He also rejected the use of sugar in any dish but dessert courses. A few spices survived: pepper, nutmeg, mace and cloves. But by the eighteenth century a German writer could remark that 'lovers of spicy food will be disappointed in France'.

Three centuries on, France still drags her feet on the question of spices and a 'curried' dish on a menu usually means no more than a creamy sauce with a trickle of Indian powdered spice. Top chefs flare up if they think they see their peer group weakening and write to the press whenever they see spicy flavourings from former French colonies adapted to *haute cuisine*, such as Moroccan lamb with cinnamon, Vietnamese fish with star anise or Tahitian lobster with vanilla. It is ironic that vanilla is the one spice whose cultivation the French masterminded, first in La Réunion and then in Madagascar, Tahiti and Guadeloupe.

But spiceless France did set a new standard for mustard, taking it farther than anyone before to create the vinegary Dijon style. Dijon mustard is mild and savoury, compared with the burning-hot British style, characterised by Colman's mustard. French mustard is made by soaking the whole seed in grape juice or vinegar, prior to grinding and sieving, whereas Colman's is made from milled mustard flour.

Each country deals with mustard differently. The Italians use mustard with sugar syrup as a tear-jerking pickle to preserve fruits, known as *mostarda di Cremona*, which are eaten with a plate of *bollito misto* (boiled meats). German mustard is mild, liquid and brown, designed to be eaten with their vast range of prepared sausages, including frankfurters, *leberwurst* (liver sausage) and salami. In the UK the heat of mustard is maximised. It is eaten mainly with fatty meats such as beef, sausages and pork pies, and it has the effect of emulsifying fat and making it more digestible. In Scandinavia they utilise the preservative qualities of mustard in pickles.

Caraway and juniper characterise German cooking, but cloves and nutmeg are important, used to enrich marinades for venison, boar, pork and beef stews. Holland, home of a mild-tasting, dairy-based cuisine with masses of ham and cheese, has a spicy secret: the *rijsttafel* (rice table) is an array of spicy little dishes of curried meat, chicken, fish and

vegetables served with rice, which echoes its former colonial presence in the Dutch East Indies.

Dill is the predominant flavouring in Scandinavia, where they use both the wavy fresh fronds and the anise-like bitter seeds, which marry so well with fish. It is used to season *gravad lax* (pickled salmon) and herring with potatoes, and it's used in both spirits and soothing babies' drinks – dill contains a chemical with calming properties.

Historically Scandinavians are great seafarers and they haven't been slow to take a share of the world's spices. You will find fish pickled with peppercorns, dill, allspice and sugar everywhere in Sweden. Allspice was a late addition, only introduced in the last century in a year when the herring catch failed; they had to use a smaller fish known as *sild* instead, and found it so tasteless with the traditional marinade that they had to experiment with other spices. Allspice was a revelation and gave it the depth it lacked. When herring catches returned to normal, customers demanded the spicier marinade containing allspice, and so it remains to this day.

Paprika

In two European countries, Spain and Hungary, paprika is the dominant spice, though used in entirely different ways. In Hungary it shapes the whole cooking culture and, for almost every meal, the home cook will start a dish by frying a tablespoon or two of paprika in lard as the base, be it a *gulyash* (soupy stew), a *porkolt* (dry braised meat dish of pork, goose, red meat or game) or a *paprikas* (veal, chicken, lamb or fish cooked with paprika and sour cream).

The pimento, introduced from the New World at the beginning of the sixteenth century, came to Hungary via Turkey, initially prized as a decorative plant for gardens, and then for its medical properties. They gave it the name 'paprika', a word of Serbian origin. The Hungarians invented the powdered form, drying the ripe, red fruit and then milling it to provide finer and finer grades of paprika 'flour' with milder flavours: *kulonleges* (meaning 'delicate') and the most famous *edesnemes* (meaning 'delicate noble-sweet'). In Spain *pimenton* (as they call paprika) is the essential ingredient in their vast range of pork *embutidos*, the name given to their salt-cured, air-dried

CANADA

UNITED STATES OF AMERICA

sausages, such as *salchichon*, *chorizo*, *fuet* and *sobrasada* (a brightly coloured savoury pork pâté unique to the Balearics).

Britain has been a major user of spices since the Romans invaded in 55BC. The Romans planted mustard, which suits this damp climate so well, although today the biggest company, Colman's of Norwich, imports most of its brown mustard seed from Canada. The Normans created a spice platform in Britain, and English traders bought in the spice markets of Champagne and Flanders. By Elizabethan times British cooking was the spiciest in Europe, with mixed spices used in court to fashion festive dishes such as mince pies and Christmas puddings, and gingerbreads for fairs. Chefs were using expensive saffron washes to gild pie-crusts; for several centuries, in Essex and Cambridgeshire, England even supported its own saffron crocus fields until it became too expensive to harvest the stigmas.

The USA inherited a similar attitude to spices, thanks to the Pilgrim Fathers. But over time other cultures have contributed to the national cuisine. From three compass points the USA draws upon foreign influences: European in New York, especially Italian and Jewish; the west coast looks to China and Japan; and the southwest, acknowledging its Mexican roots, has a love affair with the chilli. Louisiana is something else, with unique dishes influenced by Creole cooking (a combination of Spanish and Caribbean) and Cajun (the French-speaking community, who are descendants of immigrants from Brittany in France).

It is in southern USA that the chilli is fêted. At annual fairs, macho characters compete to eat the fieriest raw chillies and hot sauces. Tabasco is the invention of a Chicago banker, Paul McIlhenny. He married the daughter of Judge Avery, whose estate sat on top of America's deepest salt mine. McIlhenny salted the tabasco peppers which grew on the estate for three years before diluting them with vinegar to produce a world-beating chilli essence. Initially, he acquired a supply of scent bottles to contain it and sent them to friends. The style has been retained to this day and, thanks to the company's marketing skills, Tabasco is almost as famous as Coca-Cola. Can you imagine a Bloody Mary without it?

But to enjoy Tabasco in its element, you need to take a motor launch in the humid, steaming swampland to a wooden lodge on stilts in the bayous. Here you can share in a Cajun crayfish feast cooked in a metal bucket and served with another bucketful of boiled potatoes in their skins, tipped out on to a wooden table, with no more relish than Heinz tomato sauce spiked with Tabasco.

goulash soup (HUNGARY)

This classical dish is imbued with the colour and fragrance of paprika. The cooked potato chunks absorb the warming liquid. In Hungary goulash is often made with lard, but olive oil is as tasty, and healthier. Small dumplings can also be added and cooked in the soup.

SERVES 4

1 tablespoon olive oil
1 onion, finely chopped
2 dessertspoons mild paprika
500g beef brisket, cubed
1 red pepper, deseeded and roughly chopped
250ml dry white wine
Salt
500g potatoes, quartered

Heat the olive oil in a saucepan, add the onion and fry for about 6 minutes until golden brown.

Sprinkle with the paprika, stir well and add the beef and red pepper. Cook gently, stirring often to prevent the paprika from burning.

Add the wine, season with salt and cook slowly for about 45 minutes or until the beef is tender.

Meanwhile, boil the potatoes in salted water until cooked through but still firm. Add the potatoes to the beef with some of the potato liquid – enough to make a soup. Cook for about 10 minutes to combine the flavours.

borscht (RUSSIA)

In Russia every family has their own version of this colourful, sustaining beetroot soup, a vital dish in their repertoire since beetroot lasts the winter through. Its warm sweetness needs to be balanced with acidity and a good combination of spices.

SERVES 6

450g stewing beef
1.8 litres water
4 uncooked small beetroot
375g white cabbage, shredded
2 carrots, cut into matchsticks
2 stalks of celery
250g tomatoes, peeled and sieved
1 tablespoon red wine vinegar
1 tablespoon caster sugar
2 bay leaves
5 allspice berries or 2 teaspoons ground allspice
1½ teaspoons salt
½ teaspoon freshly ground black pepper
1 tablespoon lemon juice
1 tablespoon dill
1 tablespoon chopped parsley
Soured cream, to serve

Trim any surplus fat from the beef. Cut the meat into 2.5cm pieces and place in a saucepan with the water.

Bring to the boil, skim off any scum that rises to the surface, reduce the heat, cover and simmer for 45 minutes.

Reserve one beetroot. Cut the others into matchsticks and add to the saucepan together with the cabbage, carrots and celery. Simmer for a further 25 minutes.

Add the tomatoes, vinegar, sugar, bay leaves, allspice, salt and freshly ground black pepper. Simmer for a further 15 minutes.

Grate the reserved beetroot and put it in a small saucepan with a cupful of the stock from the beef pan. Simmer for 5 minutes and strain the liquid into the *borscht* just before serving.

Check the seasoning and sharpen with the lemon juice. Sprinkle with the dill and parsley.

Serve the soured cream separately, each person adding a spoonful or so to their bowl of soup according to taste.

marinated herrings (DENMARK)

Peppercorns are an essential ingredient in this Danish classic. Fresh herrings are unsuitable; you need raw salted herrings out of a barrel from a delicatessen and then desalinated by soaking overnight. As a substitute, you can use plain roll-mops, unrolled and rinsed under cold water. Prepare the dish 2–3 hours in advance.

SERVES 6

6 salted herrings, soaked overnight in water
200ml white wine vinegar
100g caster sugar
20 black peppercorns
2 onions or shallots, sliced into rings

Drain and fillet the soaked herrings. Wipe dry with kitchen paper.

Put the vinegar, sugar and peppercorns in a small saucepan. Boil for a few minutes, then leave to cool.

Place the herring fillets in a dish. Pour over the vinegar mixture and refrigerate for at least 2 hours.

Serve with the onions or shallots on top.

As a tasty alternative, you can drain the herrings, cut them into thick slices and serve tossed in mayonnaise seasoned with lemon juice and a tablespoon of curry powder.

florida bean soup (USA)

Florida has a unique cooking style, a mixture of Spanish and Caribbean. This rich, savoury soup has its own special combination of flavourings. You need to soak the beans in advance. The pig's trotter adds a gelatinous character.

SERVES 4

250g dried black beans, soaked overnight
2.5 litres water
250g beef, cubed
1 pig's trotter
2 onions, chopped
½ lemon, cut in half
2 cloves
Pinch of ground allspice
1½ tablespoons salt
Freshly ground black pepper
About 4 tablespoons sherry
Slices of lime or lemon

Drain the black beans. Put them in a saucepan, add 1 litre of the water, bring to the boil and boil for 10 minutes. Drain again. Place in a large saucepan with the beef, pig's trotter, onions, lemon, cloves and allspice. Add the remaining water, the salt and plenty of freshly ground black pepper.

Bring to the boil and then lower the heat and simmer for about 3 hours or longer, until the beans are very soft. Remove the meat and and set aside. Discard the pig's trotter bone, lemon and cloves.

Purée the soup in a blender. Return to the saucepan and shred the beef into the soup. Add the sherry to taste and simmer for 5 minutes.

Serve with lime or lemon slices placed in each dish.

poppy seed roll (POLAND)

This classic recipe combines tiny crunchy poppy seeds with a light, mouth-watering, sweet dough. Serve it with morning coffee, afternoon tea or at the end of a meal. Be sure to use real vanilla essence, not the cheaper vanilla flavouring.

SERVES 8

450g plain flour, plus extra for dusting
7g packet dried yeast
Pinch of salt
425ml milk
300g poppy seeds
6 tablespoons honey
6 drops vanilla essence
1 teaspoon ground cinnamon
125g butter, melted, plus extra for greasing and brushing
2 eggs, beaten

Warm a large mixing bowl and sift in the flour, yeast and a pinch of salt.

Warm half of the milk until tepid. Make a well in the centre of the flour and pour in the warm milk. Stir in the flour and knead to make a smooth dough.

Cover the bowl with a cloth and leave in a warm place for 1½–2 hours, until the dough has doubled in size.

Rinse the poppy seeds with hot water and drain well, preferably using a piece of muslin. Grind the seeds in a blender or use a pestle and mortar.

Heat the rest of the milk in a small saucepan. Add the honey and bring slowly to the boil. Add the ground poppy seeds and vanilla essence and cook, stirring often, until the mixture thickens. Stir in the cinnamon and melted butter. Remove from the heat and leave to cool.

Knock down the dough and work in the beaten eggs, stirring well. Turn out the dough and knead on a floured board. Roll the dough into a rectangle just over 5mm thick, about 30 x 20cm. Moisten the edges and spread the poppy seed mixture thickly over the dough almost to the edges.

Roll up the dough in the shape of a Swiss roll, place on a greased baking tray and cover with a cloth. Leave to rise in a warm place for a further 1½–2 hours. Preheat the oven to 190°C/375°F/gas 5.

Brush the top of the poppy seed roll with more melted butter and bake in the preheated oven for 35–45 minutes.

fish stew (PORTUGAL)

This traditional stew makes use of whatever fish the fishermen catch on the day, and you can adapt this recipe to include your favourites, including shellfish. Its authentic flavour comes from the mixture of spices. *Piri-piri* sauce is a very hot sauce of Portuguese-African origin, based on chillies infused in hot oil. It is usually soured with lemon juice; commercial varieties use vinegar.

SERVES 4

225g each of fresh sardines, eel, whiting and tuna
Sea salt
6 tablespoons olive oil
2 onions, chopped
8 tomatoes, peeled and chopped
1 green pepper, deseeded and chopped
4 cloves garlic, chopped
A little grated nutmeg
½ teaspoon ground allspice
3 teaspoons *piri-piri* sauce
1 small glass of dry white wine
4 tablespoons water
Bunch of coriander leaves, chopped
3–4 slices of bread, crusts removed

Preheat the oven to 180°C/350°F/gas 4.

Clean the fish, remove all the bones and cut into small pieces. Sprinkle with sea salt and set aside.

Heat 3 tablespoons of the olive oil in a pan, add the onions, tomatoes and green pepper and cook for about 10 minutes until they soften. Add the garlic, nutmeg, allspice, *piri-piri* sauce, wine and water. Cook for about 5 minutes, stirring, then remove from the heat.

Put 2 tablespoons of the oil in a shallow, ovenproof dish. Add a layer of the fish, then a layer of the sauce and sprinkle with some of the coriander. Repeat the layers until you have added all the ingredients. Cover with the bread slices and sprinkle with the remaining oil.

Cook in the preheated oven for about 30 minutes, until the fish is cooked through.

Serve with boiled or mashed potatoes or chunks of fresh bread.

stuffed peppers and tomatoes

(MEDITERRANEAN, MIDDLE EAST
AND BALKANS)

All over the Mediterranean, the Middle East and the Balkans, wherever peppers and tomatoes grow, you will find a version of this dish. Mint and paprika combined with lamb and rice give great character to the vegetables.

SERVES 4

4 green peppers
4 large tomatoes
3 teaspoons flour
25g butter
2 teaspoons tomato purée
½ teaspoon paprika
5 tablespoons water

FOR THE STUFFING
2 tablespoons olive oil
1 onion, finely chopped
250g lean lamb or beef, minced
25g short-grain rice (or Italian risotto or Spanish paella rice)
1 teaspoon salt
1 teaspoon paprika
4 tablespoons stock or water
2 tablespoons chopped parsley
1 tablespoon chopped mint
½ teaspoon ground black peppercorns

Carefully cut off the stalks from the peppers and remove the seeds and inner ribs, leaving the peppers whole. Cover with boiling, salted water and leave to soak and soften for 15 minutes. Rinse and drain.

Slice off the tops of the tomatoes and scoop out the pulp and seeds. Chop the pulp and seeds and set aside. Turn the tomato shells upside down to drain.

Preheat the oven to 180°C/350°F/gas 4.

Meanwhile, make the stuffing. Heat the olive oil in a saucepan and brown the onion. Add the lamb or beef and fry for a few minutes until it browns. Add the rice, the chopped tomato pulp, salt, paprika and stock or water. Cover and simmer for 15 minutes until most of the liquid has been absorbed. Add the parsley and mint and sprinkle with the black pepper.

Oil an ovenproof dish of sufficient size to hold all the tomatoes and peppers standing upright. Loosely spoon the meat mixture into them. Sprinkle the flour over and dot with the butter.

Mix the tomato purée and paprika with the water, add a little salt and pour around the stuffed peppers and tomatoes.

Bake in the preheated oven for about 50 minutes until tender.

beetroot and horseradish salad (POLAND)

This classic combination of earthy flavours dates back at least to the Middle Ages. Prepare a day in advance.

SERVES 4

4 uncooked small beetroot
2 tablespoons freshly grated or preserved horseradish
Salt
Juice of 1 lemon (or 1½ tablespoons white wine vinegar, diluted with a little water)

Place the beetroot in a small saucepan, cover with cold water, bring to the boil and cook for about 30 minutes until tender.

Peel and roughly grate the beetroot. Arrange alternate layers of beetroot and sprinklings of horseradish in a small salad bowl. Add a sprinkling of salt and the lemon juice (or diluted vinegar). Place in the fridge for 24 hours to blend the flavours.

**Beetroot: northern
Europe's sweet secret.**

mixed vegetable casserole
(BALKANS)

This is a baked equivalent of a *ratatouille*, the vegetables keeping their individual character, but also blending flavours with each other. It is a classic all over the Balkans. It can be cooked on the stove but has added richness when baked in the oven in a *guvec* or flat earthenware dish. In Greece they add garlic; in Bulgaria, green chilli peppers. This version includes both. Vary the vegetables according to taste and availability.

SERVES 4–6

1 large aubergine, cut into cubes
3 teaspoons salt
450g potatoes, cut into 2.5cm chunks
450g onions, chopped
450g courgettes, sliced into thick rounds
225g green beans, each cut into 3 pieces
225g shelled fresh (or frozen) peas
1 green pepper, deseeded and sliced
125g okra (optional)
2 tablespoons tomato purée
2 cloves garlic, crushed (optional)
1 green chilli, chopped (optional)
Bunch of parsley, chopped
4 tablespoons olive oil
2 teaspoons paprika
450g tomatoes, sliced

Preheat the oven to 200°C/400°F/gas 6.

Sprinkle the aubergine cubes with the salt and leave to drain in a colander for 1 hour. Pat dry with kitchen paper.

Mix all the vegetables, apart from the tomatoes, in to a wide, flat casserole dish with the tomato purée, garlic and green chilli (if using), parsley and 2 tablespoons of the olive oil. Season with the paprika and salt to taste. Cover with the tomato slices and sprinkle with the remaining oil.

Cook in the preheated oven, uncovered, for 10 minutes. Lower the heat to 190°C/375°F/gas 5 and cook for about 1½ hours until the vegetables are tender.

Serve hot or cold.

aubergine moussaka (GREECE)

Variations of this dish enriched with paprika and sweetened with cinnamon are served throughout the Balkans.

SERVES 6

2 aubergines, cut lengthways into thin slices
Salt
Olive oil, for frying
500g courgettes, cut into 1.25cm rounds
4 onions, finely chopped
750g potatoes, cut into thin slices
200g tomato purée
1kg lean lamb, minced
2 teaspoons paprika
2 bunches of flat-leaf parsley, finely chopped
1 teaspoon crushed black peppercorns
2 teaspoons ground cinnamon
2–3 eggs, lightly beaten

Sprinkle salt on the aubergine slices and drain in a colander for 1 hour to remove the bitter juices. Pat dry with kitchen paper.

Preheat the oven to 190°C/375°F/gas 5.

Put some oil in a frying pan and separately fry the aubergines, courgettes, onions and potatoes, transferring to plates as they are cooked.

Heat a little more oil and add the tomato purée, stirring as it cooks and turns dark red. Add the lamb and season with salt and the paprika. Stir-fry for about 5 minutes to brown the lamb. Add the parsley, onions, crushed peppercorns and cinnamon, and stir well.

In a large baking dish, arrange a layer of potatoes, then alternate layers of lamb and vegetables, finishing with a layer of potatoes. Sprinkle each layer with salt.

Bake in the preheated oven for 30 minutes. Pour the beaten eggs over the moussaka and return to the oven for a further 15 minutes until the top is golden brown.

Serve hot with natural yoghurt.

louisiana jambalaya (USA)

This classic Creole rice dish contains all the heat and spice of its Caribbean origins. Its name comes from the French word for ham – *jambon* – and it is traditional to begin the cooking in bacon or ham fat or lard.

SERVES 4

2 tablespoons olive oil, butter or bacon fat
2 onions, chopped
4 smoked pork sausages
1 tablespoon plain flour
2 cloves garlic, crushed
200g smoked ham, diced
2 medium tomatoes, peeled, deseeded and chopped
200g long-grain rice
375ml chicken stock or water
1 green chilli, deseeded
1 green pepper, deseeded and chopped
Pinch of dried thyme
½ teaspoon Creole or cayenne pepper
400g cooked prawns (or 8 cooked crayfish or king prawns), peeled
3 tablespoons chopped parsley
Salt

Heat the olive oil, butter or bacon fat in a heavy saucepan. Fry the onions and sausages for about five minutes until browned.

Stir in the flour and cook for a minute or two until it browns slightly. Stir in the garlic then add the ham and tomatoes. Cover tightly with a lid (and crumpled foil to make a good seal) and simmer for 30 minutes on the lowest heat.

Add the rice, stock or water, chilli, green pepper, thyme, Creole or cayenne pepper and salt to taste. Cover tightly and continue simmering for about 20–25 minutes until the rice is cooked but not soft. Do not lift up the lid or stir the rice during this time.

When the cooking time is over, add the prawns (or crayfish or king prawns) and cook for a few minutes more to heat through. Sprinkle with the parsley and serve very hot.

pork terrine with quatre épices (FRANCE)

Country pâtés are among the glories of French cooking, a world away from *haute cuisine*; robust and generous, the produce of practical farming people, who know how to spoil themselves. The spicing intensifies the rich flavours and cuts into the fat.

SERVES 8 AS AN APPETISER

750g boned shoulder of pork
250g pork belly (or sausage meat)
2 teaspoons *quatre épices* (see page 134)
1 teaspoon dried thyme
10 juniper berries, plus extra to garnish
2 cloves garlic, crushed
2 teaspoons salt
5 tablespoons dry white wine
3 tablespoons cognac or calvados
3 tablespoons sherry
40g butter or pork fat
2 onions, finely chopped
1 egg beaten
15g flour
250g streaky bacon
3 bay leaves, to garnish

Cut up the shoulder and belly pork finely and either put through a mincer or process in a food mixer, using the sharpest blades. The texture needs to be coarse, so be careful not to reduce it to a paste. Transfer to a bowl and stir in the *quatre épices*, thyme, juniper berries, garlic, salt and the alcohol. Cover with clingfilm and leave to marinate overnight in the fridge.

Preheat the oven to 220°C/425°F/gas 7.

In a frying pan, melt 25g of the butter or pork fat and fry the onions for about 10 minutes until soft but not brown.

Beat the egg and flour together. Stir the onions and the egg and flour mixture into the pork mixture.

Rub a 1 litre terrine or ovenproof dish with the remaining butter or pork fat and line it with the streaky bacon, letting the ends hang over the edges. Fill the terrine or dish with the pork mixture and cover with the overlapping bacon.

Place the terrine or dish in a larger container (using it as a *bain-marie*), carefully filling it to half-way up the side of the terrine with boiling water from a kettle. Cook, uncovered, for 1½ hours in the preheated oven until the top browns (cover if it starts to burn).

Test with a skewer for doneness: if it comes out clean, it's ready; if not, cook for about 30 minutes more.

Remove the terrine or dish from the *bain-marie* and leave to cool for several hours. You may need to pour off some of the surplus fat. Cover with foil and arrange small weights or cans of food on top to compress the pâté as it sets. Leave to chill in the fridge for a day. It is best eaten within a few days, but in the countryside it's often kept for several weeks, covered with a thick layer of lard, which keeps it from spoiling.

The pâté is great as an appetiser with toast, gherkins or pickled onions. Garnish with bay leaves and juniper berries before serving.

rabbit with mustard (FRANCE)

Mustard was a very important spice in Roman cooking and, when they conquered Gaul and introduced their cooking techniques, the French improved their recipes. Dijon is the world capital of mustard and the leading French company, Maille, makes dozens of flavours and styles. British mustard is made with dry mustard flour; the French is from whole seeds, which are macerated in white wine and crushed, then sieved to make a smooth mustard with a milder taste. The tartness of Dijon mustard perfectly lifts the bland, soft meat of the rabbit.

SERVES 4

2 loins of rabbit (4 if very small)
Salt and freshly ground black pepper
1 tablespoon olive oil
25g butter
5 shallots, chopped
1 glass of dry white wine
3 tablespoons Dijon mustard
6 tablespoons crème fraîche

Preheat the oven to 200°C/400°F/gas 6.

Season the rabbit with salt and pepper and fry in the olive oil and butter in an iron or ovenproof pan to brown on both sides. Place the pan in the preheated oven and cook for 20 minutes.

Using oven gloves to remove the pan, add the chopped shallots and wine, and return to the oven. Cook for 10 minutes, then turn down the heat to 150°C/300°F/gas 2, cover with foil and cook for a further 30 minutes, basting several times.

Beat the mustard and crème fraîche together and stir into the juices in the pan. Divide the rabbit into four pieces, and pour the sauce around. Serve with mashed potato.

paella valenciana (SPAIN)

Saffron, the world's most expensive spice, is an essential ingredient in a Spanish paella, as is paprika. Paella originates in the rice-growing plains around Valencia and they are very precise about the recipe, frowning upon variations common in other parts of Spain. For example, they don't accept the inclusion of seafood in an authentic paella Valenciana; they would call it an *arroz a la marinera* but not a paella. There's no reason why you shouldn't garnish your own paella with langoustine or prawns, mussels and squid; it will be delicious but not, so they say, a true paella. So here, for the record, is the true paella Valenciana. It is essential to use *calasparra* rice, which absorbs four times its weight in water. If you don't want snails or can't obtain them, the Spanish substitute rosemary, adding it towards the end of cooking to give an earthy taste.

SERVES 4

500g corn-fed chicken, jointed
500g rabbit, cut into small pieces
2 tablespoons olive oil
Salt
100g green beans, cut into 2cm pieces
16 cleaned snails (or a sprig of rosemary)
20 strands of saffron
1.5 litres water or light chicken stock
1 tablespoon paprika
1 medium tomato
100g cooked *tabella* or butter beans
100g cooked lima beans or canned borlotti beans, drained
400g *bomba* (round-grain) Spanish paella rice

Trim the chicken and rabbit, leaving in the bones.

Heat the olive oil in a 40cm paella pan, or your widest shallow frying pan, with a pinch of salt. When hot, add the chicken and rabbit and fry over a medium heat until golden brown on all sides. Add the green beans and fry for 5 minutes. If using, boil the snails in a separate saucepan for 5 minutes, then Drain.

Crush the saffron strands in a cup with the back of a spoon. Add a little boiling water and continue crushing until the colour becomes dense orange.

Bring the water or chicken stock to the boil. Sprinkle the paprika over the chicken and rabbit and stir for 30 seconds. Crush the tomato into the pan, and cook for a further 30 seconds. Add the *tabella* or butter beans and the lima or borlotti beans and all the boiling water or stock. Add the snails (if using), saffron and 1 teaspoon salt.

Cover with foil and simmer for 20–30 minutes until the meat is tender. Add enough boiling water to return to the original level. Sprinkle the rice into the boiling liquid and cook over a high heat for 5 minutes.

Turn down the heat and leave to cook, without stirring, for about 10 minutes until the liquid evaporates. Now add the rosemary, if using. If the liquid evaporates too quickly during the cooking, add a little more boiling water.

Remove from the heat, cover with newspaper or a damp, folded cloth and leave for a further 5–10 minutes, while the rice continues to cook and absorb the liquid. The final texture should be moist. If the rice sticks at the bottom, this is considered desirable – indeed the best part. It is known as the *soccorat* – named after a nearby town burnt down by the Romans!

peppered steak (FRANCE)

This relatively recent dish – it didn't come into fashion until the beginning of the twentieth century – now appears on practically every French menu. The hot, rich coating of crushed peppercorns gives flavour to the succulent meat.

SERVES 4

4 thick slices of rump steak
30 black peppercorns, crushed
Salt and freshly ground black pepper
75g butter
50ml olive oil
50ml brandy or cognac
100ml veal or chicken stock
100ml cream

Season the steaks with the crushed peppercorns, patting them into place. Season with salt. Heat the butter and olive oil in a very hot frying pan, quickly brown the steaks, then cook as preferred – 2 minutes each side for rare, 3 minutes for medium to well-done.

Remove from the pan and place on a shallow serving dish. Cover and keep hot.

Pour off the excess fat from the pan. Add the brandy or cognac to the remaining juices, and then *flambé*, setting the spirit alight. Add the stock and boil rapidly for 5 minutes to reduce. Add the cream and simmer until the sauce is thick and smooth. Check the seasoning. Add more pepper if desired. Pour the sauce over the steaks.

Serve immediately with chips or sauté potatoes.

Pickled pork with sauerkraut
(GERMANY)

This is a celebrated dish from the time of the Prussian Empire. The correct balance of spices is essential. You need to give the butcher notice that you want salted knuckles, so that he can prepare them for you. *Sauerkraut* is pickled cabbage, and is widely available.

SERVES 4

3 onions
4 salted knuckles of pork, 500g each
1 bay leaf
5 coriander seeds
5 black peppercorns, coarsely ground
4 teaspoons salt
1kg *sauerkraut*
50g pork dripping
5 juniper berries
300ml white wine
1 potato, grated
2 teaspoons caster sugar

Cut 1 of the onions in half and brown the cut surfaces in a frying pan. This will give added colour to the gravy. Chop the remaining onions and set aside.

Place the pork in a saucepan and cover with water. Add the browned onion, bay leaf, coriander seeds, ground peppercorns and salt. Bring to the boil and simmer for 1½ hours.

When the pork is almost cooked, roughly chop the *sauerkraut* and bring to the boil in a separate pan with about 500ml of the cooking liquid.

Melt the pork dripping in another pan and fry the chopped onions until golden brown. Add to the *sauerkraut* together with the juniper berries and wine. Cook gently for 40 minutes, then add the potato and mix well. Cook for 10 minutes. Finally, add the sugar to balance the sourness.

Arrange the *sauerkraut* and pork on the same dish. Serve with mashed potatoes.

midwest spare ribs (USA)

Pork spareribs are served from one end of America to the other. In Canada they eat them with *sauerkraut* and in Pennsylvania they often add a layer of apple stuffing to the centre. Chinese workers, who helped to build the railroads, introduced the 'sweet-and-sour' flavour. Tomato ketchup and Worcestershire sauce are perfect for this dish; both are good ready-made spice mixtures.

SERVES 4

1 tablespoon sunflower oil or bacon dripping
1 onion, chopped
250ml tomato ketchup
3 tablespoons Worcestershire sauce
2 tablespoon malt vinegar
2 tablespoons caster sugar
4 tablespoon lemon juice
2 teaspoons ready-made English mustard
125ml water
1 teaspoon dried basil
1 teaspoon chilli powder
3 tablespoons chopped parsley
2kg pork spareribs
Salt and freshly ground black pepper

Preheat the oven to 230°C/450°F/gas 8.

Heat the sunflower oil, or dripping in a saucepan and fry the onion for about 5 minutes. Add the tomato ketchup, Worcestershire sauce, vinegar, sugar, lemon juice, mustard, water, basil, chilli powder and parsley. Simmer for 30 minutes on the lowest heat.

Meanwhile, wipe the ribs using kitchen paper and season with salt and freshly ground black pepper. Place on a rack in a shallow roasting tray and bake in the preheated oven for 30 minutes.

Remove from the oven, drain away the fat and remove the rack. Put the ribs back in the tray and brush them with the cooked sauce.

Turn down the oven to 150°C/300°F/gas 2. Bake the ribs for at least 1½ hours more, brushing often with the sauce, until tender.

deep-dish apple pie (USA)

Apple pie is so much a part of American national life, there are very few early recipes recorded as it was assumed every home had their own. It is likely that the Pilgrim Fathers introduced the dish, but Americans made it their own with abundant use of cinnamon – for many years, Boston was one of the world's leading spice importers.

A deep pie dish is lined with pastry, filled, then covered with a pastry layer before baking – European versions usually dispense with the lining. Either shortcrust or flaky pastry are suitable, both of which can be bought frozen.

SERVES 4

225g shortcrust pastry (homemade or frozen)
Flour for dusting, plus extra for sprinkling
1kg cooking apples
Juice and grated rind of 1 lemon
100g caster sugar (more if the apples are very sour)
1 tablespoon ground cinnamon
½ teaspoon mixed spice (see page 135) or 1 nutmeg, grated
    and mixed with 2 cloves, ground
15g butter, cut into small dice
1 egg white, beaten

Roll out the pastry on a floured surface to make the lining and lid for a deep 23cm ovenproof glass or ceramic pie dish. Chill the pastry for 30 minutes in the fridge while you prepare the apple filling.

Peel and core the apples and slice into segments, transferring to a bowl of water containing a few drops of the lemon juice to prevent them turning brown.

Preheat the oven to 200°C/400°F/gas 6.

Line the pie dish with some of the rolled pastry. Drain the apple slices and mix with the sugar, cinnamon, mixed spice or ground nutmeg and cloves, lemon rind and remaining lemon juice. Fill the pie and dot with the butter.

Moisten the edge of the pastry lining and cover with the pastry lid. Pinch into place, marking with the tines of a fork to give a decorative effect. If you like, cut any leftover pieces of pastry into leaf shapes and, moistening them, arrange on the lid.

Brush the surface with the beaten egg white and sprinkle with caster sugar. Make several cuts in the lid for the steam to escape while baking.

Bake in the preheated oven for 40 minutes.

saffron buns (SWEDEN)

Saffron is associated mainly with Mediterranean and Middle Eastern cookery, but its use has also crept into northern Europe. Cornwall in England to this day maintains a long tradition of baking saffron bread and cakes, and the Swedish use saffron for buns and plaited loaves for festive occasions such as Santa Lucia (a Swedish advent festival celebrated on 13 December) and Christmas.

MAKES ABOUT 30 BUNS (OR 3 PLAITED LOAVES)

About 30 strands of saffron
225g caster sugar
250ml milk
200g butter, melted
1 egg, beaten
750g plain flour, plus extra for dusting
2 x 7g packets dried yeast
½ teaspoon salt
50g blanched almonds, roughly chopped
100g raisins
100g candied peel, chopped
1 egg yolk, beaten with 2 teaspoons milk,
    to make an egg wash
Blanched almonds, sliced, and raisins, to decorate (optional)

Dry the saffron strands in a frying pan over the lowest heat, being careful not to let them burn. Put them in a mortar with 1 teaspoon of the sugar and grind with a pestle.

Warm the milk until tepid and add the melted butter. Stir in the ground saffron and the egg.

Sift the flour into a mixing bowl and stir in the yeast, salt and 1 teaspoon of the sugar. Pour in the warmed milk and egg mixture, and, using a wooden spoon, stir into a dough. Shape into a large ball, sprinkle with a little flour, cover with a dry cloth and put in a warm place such as an airing cupboard for up to 2 hours, until the dough doubles in size.

Knock back the dough by kneading briefly. Add the remaining sugar, almonds, raisins and candied peel and divide into about 30 pieces to make small buns. If making loaves, roll into nine long strips, plaiting three together to make each loaf.

Place on a greased baking sheet, cover with a cloth and leave to rise a second time. Preheat the oven to 200°C/400°F/gas 6.

Brush with the egg wash and, if liked, stud with extra almond slices and raisins. Bake the buns for 6–10 minutes and the plaited loaves for 20–25 minutes. Remove and leave to cool on a wire tray.

christmas pudding (UK)

In the sixteenth century, this dish was known as Christmas broth or porridge and included meat, herbs and plums. But over time the meat was phased out, leaving suet in its place. Prunes and sultanas replaced the plums, and peel and glacé cherries crept into the recipe, together with a rich mix of spices that gave the taste we know and love to this traditional, textured pudding. It's best when made at least 6 weeks in advance.

TO MAKE 3 PUDDINGS

250g self-raising flour
250g shredded suet
250g fresh white breadcrumbs
250g candied peel, chopped
125g glacé cherries, rinsed and chopped
Grated rind of 1 lemon
250g currants
250g sultanas
250g seedless raisins
50g almonds, blanched and chopped
500g dark soft brown sugar
3 teaspoons mixed spice (see page 135)
¼ teaspoon salt
6 eggs, beaten
Butter, for greasing
300ml stout (such as Guinness) or ale
Generous dash of brandy or whisky

As pungent as any spice – the sour juice and bitter zest of the lemon adds a zing to every recipe.

Mix together the flour, suet, breadcrumbs, candied peel, glacé cherries, lemon rind, currants, sultanas, raisins, almonds and sugar in a large bowl. Add the mixed spice and salt, and stir well.

Beat in the eggs and stout or ale, and stir vigorously – traditionally, get everyone in the house to lend a hand. Add more alcohol if the mixture is too stiff; it should be quite loose.

Grease three 1-litre pudding basins. Divide the mixture between each, leaving about 5cm space at the top to allow the puddings to rise. Cover each pudding with a large circle of greaseproof paper, tied in place with string.

Place each basin in a lidded saucepan with enough boiling water to come half-way up the side of the basin. Cover the saucepans with tight-fitting lids and steam for 7 hours, topping up the water from time to time to keep it at the necessary level.

Lift out the basins and leave to cool. Cover with fresh greaseproof paper or foil and tie in place with string. Store in a cool dry place. They will keep for up to a year.

Before serving, steam again for another hour or two to heat through. Serve with brandy butter.

rice pudding (GREECE)

A smooth, creamy pudding laced with lemon and sprinkled with cinnamon.

150g short-grain rice
3 strips of lemon rind
1 litre milk
2 teaspoons cornflour
150g caster sugar
1 teaspoon ground cinnamon

Put the rice and lemon rind in a heavy saucepan and cover with the milk. Stir well and simmer gently for about 30 minutes until the rice is soft.

Mix the cornflour and sugar together and add to the rice. Stir well and continue cooking, stirring occasionally, for a further 20–30 minutes until the pudding is like thick cream.

Discard the lemon rind and leave to cool to room temperature. Sprinkle with the cinnamon.

ginger beer (UK)

This popular, refreshing drink was once a favourite among farm labourers, especially at harvest time.

MAKES 4.5 LITRES

5cm ginger, finely grated
325g granulated sugar
25g cream of tartar
Juice and rind of 1 lemon
4.5 litres boiling water
25g wine yeast (from a specialist shop) or dried yeast

Put the ginger, sugar, cream of tartar and lemon rind in a clean plastic bucket or suitably large bowl. Add the boiling water and lemon juice, and stir well. Leave to cool until just warm.

Cream the yeast with a little water and stir into the ginger liquid. Cover with a cloth and leave in a warm place for 1 day.

Skim off the froth, strain the ginger beer through a sieve and pour it through a funnel into sterilised beer bottles. Put corks in the bottles and, with a short piece of fine wire, secure the cork round the neck of the bottle. Store in a cool place for at least 2 days before drinking. Check the bottles from time to time, and if they are starting to bubble and ferment too rapidly, recork them.

apple, date and walnut chutney (UK)

Chutney makes a sharp accompaniment to meat and especially cheese. This recipe makes enough to keep you well supplied through the year.

MAKES ABOUT 6–8 JARS

500g onions, chopped
1kg cooking apples, peeled, cored and chopped
750g dates, stoned and chopped
75g walnuts, chopped
1 teaspoon salt
1 teaspoon ground ginger
1 teaspoon cayenne pepper
600ml malt vinegar
250g brown sugar

Simmer the onions in a little water until soft. Add the apples and cook gently for about 20 minutes until completely soft.

Add the dates, walnuts, salt, ginger, cayenne pepper and half of the vinegar, and bring to the boil. Stir from time to time and cook on a medium heat for about 20 minutes until the mixture thickens.

Add the sugar and the rest of the vinegar and keep stirring until the sugar dissolves. Simmer until the chutney thickens, stirring often. It must not stick.

Spoon the chutney into sterilised jars, seal and keep until needed. The chutney is best when left to mature for several months.

cajun spice mix (USA)

Cajun cooks are notoriously secretive about their individual spice mixes, and no two will be the same. Most will contain plenty of chilli, pepper, wild thyme, sage, oregano and, uniquely, *gumbo filé* powder, the dried bitter young leaves of the sassafras tree, long treasured by the native Indians in Louisiana; and perhaps garlic or onion powder, although it's preferable to use fresh. Like Jamaica's jerk seasoning, the mixture is rubbed into meat, poultry and fish hours in advance of cooking.

MAKES 1 JAR

½ tablespoon cayenne or chilli pepper
1 tablespoon freshly ground white or black pepper
1 tablespoon cumin seeds, roasted and ground
1 tablespoon dried wild thyme, rubbed
1 tablespoon dried oregano, rubbed
½ tablespoon dried sage, rubbed
½ tablespoon mustard powder
½ tablespoon *gumbo filé* powder, if available

Mix all the ingredients together and store in an airtight jar. It keeps for several months.

quatre épices (FRANCE)

The French have been reluctant, historically, to embrace spices, preferring dried and fresh herbs in cooking. But this mixture is an exception, often used to cut into the very rich flavour of fat in pork, duck and chicken liver pâtés and other *charcuterie*, such as *rillettes* and *saucissons*. The blend sometimes includes more than four spices as extra or alternative options. This is the basic mixture as given in the bible of French cooking terms, *Larousse Gastronomique*.

MAKES 1 JAR

125g freshly ground white pepper
25g grated nutmeg
25g ground ginger
15g ground cloves

Prepare the mixture using fresh whole spices if possible. Mix well, and keep in an airtight jar. It is best used within a few weeks, as spices lose their piquancy after being ground.

mincemeat (UK)

At one time mincemeat really did contain meat, but over the years it was replaced with beef suet. Spices were always part of this mixture, which is traditionally used to fill tarts and pies at Christmas. It tastes best when left to mature for at least 2 weeks.

MAKES ABOUT 1.5KG

4 lemons
375g Cox's apples, peeled, cored and sliced
250g seedless raisins
250g sultanas
250g currants
250g candied peel, chopped
250g soft brown sugar
Pinch of salt
250g shredded suet
2 teaspoons mixed spice (see page 135) or 1 teaspoon allspice
½ nutmeg, grated
½ teaspoon ground mace
½ teaspoon ground ginger
½ wine glass of brandy, whisky or rum

Grate the lemons, reserving the rind, then remove the pith with a potato peeler or knife. Chop the flesh of the lemons and cook with the apple slices on a low heat for 10 minutes until slightly soft.

The rainbow col
of a spice stall at
en-Provence, Fra

Remove from the heat, allow to cool, then add the raisins, sultanas, currants, candied peel and grated lemon rind, and chop finely.

Transfer to a bowl and add the sugar, salt and suet. Stir in the mixed spice or allspice, nutmeg, mace, ginger and alcohol. Spoon into sterilised jars, seal and store for at least a fortnight to mature. The mincemeat will keep for months.

piccalilli (UK)

For centuries mustard was one of the few home-grown spices in Britain and therefore the cheapest. Nobody knows how this attractive, yellow relish got its name, but it is an ideal way to use up vegetables at the end of the season. Cauliflower is traditionally included, but you can use equal quantities of any variation of vegetables to make up the total amount. It is ideal served with cold meats or cheese.

MAKES 6 JARS

2.5kg vegetables (for example, cauliflower, green tomatoes, cucumber or gherkin, courgette, green beans, onion, carrot, green or red pepper)
425g cooking salt
1 litre white wine vinegar or malt vinegar
15g turmeric powder
25g ground allspice
25g mustard powder
25g ground ginger
175g granulated sugar
2 tablespoons cornflour

Prepare your selection of vegetables and cut into very small pieces. Spread all the vegetables out on a large dish and cover with the salt. Weight a plate on top of the vegetables and leave for 1 day to extract any moisture. Drain the vegetables, wash and rinse them. Pat dry with a clean cloth.

Reserve about 25ml of the vinegar and pour the rest into a large saucepan. Stir in the turmeric, allspice, mustard, ginger and sugar. Stir over a low heat until the sugar is dissolved. Add the vegetables and cook gently for about 10 minutes until they are cooked through but still whole.

Mix the cornflour with the reserved vinegar and add to the pan. Bring to the boil, stirring, and then simmer for about 3 minutes.

Spoon the mixture into sterilised jars, seal, and leave the piccalilli to mature for at least 6 weeks.

mixed spice (UK)

A highly perfumed, pungent and warm spice mixture, used by the British since Tudor times to flavour rich fruit puddings and cakes, mincemeat for mince pies, and mulled wines and warm winter punches. It is sold ready-made, but you can make your own, adjusting the balance to taste. To make the mixture hotter, add 1 teaspoon ground ginger; to make it sweeter, add 1 teaspoon ground cinnamon. To add a lemony note, add 1 teaspoon ground coriander.

MAKES 1 JAR

1 tablespoon ground allspice
1 teaspoon grated nutmeg
12 cloves, ground
1 teaspoon ground mace
1 teaspoon ground ginger, cinnamon or coriander, to taste

Mix the ingredients well and keep in an airtight jar.

pickling spice (UK)

This warming spiced vinegar is used for pickled onions and other fresh young vegetables to see you through the winter months. It can also be used with ripe summer fruits, such as plums. Make the vinegar at least 2 months before you want to use it and always use whole spices.

MAKES 3 JARS

1 litre malt vinegar or cider vinegar (use cider vinegar when pickling fruit)
5g cloves
5g blade of mace
5g allspice berries
5g stick of cinnamon
A few black peppercorns
3cm ginger, grated

Mix all the ingredients together and leave to steep in a glass bottle for at least 8 weeks. Shake the bottle from time to time.

Strain, and remove the spices before use. Alternatively, tie the spices in muslin and leave them hanging in the vinegar to steep. Remove the muslin and spices before use.

Exotic spices have not been a main feature of cooking Down Under, but all that has changed in the last two decades. Aussie and Kiwi cooks are today among the most innovative users of spices, herbs and flavourings on the planet.

The modern style of cooking, which some have called Pacific Rim, has a debt to Thailand, Malaysia and Indonesia, and China and Japan too. But it also looks to the Mediterranean, using Asian ingredients to spice up south European dishes – a style which has been dubbed Mediterrasian, which is clever if not catchy.

But, inspiringly, Australia has also tapped into its own unique spice resource. They have rediscovered a 6000-year-old Aboriginal tradition of using bush berries, roots, barks, seeds and leaves to season a survival diet of small animals and birds.

Vic Cherikoff, who runs the Rare Spices Company in Sydney, has to be credited with this mould-breaking step back. Of the many herb and spice leaves and seeds he identified, none has been so successful as wattle seed.

Wattle seed is one of only a few edible seeds from the worldwide family of acacia trees. Roasted and ground, it tastes like a cross between hazelnut and chocolate. Wattle seed has been enthusiastically adopted by Australasian cooks as a flavouring for creamy desserts such as *crèmes brûlées* and ice cream.

Unusually, Cherikoff has also tracked down numerous leaves from different kinds of eucalyptus (there are over 1000 different varieties) and myrtle bushes; some have the flavours of thyme, basil, lemon and cinnamon. Sold freeze-dried, they deliver very fresh, tingling spice notes into the kitchen.

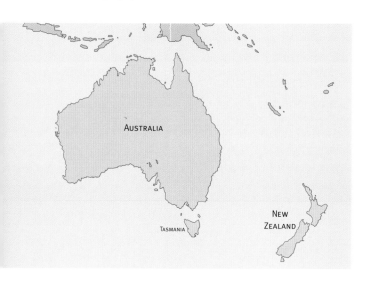

Only a very receptive cuisine would be open to these new possibilities. Until about 30 years ago, both Australia and New Zealand had limited aspirations as far as fancy cuisine was concerned. The Australian national dish was meat pie, and the national drink, beer. The same was true of New Zealand. Socialising in both countries revolved around a beer culture. It has to be admitted that, nowhere in the world is glugging beer particularly associated with fine dining (except Belgium whose fine-flavoured beers made by monks in the monasteries rank with wines).

Eating habits began to change in the 1970s, when Australia started to develop its own wine potential. Building on a tradition going back to the 1880s, when early European immigrants brought vines to the Barossa Valley, Australian wine-makers developed fresh-tasting wines with big, gutsy flavours. They were soon wowing the world, at the same time converting their own country to a wine culture. In a matter of years it became more common to take a wine box (an Australian invention) to a party, picnic or barbecue than a crate of beer.

The best beef, lamb and seafood

In New Zealand, too, the wine industry flowered and it brought in its wake a fledgling cuisine, where there had been none before. Kiwis discovered that their soil and climate perfectly suited the growing of grapes such as sauvignon blanc for superb white wines. They also won rapid worldwide recognition; fame, rather than commercial success, since New Zealand wines amount to less than 1 per cent of the world's production.

So, for two centuries, both Australia and New Zealand had been content to follow a mainly European pattern of eating. And who needed *haute cuisine* when the best beef, lamb, dairy food, seafood and shellfish, not to mention abundant vegetables and fruit, were there for the taking at the back door? And who wanted to toil in a kitchen in the hot summer when common sense demanded you just throw another prawn on the barbie and broach another tinnie?

Australia was first to break out of the European straitjacket. Immigrants from Pacific Rim countries who found themselves in low-paid jobs as kitchen porters brought with them a precious gift: the kitchen skills of their homelands. And a new generation of Australia's adventurous young travellers, mostly backpackers who'd trailed the street markets of Thailand and Southeast Asia, were quick to recognise the exoticism now flourishing in their own kitchens. They started to experiment.

In poor Asian countries subtle spicing lends excitement and interest to bland bowls of rice and noodles. But in bountiful

New World olives – big business New Zealand.

Australia the flavours could do much more, illuminating the glorious produce of Australian farms and shoreline. Classic shellfish dishes went into the spice kitchen and came out transformed; huge mud crabs, Moreton Bay bugs and squat yabbies glowed with a New Wave makeover.

New Zealand had even less of a tradition of eating out in restaurants. Then Corban's, one of the biggest wine companies, anxious to stimulate sales at home as well as overseas, teamed up with the restaurant trade, offering thousands of pounds by way of cash prizes to those who could produce menus which best matched the company's wines. Kiwis are very competitive, as all sportsfolk know, and this was good sport. Overnight, every restaurant was challenging for trophies and prizes, aided and betted by loyal customers.

Julie Dalzell, editing the New Zealand food magazine *Cuisine*, marvelled at the pace of change. It hadn't been many years since she had eaten her first avocado (and now New Zealand is a leading producer of superb avocado oils for salads and cooking). The wine initiative was part of it, she said, but mostly she put the success down to the Kiwi's thirst for experience and travel: there isn't a young student who doesn't plan a world tour and those interested in food make it their business to offer themselves for a *stage* in Michelin-starred restaurants, working around the clock for no money, and sleeping rough in barns, in order to build up their CVs.

Pacific Rim cooking

Australian and Kiwi cooks have become renowned around the world for their adventurous approach in fusing Anglo-Saxon, Asian and Mediterranean foods, both in spicing and cooking techniques.

Fusion isn't a word that they like; Pacific Rim is helpful. At its most bizarre it leads to an excess of imagination, such as this combination encountered in New Zealand (all on one plate): chicken with mustard and chargrilled aubergine with *rouille* and *gazpacho* – which is a heavy mixture of French, Italian and Spanish.

On the same rule-breaking menu was chilli and tequila ice cream with cinnamon and chocolate. Is it not the breathtaking equivalent of bungee jumping, another Kiwi invention?

But mixing and matching can produce some thrilling results, especially in the hands of a master like Peter Gordon, a Kiwi who worked in Sydney and then Wellington before bringing his Sugar Club to international success in London (with instructive cookery books to match). He has since made another cultural jump at his London restaurant, Los Providores – fusing Spanish products with antipodean New Wave cooking style.

Peter Gordon grew up with a grandmother who taught him to love such native foods as *kumera* (a yellow sweet potato) and *kabocha* (the dense New Zealand squash). After a tour of Thailand street markets, he realised he could enhance their warm colours and comforting textures with the tang of lemongrass, kaffir lime leaves, purple basil and chilli. He has never looked back.

He was not alone. Kiwi chefs Greg Heffernan and Warwick Brown travelled to France to make European three-star restaurants their university, introducing a higher level of sophistication to New Zealand than their country had ever experienced.

In Australia the revolution in cooking continued via a string of numerous brilliant chefs, culminating with the remarkable David Thompson, who learnt to speak Thai and brought Thai cooking to Sydney (and has written the best book on the subject as well as later picking up a Michelin star at Nahm, his Thai restaurant in London); and Sydney's Japanese star, Tetsuya Wakuda, whose fame has spread around the world, truly a fusion cook of brilliance, bestriding two cultures.

Food is not only changing through the chefs and writers; producers are evolving new ingredients, from the tropical fruits of Queensland and the golden kiwi fruit, zespri, to olives and avocado oils in New Zealand.

And who outside Australasia has heard of cervena? New Zealand is a country which considers lamb to be a laughable dish to put on a restaurant menu, so they ingeniously converted an ill-considered meat, deer (a pest in the South Island) into a worthy game cut – inventing a new name for it, cervena, and exciting new recipes to go with it.

Meat had been the staple in this part of the world, and shellfish was abundant, but now Australia and New Zealand started to take other prize fish from the ocean, discovering a range of exquisite species unknown in other waters, such as orange roughy, which is taken from the sea bed several kilometres down, a fish with firm, white, silky flesh which has been described as the fillet steak of the sea.

The recipes that follow (with one or two old favourites to put them in a historical context) reflect the influences of a new generation of cooks and writers, such as Peter Gordon, David Thompson, Tetsuya Wakuda and many more. Surely, this is a golden age.

shellfish soup with lobster wontons (AUSTRALIA)

Until 30 years ago, the national dish of Australia was meat pie, sauce and peas, and cooking was still based on the meat-and-potatoes ethos the first settlers brought with them. But modern Australian restaurants started to create a new cooking style embracing the cuisines of their neighbours on the Pacific Rim. This is a typical example.

SERVES 4

250g cooked lobster meat or prawns
4–6 spring onions, finely chopped
2.5cm ginger, grated
16–20 *wonton* skins (from a Chinese store)

FOR THE FISH STOCK

1kg heads and bones of white fish (for example, turbot,
    sole or conger eel)
50g butter
½ onion, chopped
1 leek, white part only, chopped
50g mushrooms, chopped
2 glasses of dry white wine
1.5 litres water
1 bouquet garni (green part of leek tied with a sprig each of
    thyme and parsley and a bayleaf)
Piece of dried orange peel
1 vanilla pod

FOR THE SOUP

2 tomatoes, chopped
1 carrot, grated
1 stick of celery, finely sliced
1 leek, white part only, sliced
Shell/s and head/s of the lobster or prawns, crushed
Pinch of saffron strands

First make the fish stock by soaking the fish heads and bones in cold water for 3 hours.

Melt the butter in a pan and cook the onion, leek and mushrooms gently for about 10 minutes without browning.

Chop up the fish heads and bones, add to the pan and heat through. Add the wine. Reduce over a fierce heat, then cover with the water, bring to the boil and skim well.

Add the bouquet garni, orange peel and vanilla pod, and simmer for 25 minutes. Strain through a sieve.

Now simmer all the ingredients for the soup, except the saffron, in the freshly made fish stock, for 20 minutes. Strain through a sieve.

Put the saffron in a cup with a little boiling water. Crush with the back of a spoon and leave for 10 minutes to infuse, then add it to the soup.

Chop the lobster meat or prawns into very small pieces and mix with the spring onions and ginger.

Place a teaspoon of the shellfish mixture on each *wonton* skin, fold together and seal. Poach the *wontons* in the soup for just 3 minutes and serve.

wasabi and sea-urchin butter

(AUSTRALIA)

The Japanese chef Tetsuya Wakuda is internationally regarded as one of the world's most innovative cooks. He practises his skills not in Tokyo but in Sydney, where he fuses Western and Eastern ingredients.

Use this butter sliced into discs and placed on grilled fish, chicken breasts or veal fillets, as Wakuda does. He will typically garnish it with Japanese *hijiki* (crumbled seaweed), finely shaved cucumber and pickled ginger. Sea urchins can be hard to find, but Spanish importers of canned seafood sell them as *erizos de mar*.

SERVES 4

5 teaspoons wasabi powder or paste
250g unsalted butter, cut into pieces
50g sea urchin roe (or canned sea urchins, drained)
2 tablespoons light soy sauce
2 teaspoons lemon juice
Pinch of chilli powder
2 tablespoons finely chopped chives
2 tablespoons finely chopped tarragon
Pinch of thyme leaves

Mix all the ingredients in a blender set on low, and be careful not to over-process. Shape into a ball and then roll in clingfilm to make a cylinder shape. Remove the clingfilm, wrap in greaseproof paper and store in the freezer until required.

sweet potato fritters
(NEW ZEALAND)

Top New Zealand chefs used to create their own apprenticeships by travelling in Europe, exploring Michelin-starred restaurants. Then they would offer their services and do what the French call a *stage* – unpaid work in exchange for experience, which would adorn a CV.

More recently, young would-be cooks take off as backpackers in Southeast Asia, browsing the food stalls in street markets. What they learn of exotic spices they apply to the homely foods of their childhood, such as lamb, venison, shellfish, root vegetables such as *kumera* (a yellow sweet potato), and *kabocha* (a dense-fleshed squash).

One of the most famous exponents of this style is Peter Gordon, who cooked in Sydney and prospered in Wellington, New Zealand, before establishing himself in London. This is based on one of his recipes.

SERVES 4

500g sweet potatoes, grated
250g carrots, grated
1 onion, grated
1 egg, beaten
1 tablespoon plain flour, plus extra for dusting
1 teaspoon chilli powder
2 tablespoons coriander seeds, dry-roasted and ground
1 tablespoon cumin seeds, dry-roasted and ground
Salt and freshly ground pepper
Groundnut or sunflower oil, for shallow-frying and greasing

Preheat the oven to180°C/350°F/gas 4.

Place the sweet potatoes, carrots and onion in a sieve. Press out any surplus moisture with the back of a wooden spoon. Mix the grated vegetables with the egg, flour, chilli, coriander and cumin, salt and freshly ground black pepper.

On a floured board, roll the mixture into eight balls and flatten into little patties.

Heat the groundnut or sunflower oil in a wide, non-stick frying pan and fry for a few minutes until crisp on each side.

Place on a greased baking sheet and bake in the preheated oven for 15 minutes until completely soft inside.

crab, chilli and lime spaghettini (AUSTRALIA)

This is an original fusion pairing of European pasta with Asian flavourings.

SERVES 2

200g spaghettini (or spaghetti or thin noodles)
150g crab meat
1 fresh red chilli, very finely chopped
Grated rind and juice of 2 limes
1 clove garlic, finely chopped
6 spring onions, chopped diagonally
4 sprigs of flat-leaf parsley, leaves only, chopped
Large pinch of sea salt
Freshly ground black pepper
2 tablespoons olive oil

Cook the spaghettini in plenty of boiling water until *al dente* (still slightly chewy).

While the pasta is cooking, break the crab into flakes in a bowl, and mix with the remaining ingredients. Season to taste – it should be quite savoury.

Drain the pasta and toss the crab mixture into it, reserving some to put on top.

saffron carrot soup (AUSTRALIA)

This unusual soup is a fusion idea, with Japanese and Mediterranean influence. Carrots, soya milk and saffron make a rich, flavoursome soup.

SERVES 4

500g carrots, finely chopped
1 onion, finely chopped
1 leek, white part only, finely chopped
2 sticks of celery, finely diced
1.25 litres chicken stock
1 tablespoon light soy sauce
About 30 strands of saffron
Salt and freshly ground white pepper
150ml soya milk
Parsley, coriander leaves, mint or chives, chopped, to garnish

Gently cook the carrots, onion, leek and celery in a non-stick frying pan without oil, until the vegetables start to soften and change colour.

Add the stock and soy sauce, and cook for about 15 minutes until the vegetables are tender.

Pour a little of the stock on to the saffron strands and crush lightly using the back of a spoon. Leave for a few minutes to develop colour and aroma. Add to the soup mixture.

In a blender, purée the vegetables, adding a little water or stock, if necessary, to keep the mixture liquid. When cool, stir in the soya milk and season to taste.

Serve chilled, sprinkled with your choice of herbs.

stewed red cabbage (AUSTRALIA)

The settlers who shaped Australia's early cuisine included the Chinese, who worked the gold mines (later creating Melbourne's Chinatown), and the Europeans, who planted the first vines. German settlers of the 1830s came to the Barossa Valley where they left their mark, bringing one of the great central European spices: piquant caraway seed.

SERVES 4

1 red cabbage, centre ribs removed, finely sliced
2 tablespoons olive oil
150g streaky bacon, finely chopped
20g seedless raisins or sultanas
2 tablespoons brown sugar
2 teaspoons caraway seeds
3 tablespoons white wine vinegar
1 glass of white wine
1 tablespoon cornflour
Salt and freshly ground black pepper

Preheat the oven to 150°C/300°F/gas 2.

Blanch the cabbage in plenty of boiling water for 4 minutes. Drain in a colander and rinse under cold water.

In a large flameproof casserole, heat the olive oil and cook the bacon until the fat starts to run. Toss the cabbage in it until well coated. Stir in the raisins (or sultanas), 1 tablespoon sugar, caraway seeds and white wine vinegar, and heat through. Cover with a lid and cook in the preheated 1 for one hour.

Stir in the remaining sugar and wine and cook for a further 30 minutes.

Dissolve the cornflour in an equal volume of cold water and stir into the red cabbage mixture to thicken. Check the seasoning and texture. If necessary, cook for up to 30 minutes more. The dish can be reheated successfully, if required.

raw tuna with goat's cheese

(AUSTRALIA)

An inspired flavour combination using raw tuna with cheese, together with piquant flavourings. Raw tuna is a delicacy introduced from Japan, where they rarely use dairy products. Cutting raw fish finely is considered the basis of cooking skills in Japan.

SERVES 4 AS AN APPETISER

250g best tuna, finely diced with a very sharp knife
75g mild soft goat's cheese, crumbled
2 salted anchovies, drained of oil, chopped
2.5cm ginger, grated
2 teaspoons light soy sauce
1 teaspoon *mirin* (Japanese cooking wine) or sweet sherry
1 clove garlic, very finely chopped
Tiny pinch of chilli powder
Pinch of salt
Freshly ground white pepper
5 chives, chopped, to garnish
Watercress (or rocket), to garnish

In a bowl, mix all the ingredients well. Chill in the fridge. To serve, spoon neatly into four bowls and garnish with the chives and watercress or rocket.

cervena steaks (NEW ZEALAND)

New Zealanders have eaten well for several hundred years, with some of the finest food in the world, but a restaurant cuisine did not emerge until the 1990s, when Corban's, a wine company, offered prizes to restaurateurs to use their skills to match wines and food.

Putting lamb on the menu is not a challenging option for the New Zealand restaurateur, but to embrace venison was verging on the foolhardy – the wild deer introduced to the South Island had become as welcome as large vermin, stripping hillsides (and private gardens) of their greenery and blooms. Enterprising farmers in the North Island, however, conspired to farm them (there's an excellent trade to Germany).

To persuade New Zealanders to try the new farmed venison, they launched a competition to find a name for the tasty, tender meat (especially from the loin) and they came up with the Latinate cervena (Italian *cerva* is a doe or hind).

roast peppered cervena

In this recipe the cervena is treated much as a French peppered steak, but using a chef's roasting trick to keep it tender and pink. Avocado oil – also a product of New Zealand – has a high burning point and is excellent for frying without smoking or burning.

SERVES 2

400g venison loin (or 2 x 200g steaks)
1 tablespoon black peppercorns
2 tablespoons avocado oil or olive oil
30ml beef or chicken stock
1 tablespoon soy sauce
Knob of butter
Salt

Cut the venison into two neat cylinders, about 12 x 4cm, if possible, or as neat as you can.

Place the peppercorns on a board and cover with a scrap of cloth or a sheet of clingfilm to stop pieces flying. Use a wooden mallet or similar implement to bash the peppercorns to small flakes (you can use a peppermill but you don't get the same explosive intensity of flavour).

Roll the venison in the crushed peppercorns, pressing them in firmly, and wrap in clingfilm. Keep in the fridge until ready to use – overnight, if you want.

When you are ready to cook, preheat the oven to 200°C/400°F/gas 6.

Using a heavy iron frying pan, heat the avocado oil (or olive oil) until hot and fry the venison for 2 or 3 minutes on both sides to seal.

Transfer the pan to the preheated oven or place the venison on an oven tray and roast for 8 minutes. Remove from the oven, cover with a lid or another pan, and rest the meat for 15–20 minutes.

Heat the stock with any remaining peppercorns and the soy sauce. After removing the venison from the pan, pour the stock into the pan and stir to take up the juices. Strain into a small saucepan and keep warm. Whisk in a knob of butter before serving poured alongside the venison, cut into thin discs to reveal its pink inside.

Serve with mashed *kabocha* (squash) and *kumera* (sweet potato) and a green vegetable.

marinades (NEW ZEALAND)

One of the new developments in Australasian fusion cooking has been the use of spicy marinades for chicken, lamb, cod and salmon. They are typical of the eclectic tastes of pioneer chef Peter Gordon using, as he does, smoked Spanish paprika powder from Extramadura with its smoky bacon flavour.

Here are some delicious examples; each will marinate 1kg meat, fish or chicken.

smoked paprika and rosemary marinade

2 tablespoons smoked Spanish paprika
1 tablespoon finely chopped rosemary
½ onion, finely chopped
150ml olive oil
Large pinch of salt
Freshly ground black pepper

Whisk all the ingredients together. Place in a bowl with meat, chicken or fish, cover with clingfilm and leave in the fridge overnight to marinate. Pour off excess marinade before grilling, roasting or frying.

cardamom, coriander and ginger yoghurt marinade

This New Zealand fusion recipe is inspired by Indian yoghurt marinades. Vary the flavours to taste, adding fennel seeds, for example, or other spices or herbs, such as mint, coriander leaves and parsley.

About 400ml Greek-style yoghurt
Cardamom seeds, scraped from 6 pods, dry-roasted
**   and ground**
1 tablespoon coriander seeds, dry-roasted and ground
5cm ginger, grated
Large pinch of salt
Freshly ground black pepper
2 stems of coriander (or mint or parsley), leaves chopped

In a bowl, combine all the ingredients. Dip chicken legs, small pieces of pork or chunks of fish into the mixture and coat well. Cover with clingfilm and leave to marinate overnight in the fridge.

Before grilling, roasting, frying or barbecuing, shake off excess marinade.

cumin, thyme and maple syrup marinade

A marvellously mixed trio of flavours, daringly combined, to evoke the tastes of baking-hot India, Mediterranean hillsides and the maple forests of wintry Canada.

2 teaspoon cumin seeds, dry-roasted and ground
2 teaspoons chopped thyme leaves, or dried thyme
100g olive oil
2 tablespoons balsamic or cider vinegar
1 tablespoon maple syrup or honey
Large pinch of salt

Whisk all the ingredients together. Brush on to duck or chicken legs and keep in a bowl, covered in clingfilm, overnight in the fridge.

The maple syrup or honey will cause the meat to caramelise slightly, either in the oven, under the grill or on the barbecue.

lamingtons (AUSTRALIA)

Vanilla was one of the flavours early Australians regarded as a significant contribution to the cakes, sweets, puddings and desserts that would give the new colonial society distinction. The Lamington is regarded as a uniquely Aussie creation, commemorating the 2nd Baron Lamington who became Governor of Queensland in 1896. They are dainty little sponge squares, topped with chocolate icing and rolled in coconut.

MAKES 12 CAKES

200g butter
150g caster sugar
3 eggs
1 teaspoon vanilla essence
75g plain flour
1 teaspoon baking powder
125ml milk
150g self-raising flour

FOR THE CHOCOLATE ICING
200g icing sugar
5 tablespoons cocoa powder
25g butter, softened
1 teaspoon vanilla essence
100g desiccated coconut or grated fresh coconut

Preheat the oven to 150°C/300°F/gas 2.

In a large bowl, beat the butter and sugar to a cream. Beat in 2 of the eggs, 1 at a time. Stir in the vanilla essence. Beat in the plain flour and the baking powder. Beat in the milk and the self-raising flour, and then the third egg. Pour into a sponge tin about 20 x 15cm and 5cm deep.

Bake in the preheated oven for 30 minutes or until a knife inserted into the cake comes out clean. Turn out on to a wire rack and leave to cool.

To make the chocolate icing, mix the icing sugar, cocoa powder, butter and vanilla essence with a little boiling water in a bowl.

Cut the cake into 12 squares and spread each one with chocolate icing. Stand the bowl in a saucepan of boiling water to keep the icing soft while you work.

Finally, dip the Lamingtons in the desiccated or grated coconut to coat.

wattle seed desserts

(AUSTRALIA)

Wattle seeds are among the newest spices on the Australian restaurant scene, but usage, among Aborigines, may go back 6000 years, according to Vic Cherikoff, the founder of the Rare Spices Company. Of the 600 or so varieties of wattle (a member of the acacia family), the Aborigines regard the seeds of only about fifteen suitable for eating. Cherikoff has developed one particular strain to capitalise on its unique flavour which, when roasted, tastes like chocolate and hazelnut. Australian chefs use it in desserts and the seeds are now widely available.

wattle ice cream

SERVES 4

500ml milk
175g caster sugar
4 egg yolks, beaten
1 heaped tablespoon wattle seeds
250ml double cream

Heat the milk and sugar in a saucepan, stirring until the sugar is dissolved. Remove from the heat. Slowly pour over the beaten egg yolks, while beating with a whisk.

Add the wattle seeds and stir over a low heat for 5–10 minutes until the mixture begins to thicken. Leave to stand for 15 minutes, then add the cream and mix well. Cool, and churn in an ice cream machine.

Alternatively, pour the ice cream mixture into a shallow tray and place in the freezer. Remove from the freezer every hour (for up to 6 hours) and beat it to break up any large ice crystals. Continue until the ice cream freezes to a perfectly smooth consistency.

wattle crème brûlée

SERVES 4

425ml double cream
¼ teaspoon vanilla essence
6 egg yolks
1 tablespoon caster sugar
4 tablespoons wattle seeds
50g brown sugar
1 tablespoon raw sugar

Warm the cream with the vanilla essence in a double boiler.

Whisk the egg yolks and caster sugar to a light and creamy consistency. Slowly pour the egg mixture into the warm cream. Stir in the wattle seeds.

Return the mixture to the double boiler. Cook over hot, but not boiling, water, stirring the mixture for about 6 minutes until it coats the back of a wooden spoon. Pour into individual moulds and chill for at least 1½–2 hours.

Sift the brown sugar evenly over the top of the custard and sprinkle the raw sugar over it.

Place the dishes in a tray of iced water and grill under a moderate heat until the sugar caramelises. Refrigerate again until ready to serve.

wattle shortbread

SERVES 4

250g butter
125g caster sugar
2 heaped tablespoons wattle seeds
350g plain flour
75g rice flour

Preheat the oven to 180°C/350°F/gas 4.

Cream the butter, sugar and wattle seeds. Mix in the plain flour and rice flour.

Spread the mixture on to a large, non-stick baking sheet, cover with greaseproof paper and press until about 1cm thick. Remove the paper.

With a knife, make a criss-cross pattern on the top and bake in the preheated oven for 30 minutes. Slice into fingers while still hot. Leave to cool on a wire rack. Store in an airtight container.

pavlova (AUSTRALASIA)

Both Australia and New Zealand count pavlova as their own, a glorious meringue confection created in honour of (and there is no argument about this) Anna Pavlova, the great ballerina, who thrilled appreciative Australian audiences in the early 1930s. You can use any fruit, including kiwi fruit, passion fruit and banana slices.

SERVES 4–6

4 egg whites
Pinch of salt
225g caster sugar
2 teaspoons vanilla essence (not vanilla flavouring)
1 teaspoon white wine vinegar (or lemon juice)
1 teaspoon cornflour, sifted
200ml thick cream
500g strawberries, hulled

Preheat the oven to 140°C/275°F/gas 1.

In a large bowl, whisk the egg whites with the salt, until stiff. Gradually whisk in half of the sugar, a little at a time. Add 1 teaspoon of the vanilla essence, the vinegar (or lemon juice) and cornflour. Fold in the rest of the sugar with a spatula.

Line a deep cake tin with non-stick baking parchment, or place a piece of baking parchment on a large baking sheet.

Pile the meringue mixture into the cake tin or spread it in a circle on the baking sheet. Bake for 1–1¼ hours until the outside is crisp and starting to colour. Leave to cool in the oven to prevent cracking. When cool, refrigerate overnight.

To serve, cut lengthways in half. Whip the cream with the remaining vanilla essence until light and fluffy, and sandwich between the two layers, reserving some to spread on top.

Arrange the strawberries artistically on top of the pavlova.

mango, beetroot and ginger vodka cocktail (NEW ZEALAND)

This is another wild, original flavour combo from the Kiwis, fearlessly pitching the fruits of several continents into one pot. It marries the sweet earthiness of north European beetroot with the sharp sour sweetness of tropical mango, and blasts them both with the punch of fresh ginger. You will need a juicer for this recipe.

SERVES 4

100ml plain vodka
Juice of 1 uncooked large beetroot
Juice of 2 ripe mangoes
Juice of 5cm ginger
Grated rind of ½ lime
Ice cubes

Combine the vodka and juices in a jug and add the grated lime rind. Fill with ice cubes. Stir to chill. Strain, and pour into four glasses, with a cube or two of ice in each.

anzac biscuits (AUSTRALASIA)

One of the most dramatic rites of passage in Australia's history was the part its troops played in the 1914–18 war, when it sent its soldiers to fight in Gallipoli in the Dardanelles. The Australian soldiers, joining those of New Zealand, were known as Anzacs (an abbreviation of Australian and New Zealand Army Corps). To maintain the morale of the young men, families at home prepared food parcels with cakes and biscuits, which became known as Anzacs.

MAKES 18–24 BISCUITS

150g plain flour
225g rolled porridge oats
2 teaspoons ground ginger
Pinch of salt
225g desiccated coconut
200g brown sugar
125g butter, plus extra for greasing
1 tablespoon golden syrup
1 teaspoon bicarbonate of soda

Preheat the oven to 180°C/350°F/gas 4.

Sift the flour into a mixing bowl and stir in the oats, ginger, salt, coconut and sugar.

In a small saucepan, melt the butter and, off the heat, stir in the golden syrup.

Dissolve the bicarbonate of soda in a tablespoon of boiling water and stir it into the syrup mixture. Using a wooden spoon, combine with the oats and flour mixture until well mixed.

Butter a non-stick baking tray (two, if necessary) and, using a teaspoon, drop blobs of the mixture on to the tray, leaving space for them to spread as they cook. Bake in the preheated oven for about 12 minutes until golden and firm.

spiced aubergine pickle

(AUSTRALIA)

The Spice Queen of Sydney is surely Christine Manfield – one of Australia's most innovative cooks. One of her successful books was *Spice Paramount Cooking*, named after Paramount, her seminal, highly fashionable restaurant. This recipe is based on her delicious eggplant pickle.

MAKES SEVERAL JARS

2 dried bird's-eye chillies
½ onion, finely chopped
2 cloves garlic
2.5cm ginger, grated
2 teaspoons turmeric powder
5 tablespoons groundnut or sunflower oil
500g small aubergines, cut into 1cm slices
150ml wine vinegar or cider vinegar
100g jaggery (palm sugar) or brown sugar
1 tablespoon brown mustard seeds, dry-roasted
Juice of 1 lime
1 tablespoon *garam masala* (see page 31)
Olive oil, to seal

Put the chillies in a cup, cover with boiling water and leave for 30 minutes. Drain and chop. Put in a food processor and blend with the onion, garlic, ginger, turmeric and groundnut or sunflower oil to make a paste.

In a wok, fry the paste gently for a minute or two, then stir in the aubergine slices. Stir-fry for about 5 minutes until well coated in the spice mixture and the pieces are tender. Mind the chilli fumes.

Stir in the vinegar and sugar, and continue stirring until the liquid thickens slightly.

Off the heat, stir in the mustard seeds, lime juice and *garam masala*. Pour into sterilised jars and top up with a little olive oil to seal. Cover and keep in the fridge. Use within 2 months.

Serve with Asian and Indian dishes.

sweet chilli sauce (AUSTRALIA)

This sauce has been adopted by many Australians as a piquant condiment to accompany New Wave spicy dishes.

MAKES 1–2 SMALL JARS

100g dried bird's-eye chillies
100g dried tamarind fruit
100ml boiling water
2–3 fresh hot red chillies, chopped small
2 onions, finely chopped
2 cloves garlic, chopped
4 tablespoons olive oil
100g jaggery (palm sugar) or brown sugar

Put the dried chillies in a cup, cover with boiling water and leave for 30 minutes. Drain and chop finely.

Soak the tamarind fruit in the boiling water. Leave for 30 minutes, then press the liquid through a fine sieve. Reserve.

In a food processor, blend the dried and fresh chillies, onions, garlic and olive oil to make a paste.

In a wide frying pan, cook the mixture very slowly for 30 minutes, stirring to avoid burning. Add the tamarind juice and sugar, and simmer for a further 30 minutes. Make sure it doesn't burn.

Pour into small airtight jars. Oil will settle on top, acting as a preservative. The sauce will keep for up to 2 months in the fridge.

the essential flavourings

Two essential flavourings for the cook, sugar and salt must be considered as spices.

Sugar

Normally sold as the refined white grain extracted from sugar cane (or sugar beet), either medium crystals (granulated), fine (caster sugar) or powdered (icing sugar). From a cook's point of view, refined sugar is the basic sweetener, yet for flavour it has the least to contribute compared with, say, jaggery (palm sugar), maple syrup or complex-flavoured honeys from around the world. Here are some sweet options for the cook.

Barbados sugar. Unrefined, soft, moist, dark brown sugar from Barbados in the West Indies, with an intensely rich flavour. A good substitute in Southeast Asian dishes for jaggery (see below).

Demerara sugar. Large crystals of refined sugar from Guyana, flavoured with some unrefined brown sugar.

Maple syrup. Nutty, smoky, dense liquid syrup, made by boiling the sap of the Canadian maple tree to concentrate it. The only sugar harvested in the depth of snowy winter. Also an alternative to jaggery (see below).

Jaggery (palm sugar). The sap of palm trees, collected and boiled down to a dense, sticky substance, intense and rich in flavour. Common in India (also known as *gur*) and Southeast Asia.

Treacle. Dark, burnt-flavoured molasses, a by-product of refining sugar. Sometimes added to pork and bean stews to enrich them in the USA.

Golden syrup. The highly refined, intensely sweet, honey-like syrup made from cane sugar, special to the UK and the southern states of the USA. Essential to making certain sticky desserts and tarts (such as treacle tart and pecan pie).

Honey. The best honeys have the perfume of the flowers from which the bees collect nectar to make it: for example, the scent of thyme in *hymettus* from the Greek hillsides; orange blossom honey from Mexico; the pungent *manuka* and sandalwood honeys from perfumed tree-blossom in Australia and New Zealand; and spicy heather honey from Scotland.

Sugar syrups. In the Middle East and India, sugar syrup is used to dip pastries like *baklava* or little rice or lentil-flour cakes. It is made by dissolving sugar in water and adding various flavourings, such as rose water or orange flower water in the Middle East; or, in India, perfumed *kewra* water. Very dense syrups are used in Greece, the Lebanon and Turkey to preserve all kinds of fruits, from lemon and melon rind to aubergine and green pistachio nuts.

Salt

Food is unimaginable without salt. It is the substance which, above every other, confers a savoury, appetising flavour to the dullest food. But it has great importance as a preservative, too, drawing out moisture from foods such as hams and fish and therefore inhibiting the growth of airborne bacteria.

Salt is an essential part of our physical make-up – 0.9 per cent of the human body is salt, and we need sufficient to survive. However, in the West salt is over-used by the food industry (as is sugar), and we mostly suffer from an excess of it, which can lead to hypertension (high blood pressure).

In the Mediterranean salted foods have long been highly prized, from salted cod (*bacalao* in Spain and *bacalhau* in Portugal) to the exquisite, salted, dried hams of Parma in Italy and the *serrano* and *Iberico* hams of Spain; from the salted olives, capers and anchovies of Spain, France, Italy and Greece to Italy's salted, sun-dried tomatoes. A classic Piedmontese dish is *crudités* dipped in a bath (*bagna caode*) of hot oil, garlic and melted salt anchovies.

Soy products are the salt relish of the east; soy beans are salted down and fermented (sometimes with wheat) for nine months to a year in barrels. The liquid which is drained off is soy sauce. Sometimes fermented soy beans are sold dry (quite often chopped into Chinese stir-fries with chilli and ginger,) or made into salty, fermented bean pastes (sold in packets or jars). Because of the soy element, it is a particularly nutritious way of taking your salt.

Fish sauce, which looks like soy sauce but is not, is also made by fermentation, salting down small fish, leaving them in barrels in the sun, and straining off the highly savoury liquid. This is known as *nam pla* in Thailand, *nuoc nam* in Vietnam and Laos, and *ngapi* in Myanmar (Burma). In ancient times it was an important condiment in Roman cooking, known as *garum*.

Shrimp paste is another salty ingredient and of great importance to cooks in Southeast Asia, as a pungent seasoning for curries. Salted shrimps or prawns are dried in the sun, then pounded into a stiff paste. It is known as *balachan* and *blachan* in Malaysia, and as *terasi* or *trasi* in Indonesia. It is never eaten raw but is grilled or fried in a pan before mixing with other spices. The smell is so overpowering that, unless you don't mind the house reeking for hours, it is best wrapped in foil before cooking to contain the odours.

Common salt, with added magnesium to make it free-running, is a form of rock salt, obtained by flooding underground salt deposits in caves and reducing the brine by heating until it forms crystals.

The tastiest salt for the kitchen is sea salt (occasionally referred to by its French name *gros sel*), collected from salt pans bordering the sea (sometimes in bays, when it is called bay salt), dried by wind and sun. Some is collected during high tides from salt marshes adjacent to the sea, such as Maldon Sea Salt from Essex. The process was introduced by the Romans. After boiling, the salt crystallises into star shapes, resembling pretty snowflakes; indeed, Maldon Sea Salt is the ballerina of the saline world. Most sea salt comes in coarse, chunky crystals like crushed glass, though some is milled fine for sale.

roots and barks / roots an

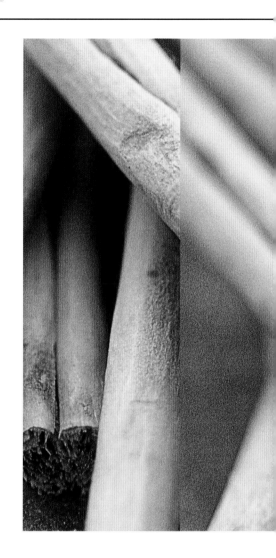

alpinia galanga / alpinia officinarum (galangal)

A fierce, raw flavour bringing to mind the medicine cabinet, cough mixtures and chest salves. Its potent, serious taste makes you feel it will do you good, cure your cold and overcome toxins.

What does it look like?
Galangal is the rhizome of plants belonging to the *Alpinia* family (which also contains ginger). Greater galangal has big knobbly roots like ginger and is cream in colour. Lesser galangal is a reddish colour and smaller, but has a stronger flavour. Ground galangal looks like ground ginger and tastes like ginger mixed with pepper.

How do you use it?
Galangal is used mostly in Thai, Malay and Indonesian cooking. It adds a mysterious flavour to Thai sweet and sour soups, a posse of flavours which also include hot ginger, tangy lemongrass, bitter kaffir lime leaves, sour lime juice and piquant red and green chillies. In Indonesia it is added to *nasi goreng* (fried rice with meat and vegetables), and also to *rendang* (see page 63), a spicy paste for meat. Lesser galangal is used like a vegetable. It is peeled and shredded, then added to stews. *Kempfera* galangal is used in liqueurs and bitters.

Where does it grow?
Galangal originated in China but was well known in the Arab world by the ninth century and became popular in medieval Europe.

Medicinal and other uses
In China galangal is mostly used for its curative effect. In medicine its power to generate a sense of warmth has led to it being used to treat rheumatism and catarrh, especially in India.

armoracia rusticana (horseradish)

The most eye-watering of spices and, in its raw state, a taste which few but the macho can tolerate. It's the north European substitute for chilli. Mixed with mustard, it's a double whammy; although it's hard to believe, mustard is the milder partner.

What does it look like?
A whole horseradish root looks like a carrot in shape but is usually rough and creamy in colour, about 45cm long and white inside. Its name refers to a radish that is 'hoarse' or coarse and strong, and it used to be called 'red cole' (cole is a Middle English word for cabbage). It belongs to the same family as turnip, cabbage and mustard (the crucifer family).

How do you use it?
Wash and peel the root, grate the flesh and discard the core. It has no bite or aroma until it is grated and the root cells are crushed. Then volatile oils called isothiocyanate are released. Vinegar quickly stops the reaction and stabilises the flavour.

Most people buy horseradish ready-prepared and preserved. Its affinity with beef is remarkable, cutting into the fat and stimulating the appetite. Grated and mixed with cream to temper its fire, it equally suits both a plate of English cold beef and a *pot-au-feu*, the French family classic (slow-simmered brisket and shin of beef with oxtail and veal knuckle). It also goes well with rich, smoked eel. It is very popular in Russia and eastern Europe, where it is called *khrine*, is often mixed with beetroot and served with fish and cold meats.

Where does it grow?
Horseradish is a hardy perennial that grows wild in eastern Europe and west Asia but is now cultivated in many parts of the world in fertile, well-drained soils. Its rough-looking leaves shoot up in a clump, sometimes with white flowers. Under the ground the roots grow deep and strong. Once it starts to grow, it spreads and is difficult to control. It grows most in the summer and early autumn and is harvested after the first frosts have killed off the tops.

Medicinal and other uses
Horseradish is said to rid the body of excess mucus and help overcome colds and flu, respiratory problems, sinusitis and hay fever. It is a diuretic, helpful for treating bladder problems and premenstrual tension.

Cassia is the rougher, more robust form of cinnamon in its character, flavour and age, taken from the rough bark rather than the sweet, young, first-year stems (see cinnamon, page 161). The deep, rich flavour of its bark works with salty tastes, while the young quills of cinnamon suit sweet pairings.

What does it look like?

Cassia comes in the form of reddish-brown curls of bark, as opposed to the tan of cinnamon. It is considered inferior and is known as 'false' or 'bastard' cinnamon, although it sometimes goes by the name of Chinese cinnamon. It is not a good idea to buy ground cassia as it soon loses its flavour. Cassia 'buds' are dried unripe fruits.

How do you use it?

The robust bark stands up to long cooking and is ideal for Chinese braising. It is one of the ingredients in Chinese five-spice powder, the most used condiment in Chinese cooking, along with star anise and ground ginger. It is used in North African stews and in Indian curries. It is also an ingredient in Indian *paan*, the mixture of seed and spices wrapped in a betel leaf and chewed in order to freshen the breath after a meal.

In Germany it is used to flavour chocolate, and its assertiveness makes it a perfect foil for a dish of stewed rhubarb. Cassia buds are used like cloves, adding a powerful aroma to meat stews and pickles. Cassia leaves are also dried and used like bay leaves in cooking or, in Nepal, as a flavouring for sweet, milky tea.

Where does it grow?

Cassia originates in Burma and is cultivated in southern China, Indonesia and India. Like cinnamon, it is the bark of an evergreen tree, with tough, shiny leaves like laurel. Cassia is harvested during the monsoons when the trunks are wet and it is possible to scrape off the bark. The bark curls as it dries to be sold as coarse pieces or as 'quills' (coiled strips).

Medicinal and other uses

Cassia, like cinnamon, was supposed to make you live forever. Carried in a kind of pomander, it was said to frighten away disease, and all Roman emperors kept it among their treasures. To the Taoists it was the food of the gods.

Cinnamon brings the perfume and sweet scent of the boudoir to dishes, especially as a powder sprinkled at the end of cooking on biscuits, apple pastries or pies, or mixed with chocolate powder as a dusting to a frothy cappuccino.

What does it look like?

The cinnamon tree grows straight with many shoots. When the stems are about 2m high, they are harvested. The outer bark is removed and the inner sections are prised off in curled strips. The strips are cleaned, formed into cylinders, trimmed and dried. They are then cut into lengths and graded. The best cinnamon is the palest, from young shoots, making thin, delicate, coiled strips or 'quills'. Cinnamon is also ground into a fine powder.

How do you use it?

In the Middle East it is often added to sweet-sour stews; it is also added to Moroccan *tagine* (see page 88). In Europe it is mainly used in baked pies and pastries, and to flavour fruit compotes. It provides the sweet note in spice blends, too, in Chinese five-spice powder (see page 44) and in Indian *garam masala* (see page 31), a combination of warm spices. It is also used to flavour wine.

Where does it grow?

Cinnamon is indigenous to Sri Lanka and has been known since ancient times. During the sixteenth century it was considered so precious that explorers went off in search of it and countries fought battles over it. Sri Lanka was first occupied by the Portuguese, who fiercely guarded the trade routes around the African coast. Then the Dutch took over the island, followed by the British. Eventually cinnamon began to be cultivated in India, Malaysia, Java, the Seychelles, Madagascar, Mauritius and Egypt.

Medicinal and other uses

Cinnamon essential oil with its high phenol content is said to be good for circulation, digestion and respiration. It is used in cosmetics, is also a powerful bactericide and is said to promote longevity.

curcuma longa (turmeric)

One of the most brilliantly coloured spices, turmeric is a cheap substitute for saffron, but with a musty, bitter taste. It stains the fingers as surely as tobacco. Curry would be unthinkable without it, though it is more an acquired taste than a particularly delightful one.

What does it look like?
Turmeric is a herbaceous perennial plant with large leaves like those of lilies and yellow flowers. Ground turmeric resembles saffron only in colour, and derives from the rhizomes rather than the stamens. The rhizomes are bulbous in the centre and shaped like fingers. They are yellow inside due to the pigment *circumin*.

How do you use it?
In Southeast Asia turmeric is the most popular spice, added to rice, fish and shellfish dishes. It is a major ingredient in curry powder to which it adds the yellow colour. In Europe, it is used in kedgeree and in mustard pickles, especially piccalilli (see page 135). It can be bought as a root but it is usually sold in powdered form.

Where does it grow?
Turmeric is native to India and Southeast Asia and is now also cultivated in the tropics.

Medicinal and other uses
Turmeric is said to be a mild digestive and is sometimes used as a remedy for liver complaints. In parts of Asia its bright colour is believed to have magical powers and a clump is often planted in the middle of paddy fields to bring luck. In India and China it is used as a dye for cloth. In ancient Persia it was associated with sun worship and Tamil women use it to paint their hands and feet for weddings.

Sri Lankan market
der weighing fresh
zedoary root.

Even more pungent in flavour than galangal, zedoary is another root which tastes like a medicine. When zedoary slices are cut into soups, they impart a haunting, rather medical, camphorous scent and flavour, which grows on you.

What does it look like?
This perennial herb, related to ginger and turmeric, is known as 'white turmeric'. It grows to 1.5m with dark green leaves and a rhizome which is pale yellow or white inside.

How do you use it?
The rhizome is rich in starch, which is extracted as *shoti* starch. It is sold in powdered form and used like arrowroot to thicken soups and sauces. The leaves taste similar to lemongrass and are added to fish dishes. The hearts of the young plant are eaten as a vegetable. (The dried powdered rhizome has a bitter taste and is seldom used alone but is added to spice mixtures in Indonesia and Malaysia.)

Where does it grow?
Zedoary grows in Southeast Asia and northeast India, where it is also cultivated. Its musky, pungent flavour played a large part in the cooking of medieval Europe.

Medicinal and other uses
It is said to ease stomach ache and relieve flatulence. Zedoary essential oil is used for perfume and in liqueurs.

If horseradish is a tear-jerker, wasabi is a precision rifle of intensity and refinement. This green root grown in water is the big-hitter on the Japanese table, the most dramatic taste sensation they have, lifting the blandness of the everyday diet of boiled rice.

What does it look like?

Wasabi is an aquatic plant and its Japanese name means 'mountain hollyhock'. In Japan you buy the roots of the plant in pots of water. You then peel, trim and grate them into a fine green paste. Outside Japan you can buy wasabi as a powder or as a tube of paste.

How do you use it?

Small blobs of wasabi paste are smeared inside sushi rolls or dotted on top (see page 41). It also accompanies *sashimi* (raw fish) and other dishes, alongside its regular flavour partners, pink slices of pickled ginger and saucers of soy sauce for dipping. It can also be added to soups or to make wasabi pickle, where the leaves, flowers, stalks and rhizomes are chopped, placed in brine and preserved.

Where does it grow?

Wasabi is a perennial herb, a member of the *Cruciferae* family, related to cabbages. It grows wild on the banks of mountain streams in Japan and also in eastern Siberia. It is cultivated in flooded mountain terraces amid cool running streams, and grows to about knee-high with a thick stem a bit like a small Brussels sprout.

Medicinal and other uses

In Japan it is said to help prevent food poisoning and its antimicrobial properties may help prevent tooth decay.

glycyrrhiza glabra (liquorice)

The most dense and sweet of all the anise-flavoured spices, and derived from the roots of a spreading plant related to the pea family. Strangely, it was monopolised as a flavouring by the confectionery world, combining with sugar to make incomparable liquorice allsorts.

What does it look like?
Liquorice comes from a small plant like a tall shrub with bluish flowers. It has very thick roots up to 1m long and underground runners that contain a sweet compound called glycyrrhizin. Its name comes from the Greek word for 'sweet root'. In its purest form glycyrrhizin is fifty times sweeter than sugar, but bitter substances in the plant tend to hide the sweetness.

How do you use it?
In Europe liquorice extract prepared from the roots of the plant is added to sweet foods like gingerbread, Pontefract cakes and Yorkshire pennies. It is also mixed with sugar, water, gelatine and flour to make a soft black paste, which is then transformed into colourful liquorice allsorts. Liquorice is also used to flavour Sambuca liqueur, soft drinks, stouts and beers.

Where does it grow?
Liquorice grows wild in Asia and southern Europe, and has been cultivated in western Europe since the sixteenth century. The root or runner is harvested and cut into pieces. It is then dried to make a natural sweetmeat for chewing. Napoleon chewed on it and it is said to have turned his teeth black. It was grown in the UK in Yorkshire from the seventeenth century to the 1970s.

Medicinal and other uses
It has had a high medicinal reputation since ancient times when it was used for asthma, dry coughs, respiratory illnesses and to soothe stomach upsets. It is also said to promote longevity. It is an active ingredient in lipstick, boot polish and foam fire extinguishers, but 90 per cent of liquorice production now goes into tobacco, to make it burn evenly.

Fresh or dried, ginger is one of the most exciting taste sensations of all spices, delivering intense flavour as well as biting heat. Dried, it is a perfect foil for sweet things such as gingerbread, ginger cakes and biscuits. It is one of the key flavours in spice mixes too, adding aroma, as well as warmth. Fresh ginger, sliced or grated, opens up the palate and extends the taste buds.

What does it look like?
The ginger plant grows in the tropics and is about 1m tall. It has large, tapering leaves with spikes and fleshy, yellow, red-edged flowers. The spice comes from the knobbly root, and the degree of pungency is caused by non-volatile compounds called gingerols. Its aroma and flavour depend on many things such as where it was grown and the conditions when it was harvested.

How do you use it?
Ginger is used fresh, dried, grated, preserved in syrup or vinegar, and crystallised. Fresh ginger can be added to savoury and sweet dishes. In China and other parts of Asia it is added to fish dishes, especially freshwater fish to mask the earthy tang. In Japan pink, pickled ginger called *gari* is served with sushi. Dried and powdered ginger is best in biscuits, breads and desserts. It can be used to make chutney (see page 30). Ginger ale is a soft drink and ginger beer is fermented and slightly alcoholic. In Kashmir they drink ginger tea.

Where does it grow?
Ginger is believed to have originated in Southeast Asia but it has never been found growing wild anywhere in the world. It has been cultivated for millennia and was an important spice in ancient Rome. It was used in England in Anglo-Saxon times and was an extremely expensive spice throughout Europe in the Middle Ages, when it was used as a sweetmeat and often combined with cinnamon, especially in France. India now produces about half the world's crop but it is also produced in China, Taiwan, Thailand, Africa, the Americas and Australia. It likes to grow close to its cousin turmeric.

Medicinal and other uses
Ginger aids digestion and is an appetiser, stimulant and carminative. It helps treat headaches, colic, vomiting and diarrhoea, and is also said to be an aphrodisiac.

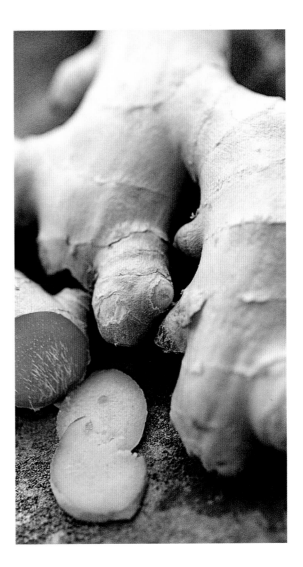

berries and seeds / berries

These small brown seeds with a hot peppery tang are called 'grains of paradise'. They are related to cardamom and have a similar aroma. (Confusingly, the small green chillies of northern Brazil are known as *malagueta* peppers – a very different spice, although a very subtle difference in spelling.)

What does it look like?
The seeds come from a tall herb, like a reed, that bears brilliant red or orange fruit 5–10cm long. Inside each fruit there are roughly 60–100 little seeds.

How do you use it?
Melegueta pepper is used instead of pepper in tropical west Africa where it grows, and it is sometimes an ingredient in the Moroccan spice mix *ras-el-hanout* (see page 96). In most cases, white pepper mixed with ground ginger creates a similar flavour. The Romans flavoured a sweet wine with it, adding ginger and cinnamon. The practice was adopted in medieval England in the fourteenth century, when it was known as hippocras. The name comes from the wine being strained through a cloth resembling, it's said, the sleeve of the gown worn by Hippocrates. It was usually mixed with the rich and cloying sweet wines from Crete, Cyprus, northern Spain and later Madeira, when the Portuguese started to grow the malvenia grape to make malmsey. Hippocras was drunk at the end of a meal with spiced biscuits.

Where does it grow?
The seeds are native to West Africa. During the Middle Ages they were very popular in Europe, and west Africa became known as 'the grain coast'.

Medicinal and other uses
In west Africa the pulp surrounding the seeds is chewed as a stimulant. In Scandinavia they use the seeds to flavour aquavit.

The feathery green fronds of dill are associated with north European cooking. Their fresh anise flavour cuts into the oiliness of raw salmon and, combined with salt and sugar as a marinade, matured under weights for several days, produces the unique delicacy _gravad lax_ (literally 'buried salmon').

What does it look like?
Dill belongs to the parsley family and is closely related to fennel, but is more aromatic.

How do you use it?
Dill is used in Scandinavia, eastern Europe, Poland and Russia as freely as parsley is in western Europe. It is chopped on to potatoes and salads, and added to yoghurt and soured cream, or poached fish. Pungent dill seeds are often used in pickles, along with the chopped green stems. Dill pickles from Poland, especially pickled cucumbers, are particularly delicious.

Where does it grow?
Dill is native to western Asia but also grows in the Mediterranean and southern Russia, and is now cultivated in many parts of the world.

Medicinal and other uses
Dill seed is used to sweeten the breath and to improve digestion and appetite. The oil is used to kill bacteria and relieve flatulence. Dill is also used for fevers, ulcers and kidney and eye problems. The Romans believed it had fortifying qualities and sprinkled it liberally over food that was given to gladiators. Its name comes from the Norse _dilla_ meaning 'to lull' and its soothing properties make it ideal in a gentle gripe water for babies.

The seeds of this cool, fresh-tasting pot-herb, as it was known in medieval times, carry tremendous wallop, trumpeting a wake-up call to the palate. It is used in India and has enjoyed a role in the West as celery salt (the seeds pounded with salt).

What does it look like?
Celery comes in three varieties: wild celery is a small hedgerow plant sometimes called 'smallage'; cultivated stem celery has thick green or white stems; celeriac has a fat base stem. Celery seeds are tiny and brown with touches of light colouring.

How do you use it?
Celery seeds are slightly bitter with a strong scent of celery. You can scatter whole seeds into salads or sprinkle them over cooked vegetables. You can also add them to stews, soups, sauces and fish dishes. In grand hotel buffets, celery salt has played a part as a salty dip for hard-boiled quail eggs and seagull eggs. Served with a Bloody Mary, the cool, saline freshness of celery salt balances the sweetness of tomato juice and cools the fire of Tabasco sauce.

Where does it grow?
Wild celery has grown in Europe and the temperate parts of Asia since ancient times. In the seventeenth century it began to be cultivated in Europe and shortly afterwards both wild and cultivated celery moved across to America.

Medicinal and other uses
Celery is said to aid the treatment of amenorrhoea (abnormal absence of menstruation), angina, arthritis and gout. It is also used as a diuretic and to treat colds and flu. Celery seed tea is good for relaxation and sleep. The ancient Greeks and Egyptians made garlands of celery for funerals.

bixa orellana (annatto)

A South American spice whose scarlet seeds have made it useful worldwide as a food colouring, adding visual richness rather than flavour, which is earthy with a hint of iodine.

What does it look like?
Annatto is a small, bush-like tree with shady leaves covered in red veins. It has pink flowers and thick, heart-shaped pods filled with about 50 brilliant red, triangular seeds, nestling in a pulp, which is used to make dyes.

How is it used?
In Britain, in the eighteenth century, annatto dyes were used to add colour to butter and cheeses, which would otherwise have been white, such as Cheshire Cheese and Red Leicester, exaggerating the colour to mimic the yellowish cream milked from cows feeding on spring grass rich in beta-carotene. In Central and South America it is made into a paste called *achiote* and used as a marinade for fish before grilling,

adding colour and acidity (see Grilled Spiced Snapper, page 104). In Jamaica it is added to the spicy sauce that accompanies the national dish, *Ackee* and Salt Cod. It is also widely used in the Philippines to make brick-red *adobo* sauces for meat and fish.

Where does it grow?
The annatto tree is native to Central and South America and the Caribbean. In the seventeenth century, it began to be imported into Europe and was used to make chocolates. The Spaniards took it to the Philippines where it became very popular. Today it is cultivated also in Asia and Africa.

Medicinal and other uses
Annatto has been used to control fever, dysentery and kidney infections, and as an insect repellent.

In the Caribbean, it was historically used as body paint, and is the reason why the north American Indians became known as 'redskins'.

The most important spice, and one of the oldest, in Europe, mustard is almost an essential condiment with beef and ham. It's especially significant in France, the UK and Germany, which are notably carnivorous populations. It's also popular in the USA, Canada and beef-conscious Argentina. It has a special affinity with beef, both cold cuts and piping hot roasts, cutting into the fat to form an emulsion as you chew, making it more easily digestible.

What does it look like?

The seeds of three plants belonging to the cabbage family go together to make mustard. White or yellow mustard (*Sinapis alba*) is a small plant with yellow flowers producing pods of large, pale yellow seeds. Black mustard comes from *Brassica nigra*, which grows to 3.5m and has small brown-black seeds. Brown or Chinese mustard comes from the small red-brown seeds of *Brassica juncea*.

How do you use it?

Mustard is made from the crushed seeds of the plant. Raw powdered mustard generates its heat within five or ten minutes of adding cold water – activating an enzyme, bringing tears to your eyes. But adding hot, instead of cold, water kills the enzyme, so mustard used in cooking rabbit dishes (see page 127), Welsh rarebit or lamb in a mustard and breadcrumb coat are mild in flavour.

No mustard is as strong as English mustard. German mustard is dark, mild and vinegary, and American mustard, piped on to hot dogs, is barely hot at all. *Savora* – a mustard made for the South American market – is mild too. French mustards are highly flavoured, often with herbs, like tarragon, and, more recently, blended with blue cheese, Chablis wine and even cassis, the blackcurrant liqueur of Beaune. Maille mustard is the leading brand.

The small black mustard seed grown in India is used differently, fried until it pops and then sprinkled on *dhal* to add a hot nutty note, or on flatbreads like *naan* for added interest.

Where does it grow?

White and black mustard originated as weeds growing among crops in southern Europe. Brown or Chinese mustard originated in Asia, but is now widely grown. Mustard has been cultivated since ancient times and has always been important in Europe, since it grows locally and is relatively inexpensive. The Romans used mustard and took it to France, where they developed their own unique style in Bordeaux, blending the whole seed with unfermented grape juice, and in Dijon, making a mustard slurry with verjuice (the juice of unripe grapes), later sieving it for smoothness.

English mustard was made in a similar way in Tewkesbury, often combined with horseradish to intensify it, until the end of the eighteenth century, when a Mrs Clements evolved the technology of milling the seed to make mustard flour, previously considered difficult because it contains a lot of oil and the rollers clog up.

Ninety years later Jeremiah Colman exploited the technology and, mobilising farmers in the fenland between Norwich and Wisbech in the UK, made his name synonymous with mustard. Adding turmeric for extra colour (mustard isn't as mustard-yellow as it's made out to be) and cornflour to stabilise it (called 'management' in the factory), he created a product unique in the world. Harnessing the infant art of press and poster advertising at the end of the nineteenth century, the Colman family made it the most famous product in the land. They said their fortune was made from the mustard left on the edge of the plate.

Medicinal and other uses

Mustard is said to be a stimulant, expectorant and diuretic. Indian folk remedies suggest using it to ease aching feet, arthritis and lumbago. In Korea the seeds are used for abscesses, colds and stomach disorders. Ancient herbals recommend mustard for epilepsy, snakebite and toothache.

carum carvi (caraway)

The bitingly hot little seed from the caraway plant delivers a concentrated explosion of aggressive flavour, not unlike anise and fennel.

What does it look like?

The caraway plant, which is grown specifically for its seeds, reaches a height of about 60cm. It has feathery leaves and cream-coloured flowers, and the seeds are the split halves of the ripe fruit.

How do you use it?

Caraway is well understood in Germany, where it challenges the sourness of rye bread, tames the raw flavours of pickled cabbage (German *sauerkraut*), and keeps smelly cheeses in

their place, such as German Tilsiter and Munster and the Hungarian cheese spread Liptauer. Ground to a powder with sugar, it may even be served on bread and butter with a ripe Gorgonzola. In Austria and Hungary, as well as Germany, it seasons sausages, roast pork, goulash and many pickles. It is ideal tossed with buttered cabbage or potatoes.

Caraway pops up in the Arab world, usually adding a mysterious note to spice mixes, such as *tabil*, and in north Africa, in *harissa* (see page 98), adding subtlety to the fierce heat of the chilli peppers. It has had its place in the UK, but the last vestige is probably caraway seed cake, made for a traditional English tea.

Where does it grow?

Caraway is indigenous to western Asia and the Mediterranean, and is possibly the oldest cultivated spice in Europe. It is now grown primarily in Europe, north Africa and the USA.

Medicinal and other uses

Caraway is used as an appetiser, expectorant and stimulant. It is also an aid to digestion and a cure for colic and nausea; you can chew the seeds at the end of a meal or use them to make a tisane.

In Shakespeare's time, it was said to prevent lovers from straying and was an important ingredient in love potions. Uniquely, the German liqueur *Kummel* is caraway-based.

coriandrum sativum (coriander)

As a leaf, coriander is one of the most universally enjoyed herbs, especially in the East and in Latin America, where it is known as *cilantro*. Its fresh, appetising flavour, however, bears no resemblance to that of the seed, which is sweet, perfumed and citrussy, echoing both orange and lemon peel.

What does it look like?
Coriander is related to parsley and is similar in appearance, although it tastes completely different. The plant, which grows 60–90cm high, has a stem with many branches, decorative leaves and pink or white flowers. The seeds are small, creamy-brown in colour, and round or oval.

How do you use it?
The seeds are an aromatic spice and must be kept whole until you are ready to use them. Dry-roast them quickly in a small frying pan, then crush or grind them. Indian cooking would be unthinkable without coriander seed, freshly ground to release the full cargo of its aromas, and almost always paired with cumin. As a herb it's also known as both Chinese and Japanese parsley, and in Thailand, in particular, the root is prized.

Though small, when it is scraped and chopped into soups, it contributes a disproportionate amount of flavour. Middle Eastern *taklia* is a spice mix combining crushed coriander seeds and eaten with spinach, chickpeas and meat balls.

Where does it grow?
Indigenous to southern Europe, the Mediterranean and the Middle East, coriander is one of the oldest spices and even has a mention in the Bible, in Exodus. It appears in the recipes of ancient Greece and to this day features in any recipe described as '*à la Grecque*' (such as mushrooms cooked in an olive oil, vinegar and spice dressing and left to cool). Its name comes from *koris*, the Greek word for bed bug; the leaves and unripe seeds have a strong odour which some people find unpleasant but which disappears by the time the seeds are ripe.

Medicinal and other uses
Since Roman times, coriander seeds have been used to encourage appetite. It is also used as a digestive, a carminative and a bactericide. The Chinese believed it granted longevity, and it was used in love potions in the Middle Ages. The ripe seeds can also be used in potpourris to add a fresh perfume.

Cumin is one of the most important spices in India, where it is known as *jeera*. As a ground spice, cumin seeds lend an acrid, sour, woody taste to a blend, but when fried the whole seeds acquire a nutty and sweet taste.

What does it look like?

Cumin is a small, annual herb that belongs to the parsley family. It grows to about 30cm with pale mauve, pink or white flowers.

How do you use it?

Its mild flavours dissipate in cooking but come to the fore when added at the end of cooking, in Indian *garam gasala* (see page 31), a mix of warm-flavoured spices including cinnamon. Cumin is also a key ingredient in the savoury version of the Persian spice mixture, *advieh* (see page 79). In Switzerland and the Netherlands it is paired with cheese, such as Munster. It is also used in North African cooking, for example, in harissa paste (see page 98) and with couscous.

Where does it grow?

Cumin is said to have originated in the eastern Mediterranean but is now also grown in many parts of Asia. It has a long history and figures frequently in the most famous of Roman cook books, by Apicius, blended with other spices in the many marinade-type mixtures used to prepare meat and fish.

Medicinal and other uses

Cumin seeds are said to stimulate the appetite, and to treat indigestion, fever and stomach upsets. Cumin essential oil is used in perfumes.

Cardamom, with its shrivelled husk and shiny black seeds like caviar, is known as the 'queen of spices'. It belongs to the ginger family and is the third most precious spice in the world, after saffron and vanilla.

What does it look like?

Cardamom is a beautiful plant, like a bushy bamboo with broad leaves, similar to ginger. It flowers on stems like an orchid, close to the ground. True cardamom pods are green, or white from bleaching. Large brown or black pods, known as 'false cardamom', come from other species.

How do you use it?

You can either grind the seeds and add them to the pan or use the whole fruit, but remove and discard it before serving. Indian cooks prize cardamom as one of the ground spices in a *garam masala* mixture (see page 31); they also use it whole to perfume rice dishes, such as pillaus and birianis. In Arab countries it is used to add a piquant note to coffee and tea, and in Europe, especially in Germany, and in Scandinavia it is added to baked foods and pickles. Sweden imports a quarter of all Indian cardamom production and regularly uses it to flavour spirits.

Where does it grow?

Cardamom has been cultivated for more than a thousand years in India and Sri Lanka, and more recently in Guatemala, Tanzania, Papua New Guinea, Thailand and Cambodia, where there is an area known as the Cardamom Mountains. It grows well only in certain highland areas and has to be kept weed-free, airy and dry. It is prone to disease, requires great care in cultivation, and its high cost is because supplies of the best quality are limited. The biggest plantations are in the fertile hills of Kerala in south-west India between the rubber and tea plantations where the cool houses of the managers, with their whirring fans and wide verandahs, evoke the colonial days.

How is it harvested?

The fruits of the plant are picked early to prevent them from splitting and so losing their powerful aroma as they ripen. The not-quite-ripe pods are gathered and taken to huge, cool barns with palm-leaf roofs to be sorted by dozens of local women in colourful saris, sitting cross-legged on the earthen floor. By eye alone, they rapidly pick over the pods, grading them by size into seven piles. The fruits are left to dry in the sun until their skins harden and become green. Some are then bleached for the market place. Each fruit contains three cells filled with seeds that ripen from white to black. The largest pods go to the demanding Indian market, used by top chefs in the Taj and Oberoi hotel chains or sold in Bombay and New Delhi's best spice shops. The rest are sold to smaller retailers and markets.

Medicinal and other uses

Cardamom has been used since Greek and Roman times to sweeten the breath, help cure sore throats and coughs, and to ease stomach disorders. The fragrant essence of cardamom, with its hint of eucalyptus, is captured in cardamom essential oil, which is used to treat flatulence, nausea and diarrhoea, and as an aid to digestion. The Greeks also mixed cardamom with wax to make solid perfume, which they placed in shells and wore in their hair or pinned to their clothes.

Fennel comes from the large family of anise-flavoured plants. Uniquely, sweet fennel has been harnessed in Italy, as 'Florence fennel' to be eaten raw as a crunchy salad item, or braised or boiled to be eaten warm or cold in an olive oil dressing.

What does it look like?

Wild fennel is a hardy perennial herb, a graceful plant with strong, bright green stems up to 2m high, with feathery leaves and golden flowers. The seeds of wild fennel tend to be bitter. Sweet fennel is similar in taste to aniseed, but more assertive in flavour and not as sweet. The third type of fennel is the vegetable Florence fennel or *finocchio*, mentioned above, which was developed in seventeenth-century Italy.

How do you use it?

Fragrant fennel seeds have a sweet, warm, aromatic flavour that marries well with fish. They are added to various breads, and in Florence the long-standing Italian fondness for fennel lives on in the salami known as *finocchiona*.

Where does it grow?

Fennel is a flavouring passed down from the Romans, featuring in the spice mixtures recorded by Apicius. Fennel plants grow freely in temperate Europe and are often found towering alongside river banks and on waste ground. They are thought to have originated along the shores of the Mediterranean then spread east to the Middle East, India and China by way of Arab traders. They are now grown in moderate climates around the world.

Medicinal and other uses

Fennel is said to give strength and courage and make people live longer. It aids digestion, relieves headaches, treats flatulence and colic, and often lends an aromatic punch to cough medicines. It is also used to ease eye strain and as a remedy for snakebite. In India they chew fennel seeds to freshen the breath; in Spain they chew them to settle the stomach. Sweet fennel is one of the soothing ingredients in babies' gripe water. Fennel seeds are also pressed into service to make alcoholic drinks, such as the famous Spanish liqueur, *Hierbas*.

Bitter cucumbers, leaf vegetables, hot radishes, limes and chillies: the exotic world of the Vietnamese street market.

illicium verum (star anise)

Its eight-pointed stars make star anise one of the most attractive spices. The dark red-brown pods enclose large oval seeds as shiny as polished mahogany. It is one of the most important spices in China, crushed and combined in a five-spice powder.

What does it look like?
Star anise grows on an evergreen tree, like a magnolia, with bright red saucer-shaped flowers. The tree grows to about 8m but doesn't begin to bear fruit until it is six years old. It then goes on fruiting for up to 100 years. Star anise contains anethole, the essential oil which gives anise its powerful taste, although it is not related to herbs in the anise family.

How do you use it?
It has a deeper, more earthy flavour than other sorts of anise and combines well with soy sauce and five-spice powder in slow-braised Chinese and Malaysian pork, duck and beef dishes (see page 44).

Where does it grow?
It is believed to have originated in China and, with its very complicated cultivation, it has tended to stay in China and parts of Asia.

Medicinal and other uses
Star anise is a stimulant and a diuretic, and can soothe sore throats. It is used in the East to relieve colic and rheumatism and to flavour cough medicines. It is also used to flavour liqueurs such as *anisette*. In Greece it flavours the best *ouzo*, from the island of Lesbos, combining star anise with locally grown aniseed to make a concentrate, which is blended with grain to soften the raw alcohol.

juniperus communis (juniper)

The pine-scented, fir-tree-forest aroma of these berries hugely excites north Europeans. It is dry and harsh, and for the hunter the closest seasoning to hand, and therefore closely associated with cooking game.

What does it look like?
The juniper berry is unique in that it takes three or four years to mature on its bush, which bears berries of different maturity simultaneously. The dark purple berries are about 0.5–1cm in diameter.

How do you use it?
Juniper is almost an essential flavouring for marinating game, such as wild boar, reindeer and venison, which is then cooked slowly to tenderise. It's also associated with the cooking of game birds, not to mention thrush and blackbird.

Where does it grow?
It is found throughout Europe and North America and also in the Himalayas.

Medicinal and other uses
It is said to be a diuretic and a stimulant; it reduces colic, is a carminative and can help with bladder disorders. But Juniper's unquestioned place in the spice Hall of Fame has to be its contribution to the flavour of gin. The name originates from the French name for Juniper, *genièvre* (*ginebra* in Spanish). If the berries themselves are unavailable, a slug of gin in a game dish may just do the trick.

nigella sativa (nigella)

Nigella provides a uniquely Indian taste and is often sprinkled on *naan* breads to give crunch, improve appearance and add a delicate, peppery flavour. The name comes from the Latin word *nigellus*, or *niger*, meaning 'black'.

What does it look like?
Nigella is a hardy annual that grows to about 60cm. The pods are gathered before they burst and release their small black seeds. The seeds resemble onion seeds.

How do you use it?
In Turkey and throughout the Middle East it is sprinkled on bread. In Europe it is sometimes used as a substitute for pepper and can be sprinkled on cooked, buttered vegetables, such as carrots, cabbage and cauliflower.

Where does it grow?
It is native to western Asia and is now cultivated in India and the Middle East.

Medicinal and other uses
It is used in India as a carminative and stimulant and to ease indigestion and bowel problems. It is also used like mothballs to repel some insects.

Lovely little poppy seeds give flavour and crunch to many east European breads. They are harvested from the opium poppy, but are entirely free of the drug (opium is extracted from the white latex gum inside the green seed case).

What does it look like?
The seeds are as tiny as pinheads and range in colour from white to gunmetal blue. The plant grows to a height of 1.2m with white, pink, red or purple flowers.

How do you use it?
Poppy seeds were used in Egyptian cooking as far back as 1500BC, so archaeological finds reveal. In Poland, Hungary and Austria the seeds are soaked so that they swell up to make a dense filling for sweet pastry rolls and cakes, such as Poppy Seed Roll (see page 122). A paler, browner poppy seed is used in Indian cooking, scattered on *naan* bread or sprinkled on potato dishes.

Where does it grow?
Native to southeastern Europe and western Asia, it is cultivated in many countries, including Iran, Turkey, Holland, Romania, parts of Asia, and Central and South America.

Medicinal and other uses
It is a major medical plant used as an astringent, aphrodisiac, expectorant, hypnotic and sedative, and to treat coughs, toothache, asthma, headache and boils.

pimenta dioica (allspice)

Allspice is the descriptive name of Caribbean seeds which mysteriously combine the forceful flavours of nutmeg, cinnamon and cloves. In fact, they contain eugenol, the essential oil which gives cloves their intense perfume and character.

What does it look like?
The seeds resemble large round peppercorns, about 7cm across, and the Spaniards, who discovered them, named it *pimiento de Jamaica*. The seeds are the dried unripe berries of an evergreen tree, that grows 7–13m high, with large leathery leaves and small white flowers, followed by green berries that then turn purple. The complete dried fruit is ground to produce allspice powder.

How do you use it?
At home in the West Indies, it plays an important role in Jerk seasoning (see page 115), used to marinate pork and goat before cooking. It is particularly enjoyed in the northern hemisphere, adding a warming touch to dishes from the USA and Canada all the way across to Germany, Sweden, Finland and Russia. In Germany it is used to add depth of flavour to beef stews, and it is much liked in Turkey. In Britain it is an important pickling spice and also finds a place in spice mixtures, indispensable in dense, rich fruit cakes and Christmas Pudding (see page 132).

Where is it grown?
It is native to the rainforests of Central and South America, and cultivated in Mexico, Central America and Jamaica.

Medicinal and other uses
Its medicinal qualities are similar to those of cloves. It is a digestive and carminative, mildly anaesthetic, and used for arthritis and stiff muscles.

The powerful flavour of the anise family makes it among the world's most popular spices, pleasantly soothing and sweet on the palate. It contains the essential oil anethole which, in concentration, has a keen, assertive taste like peppermint, overwhelming all others.

What does it look like?

The plant is an erect annual that grows to a height of roughly 60cm and has small white flowers. The seeds are tiny, about 2–4mm across, and grey-green or brown.

How do you use it?

Anise is a prime flavouring in Chinese cooking, used with rich meats such as pork and duck. But in the West its use goes back to the time of the Pharaohs of Egypt, when it was used in sweetening cakes, a practice later adopted by the Romans and, more recently, the Americans.

Its affinity to sugar appeals to the British, where aniseed enjoys an important place in the confectionery business, most famously in aniseed balls. The French roll the anise in a sugar and gum paste to make *dragées*, sugar-coated seeds that sweeten the breath. But the French also enjoy the savoury possibilities of anise, introducing its sweet perfume to Mediterranean fish stews.

Where does it grow?

Native to the Mediterranean and Egypt, it is cultivated in Europe, Asia, India, Mexico, North Africa and Russia.

Medicinal and other uses

It is used to ease flatulence and as a diuretic. It is also used against bronchitis, indigestion and lice and to treat coughs and stomach problems. Combined with raw alcohol, it is the basis of numerous liqueurs such as French *pastis*, Greek *ouzo*, Turkish *arak* and Dutch *anisette*. They have in common the curious property that in solution they are transparent but turn milky upon the addition of water.

187

A keen-flavoured, rather camphorous member of the pepper family with a dry, woody aroma. Also known as Java pepper, after its country of origin.

What does it look like?
It grows on a climbing vine similar to that of pepper. The berries are a little larger than peppercorns and have indented skins and tiny stalks. They are mostly hollow and need to be crushed or ground before use.

How do you use it?
It is used in Arab spice mixes. In Roman times it was a flavouring in an aperitif wine called *hippocras*. In Europe its hot, bitter flavour was once a substitute for pepper and it was used in the Elizabethan kitchen as both a condiment and flavouring. Its bitterness made it less attractive as a seasoning when pepper became more economical, although it is still sometimes used as a pickling spice.

Where does it grow?
It originates in Java but is also grown in Africa, the West Indies and Ceylon.

Medicinal and other uses
It is used as a source for camphor in medicine. In China and Southeast Asia the fruits are used to aid digestion and for treating sunstroke. In other parts of the world it is used as a diuretic and for lung disorders.

The acid, sour berries of the sumac plant are crushed and sprinkled on salads and kebabs instead of lemon juice.

What does it look like?
The bush (from the *Rhus* family) grows to about 3m with hairy branches and leaves, and has white flowers. The fruit appears in clusters, covered in an orange hairy coat.

How do you use it?
It was used in Roman times as a souring agent in the years before the lemon was grown. It still predominates in parts of north India, Turkey and Iraq, where lemons don't grow. In Lebanese cooking it's used to add a sour note without adding the wetness of juice. Sumac is also an ingredient in the Jordanian spice mixture *za'atar* (see page 78), together with wild thyme, sesame seeds and salt, to be sprinkled on egg dishes or eaten with bread dipped in oil.

Where does it grow?
It grows wild in the Mediterranean, especially in Sicily and southern Italy, Turkey, Lebanon, Iran and the Near East. It is also found in north Africa and India.

Medicinal and other uses
Sumac is a digestive, and refreshing. It is said to reduce fever and settle an upset stomach, such as 'Beirut belly'.

Little sesame seeds contain 50 per cent oil. They have hardly any taste until you toast them and then they are bitter-sweet and delicious.

What does it look like?
The small, oval seeds vary in colour but are usually white. The plant grows to 1–2m with pale rose, purple or white flowers shaped like little bells and fruit like small capsules. When the capsule ripens, it bursts open with a pop, discharging the seeds, hence the phrase 'Open, sesame'.

How do you use it?
They enhance any toasted bun, flatbread, *naan* or Chinese deep-fried prawn toast. Sesame oil used as an aromatic in Chinese cooking: a nutty, caramelised flavour added as a few drops before serving a stir-fry, for example. Toffee apples dipped in the seeds are also popular.

Sesame seeds are important in Middle Eastern cooking. The whole crushed seed, oily and bitter, is made into a paste called *tahina*, and used to enrich Turkish and Lebanese *mezze*. It's commonly added to *hummus*. It is also the base of a delicious, crunchy confection, *halva* which is made from the solids after the oil has been extracted, then combined with sugar and egg white.

Where does it grow?
Sesame is native to the tropics but is one of the oldest cultivated plants in the world. It was greatly prized in Babylon and Assyria more than 4000 years ago. Now it is cultivated in many places, including China, India, Ethiopia, Central America and the USA.

Medicinal and other uses
It was traditionally used as a laxative and tonic. It has been a symbol of good luck and immortality. Sesame oil, rich in protein, is used in margarine and cooking oils. It is also an ingredient in some soaps and cosmetics.

trachyspermum ammi (ajowan)

Ajowan are tiny seeds which are slightly peppery, with a hint of oregano and anise. When crushed, they have the aromatic scent of thyme and, though no relation to thyme, they contain the same chemical, thymol, which gives both their flavour.

What does it look like?
Ajowan is an annual plant, 30–70cm in height. The small hard black seeds are similar in appearance to cumin or caraway seeds. It is of the same family as caraway and lovage.

How do you use it?
Sprinkled on to *naan* breads and pastries in India, the seeds add pungency. They also give a kick to bland dishes of lentils and other pulses, and potatoes, carrots and other root vegetables. Indian fried snacks made with lentil flour are also sprinkled with ajowan.

Where does it grow?
It is native to India but also cultivated in the Near East.

Medicinal and other uses
Medically, ajowan has excellent properties. It is an antiseptic and also an antioxidant, active in suppressing free radicals which cause cancers. It is used as a remedy for indigestion and asthma and also to treat diarrhoea and wind. It is said to be an aphrodisiac and to help control a desire for alcohol.

trigonella foenum-graecum (fenugreek)

For many the savoury, meaty aroma of fenugreek is the authentic smell of curry, especially to Britons. It was one of the main spices used in the original tins of curry powder first imported to Britain in the eighteenth century, when the Raj was responsible for an early form of fusion cooking.

What does it look like?

An erect, powerfully perfumed annual herb that grows to a height of 30–80cm, it has yellowish-white flowers that become slender, pointed pods, containing the small, brown fenugreek seeds.

How do you use it?

Fenugreek has a bitter and astringent character, which tones down when it is dry-roasted, balancing its perfume with that of cumin and coriander seeds in curry spice mixtures. Great care needs to be taken not to burn fenugreek, as it quickly turns to a near-poisonous bitterness.

The juicy leaves (it's a member of the clover family), known as *methi* in India, are used both fresh and dried, and give a fresh, celery-like tang to vegetable dishes. The seeds lend themselves to sprouting, like mustard and cress, and are delicious and nutritious in salads.

Where does it grow?

It is native to southern Europe, India and Morocco and is one of the oldest cultivated medicinal plants, now grown in the Mediterranean, India, north Africa, France, the USA and Argentina.

Medicinal and other uses

Traditionally used to ease flatulence, diarrhoea, coughs and colds, fenugreek can also help treat bronchitis, sore throats, swollen glands, diabetes and ulcers. It is an aid to digestion and is said to promote lactation. It can also be used to treat inflammation and as an aphrodisiac.

zanthoxylum pipertium (sichuan or szechwan pepper)

Chew on a tiny, broken Sichuan pepper seed for two seconds and spit it out. You'll find a sensation of pins and needles on your tongue, as it starts to go numb. It is one of the strangest spices and much loved in the western Chinese province of Sichuan, where it has been known and used for centuries.

What does it look like?
It is actually the berry of a thorny bush of the *Rutaceae* family, similar to citrus and North American prickly ash. The peppercorns are rust-coloured with tiny stems and open ends, about 5mm across.

How do you use it?
It has a significant place in Chinese cookery as one of the ingredients in five-spice powder (see page 44). It has also been known as *fagara*, but this term is now outmoded. In Sichuan it is combined with fiercely hot dried chillies, numbing and pricking the palate in turn. It is also toasted and crushed with salt, to be used as a dip at table, usually with grilled or fried food. Sichuan pepper needs to be bought fresh (now possible through mail order). Stale Sichuan pepper loses its kick and should be thrown away.

Where does it grow?
It is native to the Sichuan province of China and temperate zones of Asia, especially the Himalayas, but it grows in any temperate climate.

Medicinal and other uses
Traditionally used to treat stomach pain, vomiting and diarrhoea, Sichuan pepper is also used externally to treat eczema.

flowers and leaves / flowe

Sometimes known as Mexican tea and Mexican herb, epazote is one of the trinity of Central American and Caribbean flavours, along with cumin (*comino*) and coriander leaf (*cilantro*). Its taste is strange on first encounter, shocking in fact, with a distinct resemblance to creosote, but this dissipates in the cooking, leaving an agreeable bitterness which works very well with soupy beans.

What does it look like?
Epazote grows abundantly, spreading over waste ground, with compact, mild-flavoured, fleshy leaves when young. At 0.6–1m, looking like a straggly spinach run to seed (it is of the same family), its flavour becomes distinctly strong. One of its less charming names is pigweed (because pigs like it).

How do you use it?
It is the ubiquitous flavouring used in meat stuffings for *tortillas* and especially in most bean dishes – one of its many names in Spanish translates as 'bean herb', as it is regarded as anti-flatulent.

Where does it grow?
Its name derives from the Nahuatl dialect of Oaxaca: *epatl* and *tzotle* (meaning 'smell of skunk') which gives it its least flattering name, the consumer-unfriendly 'skunk weed' (but it's not really that strong). In fact, it's prized so much that the whole plant, leaves, stem, flowers and seeds, is harvested and dried, to be reserved for out-of-season use. It also grows outside in moderate climates, including the UK.

Medicinal and other uses
It's thought to kill internal worms and another of its many names is 'worm weed'. Besides preventing flatulence and easing colic, it has properties for healing wounds and can be made into a poultice to detoxify snakebite.

Known in Thailand as the *makrut* lime, kaffir lime has almost no juice but is prized for its perfumed thick skin and leaves.

What does it look like?
It is a knobbly, pear-shaped citrus fruit with figure-of-eight leaves.

How do you use it?
Kaffir lime leaves are an almost essential addition to Thai hot-and-sour soups (see Tom Yam Kung, page 52). Their lemon-lime scent and bitter flavour combine with the medical-tasting galangal, ginger root, coriander root, fresh chillies and lime juice to create a dramatic harmony of taste and aroma. They can be bought fresh and kept in a sealed plastic bag in the fridge or deep-frozen, or bought dried. Soak dried leaves in warm water for ten minutes before using.

Where does it grow?
Kaffir lime grows in Southeast Asia where it is cultivated for its leaves rather than its fruit.

Medicinal and other uses
The outer layer of the fruit's thick rind yields an oil which is the basis of many perfumes.

A bustling fruit, vegetable, herb and spice floating market – Thai-style.

The world's most celebrated and expensive spice by weight, saffron is more costly than gold. The word 'saffron' comes from the Arabic for yellow and it casts a warm, primrose glow on everything it touches. It gives rice dishes the world over a unique character, from the paella of Valencia and the risotto of Milan to the pilaffs of Iran and the biriani of north India.

What does it look like?

Saffron is the orange-red stigma from the flower of the autumn crocus. Its high price is entirely due to the labour-intensive work involved in collecting it. The flower petals are left discarded in translucent blue mounds beside the fields where the pickers are working. They remove a mere three orange-red stigmas from each flower head. It is estimated that it takes one million stigmas to make a kilogram of saffron.

How do you use it?

Saffron's mysterious scent evokes the smell of antique varnished furniture in a musty, dusty, old stone crypt. In high concentrations it smells almost like the entire contents of a medicine cabinet. But used in tiny amounts it fuses with other aromas, wrapping itself around the coarse flavours of a rough, tough sailors' fish stew to transform it into one of the world's classic dishes, *Bouillabaisse*.

It has the ability to overcome the crudest flavours, tame them and then beautify them. It goes especially well with fish, but in India it is used with some of their classic lamb dishes. In Spain cooks use saffron freely, chucking a generous pinch into a simmering pan of rice for paella (see page 128). But in most parts of the world it is used more thriftily and made into an infusion (see page 74). The power of a tiny amount to produce an intense colour is extraordinary. It adds a dramatic flavour and colour dimension to rice, fish, mashed potatoes or bread, for example, Saffron Buns (see page 130).

Where does it grow?

The saffron crocus may have originated in China. It was encountered in Kashmir, memorably by Alexander the Great who described a scene under a full moon, the crocus harvest in full bloom, the landscape an eerie, unnatural blue.

On account of its value, it has been grown around the world. It suits a terrain with hot summers and cold winters. In Spain the 40°C summer temperatures drop to minus 30 C in winter, ideal to clear the soil of insects which feast on the juicy bulbs of the crocus, but they still have to be protected from mice, rats and game birds.

Kashmir is still a producer and so is Iran, whose saffron is a darker mahogany and with a deeper, smokier flavour.

How is it produced?

In La Mancha in southern Spain, the world's largest producer of quality saffron, it is a cottage industry. The flowers are picked over in the villages, the whole family working in unison, the young girls the deft pickers, filling a flat plate in the centre of a kitchen table, until it glows fiery-red like the setting sun. The patient *abuela* (grandmother) is usually entrusted with drying the fragile threads. They lose a third of their weight in the process. If they are not dry enough to store well, the profits from the precious crop will be lost. She holds them in a sieve high over a glowing wood-fired stove – perhaps contributing a certain smokiness to the flavour.

Left: plucking the bright orange stigm from the purple croc flowers, the La Man saffron harvest, Spa

Saffron in England

For three centuries in England, saffron cultivation flourished in Cambridgeshire and Essex. King Henry VIII bestowed the prefix of Saffron on the market town of Walden in reward for providing him with a generous supply. The ladies of the court (in his country house at Audley End) had to be warned not to use the precious substance as a hair dye. Court chefs brushed pastry with beaten milk and egg yolk coloured with saffron to make them look golden when baked, and added it to creamy desserts to create the effect of rich cream.

Saffron's medical value came under scrutiny in the eighteenth century and the practice of growing it at home faded out. Other flavours such as vanilla displaced it in the kitchen. Its use still survives in Cornwall, where bakers make saffron cakes and buns, a practice believed to go back to earliest times, when Phoenician seamen (from present-day Lebanon) traded it for Cornish tin.

How is it sold?

In Spain saffron is often sold as powder, although occasionally mixed with a colouring agent for packets of paella spice. Outside Spain it is often subject to adulteration, mixed with, but more probably replaced by, other colouring agents, such as safflower flowers or marigold petals, which offer mild colour but no scent. The price will be a guide. In some countries turmeric (often labelled 'curcuma') is offered as saffron, but more through ignorance than deception, the word saffron representing the colour yellow. However, in fifteenth-century Germany the penalty for adulterating ground saffron with turmeric was to be burnt or buried alive.

Medicinal and other uses

Saffron has long been valued as a medicine, a cure for almost everything, from headache to measles and gout. It may have been the cannabis of its day, for a little was said to induce a mild sense of pleasure, increasing to merriment and finally ending, in excess, to convulsion (so said Nicholas Culpeper, the seventeenth-century herbalist). It is also used as a dye.

lemongrass has the fresh, zippy flavour of lemon zest. It is used to impregnate dishes throughout Southeast Asia, invariably as an ingredient in the hot, sweet-and-sour soups of Thailand.

What does it look like?

It is a robust, spiky grass, a hardy perennial, which grows in clumps as freely as a weed, and many homes have it growing at the back door, ready for use. It reaches about 60cm in height with woody, fibrous outside leaves which must be discarded to expose a soft, long, bulbous heart. It looks like a spring onion or a thin leek, pale in colour and firm to the touch. It is sometimes called 'citronella' or 'sereh'.

How do you use it?

The heart is sliced into 5cm lengths and strewn into soups or pounded to release its scent. It is also crushed into a paste with chilli, shallots and other spices for Indonesian and Malaysian snacks, such as stuffed banana leaves with minced pork and prawns, steamed or grilled, often sold at the roadside and market stalls. In the West it is always available in Chinese and Asian stores, either fresh in bunches, or dried or in powder form. Keep in a plastic bag in fridge or freeze it.

Where does it grow?

It grows wild in tropical Southeast Asia and Latin America.

Medicinal and other uses

In east India and Sri Lanka it is called 'fever tea' and is mixed with other herbs to treat fever, menstrual problems and stomach aches. In Latin America and the Caribbean it is used to help digestion and calm nerves. The Chinese use it to treat headaches, stomach pains, colds and rheumatism.

The bracing and powerful aroma of a bay leaf is an invaluable agent in the professional chef's kitchen. It overwhelms less attractive tastes in slow-simmered stocks. It is particularly effective in subduing fishy flavours and is used in fish stock, fish soups and *court bouillon*, the seasoned preparation in which chefs poach whole fish such as salmon and turbot.

What does it look like?
Bay is an evergreen tree with dark, glossy leaves, growing abundantly either in small, trimmed bushes from garden centres or, if left unattended, climbing to 20m or more.

How do you use it?
In France, where for centuries herbs have been preferred to spices, its essentially spicy quality lifts a *bouquet garni*, the ubiquitous bunch of herbs used to flavour soups, stews and stocks. Usually this consists of bay leaf, thyme and celery leaf, rolled tightly in the green of a leek and tied with string, so that the *bouquet* can be fished out at the end of cooking.

Bay is mostly used around the world in savoury dishes, often in lamb kebabs between skewered items. In the UK it is added to milk puddings, such as rice pudding, to brace up the flavour and remove the sickly sweetness. In Scandinavia it is used to overcome the rather rich smell of soused herring (herring baked with bay leaf, peppercorns and sometimes juniper, in diluted wine, vinegar or cider, and left to cool in the liquid).

It is also used in marinades and is strong enough to give pork a gamey flavour, like that of boar, when combined with coarse red wine, juniper berries and chopped onion.

Where does it grow?
Bay is found all over Europe and the Mediterranean, and in most temperate climates.

Medicinal and other uses
Bay has medical and magical associations. The Romans used it for treatment of liver disorders, and in the Roman games a wreath of bay was woven into a crown to adorn the overall winner, the *Victor Ludorum*. It is a symbol of glory and reward and its Latin name comes from the word for 'renowned' (*nobilis*). It was also believed to protect you from thunder and lightning. It is said to stimulate digestion and calm a queasy stomach, sharpen memory, relieve headaches and calm hysteria. It can be used also in salves for rheumatism, bruises and skin problems.

Mint is the key ingredient of numerous dishes in the Middle East, where the herb originates. Its assertive, cooling, refreshing flavour has become prized the world over. Its essential oil, menthol, is an important ingredient in a whole range of products including chewing gum, toothpaste, confectionery (such as peppermints and after-dinner mint chocolates), drinks and even some varieties of cigarette. Dried, it is used in teas and tisanes.

What does it look like?

Mint is a perennial usually reaching a height of about 60cm. There are over 600 varieties of the herb, the most important of which are spearmint and peppermint (both major sources of commercial menthol). The range of mints is huge, embracing apple mint (common in the USA), ginger, pineapple, chocolate and citrus (bergamot mint).

How do you use it?

The important Middle Eastern mint is spearmint (*Menthus spicata*), ubiquitous in the highly sweetened, syrupy mint tea, drunk all day long in a spirit of hospitality, and also in cooling iced mint tea. It is a vital ingredient in Middle Eastern salads, too, with large amounts being chopped into the cracked wheat salad, tabbouleh (see page 68).

In Southeast Asia they use a particularly fiery and furry-leafed form of hot mint in soups and salads.

In Greece mint provides an inimitable bite to stuffed vine leaves (*dolmades*). It also gives zing to the yoghurt and cucumber dip, *tzatziki*. In India they have the same idea, using mint in a cooling *raita* to serve with hot curries. The French love their mint in *pastilles*, which are delicious breath sweeteners, and also in liqueurs. The Americans adopted the flavour for chewing gum, also embracing it for one of the world's great long drinks, the southern mint julep. A Pimm's would not be complete without a sprig of mint. Mint also goes very well with fruit salads, adding colour and an appetising scent.

Where does it grow?

Mint has its roots in Greek mythology, getting its name from the nymph Minthe, who flirted with Pluto and was accordingly turned into a plant by Pluto's angry partner, Proserpine. In Greece and later in Rome, young people wove celebratory mint wreaths.

Mint originates in the Middle East but now grows almost everywhere. The Romans introduced the herb to Britain, where it was grown extensively in monastery kitchen gardens, but it wasn't until the Crusades that returning mercenaries educated cooks as to its possibilities, especially in a sauce to serve with roast lamb. Mint and new potatoes (or peas) is a particularly British taste.

Medicinal and other uses

Mint has always been prized for its medicinal properties, especially as a digestive and breath sweetener. It has been used to treat gallstones, irritable bowel syndrome and colds. Peppermint oil is employed as a flavouring in toothpaste, cough sweets and chewing gum. It is also used in perfume, face creams and lipstick.

Curry leaves, known as *kari patta*, convey the very essence of curry. Not well known outside its native India, this plant has the amazing property of smelling exactly like the contents of a proprietary commercial tin of curry powder, although it is not one of the 30 or so spice ingredients actually used in curry.

What does it look like?
Curry leaves are the small, shiny leaves of a shrub.

How do you use it?
Curry leaves are much used by the vegetarian communities of south India, flavouring a lentil stew (*dhal*) or vegetable curry as a last-minute seasoning, usually in combination with the meaty spice, asafoetida. They are fried together in ghee with mustard seeds, and when these begin to pop, the mixture is stirred into the dish.

Where does it grow?
The leaves grow abundantly all over India and Sri Lanka, particularly in the foothills of the Himalayas. They are usually bought fresh (available in specialist shops). Place the leaves in a plastic container and keep in the fridge, or freeze them. Dried curry leaves are fine until they lose their flavour, so keep them in an airtight jar.

Medicinal and other uses
Said to be a tonic and used to treat dysentery and diarrhoea, curry leaves can be also made into a poultice to help heal burns and wounds. Eating lots of curry leaves is believed to prevent hair from turning prematurely grey.

myristica fragans (mace)

Mace has a lovely old-fashioned flavour – nutty, dry and scented; a milder, sweeter form of nutmeg.

What does it look like?
When the outer flesh of nutmeg (like that of a walnut) is cut open, it reveals the nut of the nutmeg. The mace is a lacy wrap around the nut, like a red cage, known as an aril. It is stripped off while still soft and dried in the sun, changing colour to orange. (In Grenada it is kept in the dark for some months to reduce the colour even more.) When hard, mace is sold off as pieces (blades of mace) or powdered.

How do you use it?
Use mace whenever you would use nutmeg. It is blended with butter to make the incomparable Morecambe Bay potted shrimps. It is difficult to grind whole mace into powder as it contains some oil, so grind it with a little rice or flour.

Where does it grow?
Mace originated in the Moluccas in the Spice Islands. It is also grown in Singapore, Brazil, Colombia, Central America, Madagascar and the West Indies. Grenada now produces roughly 40 per cent of the world's crop.

Medicinal and other uses
It reduces flatulence, is a stimulant and a tonic, aids digestion, helps circulation and, in Asia, is used to relieve nausea. Taken in a toddy, it was thought to cure insomnia.

ocimum basilicum (basil)

One of the most fragrant and spicy of all herbs, basil is grown in pots on Mediterranean patios for its perfume alone. The European sweet basil, a member of the mint family, evokes the smell of cloves. Purple basil is essential in Southeast Asian cooking, and has more of the scent of liquorice. There are several other varieties, which are lemon-scented and cinnamon-flavoured.

What does it look like?
Basil is a bushy plant with many variations that can grow up to 1m. Its oval leaves have pointed tips and it has spikes of white to pink or purple flowers.

How do you use it?
In Thailand, Vietnam and Cambodia basil is used in spicy soups (with ginger, lemongrass and kaffir lime leaves) and it is added to stir-fries at the end of cooking. The leaves may even be deep-fried and added as a fragrant garnish.

In Europe, Italy has more or less monopolised the use of basil. Its peppery notes and perfume added to a simple salad of sliced ripe tomatoes and creamy mozzarella cheese, with no other dressing than virgin olive oil and sea salt, lift it on to another plane.

Making pesto
Trapping and preserving basil's elusive properties is difficult. When it is dried, its flavour quickly fades and stales. But since Roman times the Italians have learnt to preserve the seasonal leaves, packing them in jars under layers of salt and covering with oil. From this grew the famous *pesto alla genovese*, the ready-made pasta dressing mixed with pounded pine nuts and pecorino cheese.

Pesto, the Latin word for 'pounded', has become synonymous with basil, but it equally relates to mixtures of many other herbs and spices. Genoese basil *pesto*, made in the home, will be a rich mixture of pounded basil leaves, good Ligurian olive oil, crushed local pine nuts, and salty, dry pecorino cheese. Commercial varieties, looking to cost, may use the whole plant rather than the individual leaves, oils cheaper than olive oil, other nuts such as peanuts, cheeses such as Parmesan imitations and others. And, bound by safety and health regulations, they must pasteurise the jars by heating and, although this is for a short time, the fresh flavour of the basil leaf is changed in this brief 'cooking' process. So, the most worthwhile *pesto* is the one you make at home using the best ingredients, employing the simple technique, as old as time – hammering them with a pestle and mortar.

Close to the border in northern Italy and in southwest France they make the famous basil-flavoured country soup, *pistou*. This usually consists of vegetables, such as potatoes, green beans, tomatoes, onions or leeks, cooked in stock, with pasta such as spaghetti or vermicelli. Just before serving, a dramatic injection of flavour is added, including fresh basil, crushed garlic, olive oil and salt, bringing zesty bite and appetising perfume.

Basil seeds are so tiny, it seems unlikely they would have a culinary role, but, in fact, they are prized throughout Asia. Soaked in water for ten minutes, they become gelatinous. They are added to savoury dishes such as cold and warm noodles, and to desserts for both decoration and flavour. Mixed with coconut milk, shredded young coconut and palm sugar, they also make a delicious drink.

Where does it grow?
Basil, which is thought to have originated in India, has a magisterial history. It was once a royal plant and had to be cut with a golden sickle. Now it is found in most parts of the world.

Medicinal and other uses
In parts of India basil is regarded as a holy plant and is used to ward off evil spirits. It is associated with funerals: basil-infused water is used to wash bodies, and a basil leaf placed on the dead person's chest. The Chinese used it to treat stomach, kidney and blood complaints. In Europe it was used to treat colds, warts and intestinal worms. It is also used as a tonic for coughs, skin complaints and earache. In Italy basil is a symbol of love.

Oregano is one of the Mediterranean's most important herbs, with its haunting, appetising aroma. It is much used in Spain, Greece and especially Italy, where it is essential to the Napolitan pizza.

What does it look like?

It is a perennial herb that grows to about 75cm with purple flowers. Oregano and its cousin sweet marjoram (*origanum majorana*) are the two most commonly used herbs of this huge and complex botanical family. They are related both to the mint family, the *Labiatae* (which also includes basil, rosemary, sage and thyme, and numbers no fewer than 3200 species, according to food scientist Harold McGee) and the *Verbenaceae*, and there's confusion over naming each variety in many countries. What they both have in common are the flavouring oils thymol and carvracol (also present in thyme).

How do you use it?

Oregano goes with grilled fish, and is good in stuffings and with sausagemeat, but its perfect partner and soulmate is the tomato. Oregano's slightly soapy, alkaline character is neutralised by the acid of the fruit, which in turn is modified by the herb, sweetening its abrasiveness. Oregano also has the effect of sharpening the blandness of mozzarella cheese, which makes it ideal for the Marguerita pizza. Fresh oregano is splendid in tomato salad.

To capture its full aroma, oregano needs to be added at the end of cooking. Its flavour on the tongue is quite peppery and bitter and disappears in a slow-cooked stew. It lends itself perfectly to drying, and dried oregano, added towards the end of simmering, enhances a tomato sauce.

Where does it grow?

Oregano is a Greek word meaning 'delight of the mountains' and it grows wild in the Mediterranean. Greece is its traditional home, but Turkey is now the major supplier. There are numerous cultivars, including golden, white, dark and variegated. Its perfume is rich and highly scented, more so when it's grown under a hot sun, which concentrates the flavour oils. From the taste perspective, the highly perfumed oreganos of Crete (known as '*rhigani*') and Mexico (wild oregano) are significant. After World War II, American GIs

stationed in Italy returned home effectively introducing oregano to the US kitchen. But further south, in Latin America, it has long been an important flavouring, linked with chilli powder to give a hit that is both fiery and perfumed.

Medicinal and other uses

Oregano is traditionally used to stop colds and indigestion, and as an antiseptic.

pandanus odorus (pandanus)

An essential flavouring in Southeast Asia, especially Malaysia and Indonesia, Pandanus has the delicate fragrance of roses and, some say, new-mown hay. Its insistent floral flavour is clinging, in a way that sweet vanilla is.

What does it look like?
It is the stiff blade of a bright green, aromatic grass, growing to 60cm. In Thailand it is known as *bay touhy* or *toey* and in India as *kewra* and *kevda*. In the West it has been known as screwpine, a name given to it by sailors describing one variety with a maze of above-ground roots.

How do you use it?
When it is pounded into a paste, it adds depth, colour and perfume to many sweet dishes. Often a blade of the grass is tied in a knot before being dropped into a dish. Pandanus is also an ingredient in paste mixes, along with green chillies and lemongrass, and it is used to stuff banana-leaf parcels of mixed pork and shrimps.

In Malaysia pandanus leaf is often simmered in sugar syrup to release its colour and flavour, and strained for use in rice, tapioca and semolina puddings. It is best used fresh (from specialist Asian shops) but it is also sold dried as a powder in 25g bags.

Where does it grow?
It grows in Southeast Asia and the Pacific region.

Medicinal and other uses
Pandanus is a good source of vitamins A and C.

rosmarinus officinalis (rosemary)

This universally loved, appetising herb enhances every food it's paired with. Its rich, sweet, fragrant scent adds dizzy delight to Provençal, Spanish and Italian roasts of lamb, pork and poultry. Sizzling on a barbecue its inviting, heady smoke has a magical effect. (The woody stems, stripped of their needle-like leaves, make ideal skewers for kebabs.)

What does it look like?
Rosemary is a small, evergreen shrub with leaves like short, sharp needles. It has pretty, mauve flowers in the spring.

How do you use it?
There is hardly any kitchen use for which one cannot recommend rosemary: in a *bouquet garni*; in marinades for meat, poultry and fish; studded into lamb with garlic for a roast; with grilled meat; and on the barbecue, where it burns to fill the nostrils with anticipation, tingeing everything with its smoky, bitter sweetness. Rosemary can also flavour a sweet-sour, pungent jelly to accompany roasts, and is even added to some desserts to provide piquancy.

Its pretty, mauve spring flowers make a delightful addition to a salad of tomato, onion and feta cheese. The flowers are a magnet for bees, and rosemary honey, containing the essence of this wonderful plant, is one of the finest.

Where does it grow?
Its Latin name means 'dew of the sea', perhaps because it flourishes in the wild on hillsides close to the sea in its natural habitat, the Mediterranean.

Medicinal and other uses
Before we came to love rosemary so much in the kitchen, it enjoyed an important role in history as a remedy for many ills. The ancients decided it was good for the brain. It was claimed to prevent nightmares and ward off evil spirits and dried rosemary, made into a tea, was used as a cure for headaches. Shakespeare reminds us that 'Rosemary is for Remembrance', and it is a herb associated with both weddings and funerals. A rosemary bush is often planted by a gravestone. It is also used to treat acne, asthma, muscular pains, bronchitis, colds, flu and stress.

Finally, rosemary has no equal as a fumigant. Dried branches may be kept in the kitchen and burnt when one wants to remove an obnoxious smell. Set light to it and, as the flames die down, wave its plume of odorous smoke around the room, masking everything that went before.

salvia officinalis (sage)

One of the most important herbs in ancient times and credited with curative and restorative properties, sage was once thought to confer wisdom. It has a beguiling perfume, pungent and pervasive, triggering the senses, but it is fierce on the palate, one of the most powerful and assertive of all herb flavours.

What does it look like?

Sage is a perennial herb with grey-green leaves growing on woody stems to a height of about 60cm. Its thick, soft, velvety and furry leaves are a delight to gardeners who can, these days, track down variegated forms in many shades, with some curious flavours including lavender, pineapple and even blackcurrant sage.

How do you use it?

Sage was thought to aid digestion, so it is often paired with fatty foods such as pork sausagemeat, and with onion in sage and onion stuffing for Christmas turkey or goose. The Pilgrim Fathers took it with them to America, where it still features in the November Thanksgiving dinner.

Used in moderation, sage marries well with some strong-flavoured foods. Its bitterness tames the powerful taste of liver (a common pairing in Italy); the French use it to spice up pork sausages and they slip it into a *bouquet garni* with other herbs to flavour soups, stocks and stews; in the Low Countries they use it in a green sauce with fish and eel dishes. One of the classic English cheeses is sage Derby, coloured green with sage leaves.

Where does it grow?

Sage originates in the Mediterranean where it gives off its best fragrance in warm sunny soils. Its main users continue to be in Europe and the USA, although beans and sage were on the menu in Mexico as long ago as the fifteenth century, when the Spanish reached the court of Monteczuma in Teotichlan. Like epazote (see page 196), the bitter herb gives bland beans the lift they need. Once you have a plant in your garden, it grows so abundantly and is so strong that it's a pity that all you'll ever need is a leaf or two.

Medicinal and other uses

Sage was an essential plant in the medieval apothecary's garden. Since the Middle Ages, rubbed sage (as it's called when dried) has been used to make sage tea and tonics, and to bring down fever. It was also used to treat liver complaints, colds, sore throats, pains in the joints, measles and nervous headaches.

A native American spice from the deep south, appropriated by Cajun settlers, sassafras is an important ingredient in the gumbos of New Orleans.

What does it look like?
Sassafras is an evergreen of the laurel family.

How do you use it?
Roots, bark, leaves and buds are all used. Its roots have long been used by native Americans, either chewed, made into tea, or mixed with maple sugar to make a sweet drink. Jelly is also made from the root to capture an alluring bitterness. But it is the leaves which interest cooks the most, pounded and sold as fine powder (sometimes as *gumbo filé*). It is added towards the end of cooking as a thickening agent, and is also put on the table as a condiment. It is not normally available in the UK, having failed to pass UK laboratory tests, and is considered to be addictive.

Where does it grow?
Sassafras grows in the deep south of America, where it was adopted by the Cajun settlers, who had been driven out of northwest France for refusing to swear allegiance to the Catholic king. They emigrated to Canada, where they termed themselves the Arcadians (pronounced 'Ar-cash-jian' in the slang of Canadian French and becoming 'Cajun'). Encountering similar religious intolerance and refusing once more to surrender their own religion, they were shipped to the humid, hot and insalubrious swamps of Louisiana, then a French colony.

Marginalised as they were, when France ceded their rights, they exploited the scant produce of the bayous, and combined rice, freshwater crayfish and tropical vegetables, such as okra, to create one of the great fusion cuisines, thanks to the kitchen craft of their homeland. They adopted local ingredients and flavourings: okra, with its gelatinous texture, often replaced blackened *roux* as the thickening agent for stews, and they discovered sassafras which produced a similar effect, also providing the mucilaginous property that makes gumbo so gooey and good.

Medicinal and other uses
Sassafras has long been used to treat high blood pressure, rheumatism, arthritis, gout, menstrual and kidney problems. It has also been used for head lice, rheumatic pains, skin problems and ulcers. The root bark is also used to extract oils for perfume.

A native Indian woman shops for spices in a Peruvian market.

One of the most powerful and pungent spices in the world, and for many years one of the most expensive, the clove has a wide range of culinary and medical uses and has commanded high prices throughout history.

What does it look like?

Cloves are the flower buds of tall evergreen trees, which flourish in the tropics. The French call them *clou de girofle* ('nail of clove') because they resemble nails. The short 'nails' are four-sided with a calyx and four sepals, pink when picked, but hardening to dark brown when dried in the sun.

How do you use it?

The clove is warm, even burning, in concentrated amounts and is one of the ingredients in Indian *garam masala* (see page 31), the warming spice often added at the end of cooking curries.

In the UK it is used to put a seasonal glow into Christmas cake, Christmas pudding (see page 132) and mulled wine, bringing a recognisable blood-stirring warmth. Such is its power, it was used in Elizabethan times to make pomanders, stuck into oranges to provide an intense perfume (drowning out other less pleasing odors). Cloves are also spiked into an onion before cooking in milk, to flavour bread sauce to go with turkey. They can be used to flavour a baked ham, the fat studded with a pattern of cloves and roasted, infusing the ham with a sense of luxurious richness. Cloves are especially linked to apple, a couple of cloves in an apple pie sends a shock wave of flavour through it (see page 130). But it is one of those spices which is overpowering unless used with restraint.

In a stock, a clove might well be a hidden ingredient, contributing its rich, earthy warmth but not its obvious flavour. 'Keep it below the level of recognition,' advises Tom Stobart in his *Encyclopaedia of Food*.

It has preservative properties, too, so it is an important element in pickling spices.

An unusual dish using cloves is to be found in Brazil: one of the dozens of desserts based on eggs, coconut and sugar is Mother-in-law's Eyes (see page 112), a children's sweet with the eyes picked out in cloves. In Turin there is a fine candied walnut flavoured with cloves.

Where does it grow?

In the thirteenth century Marco Polo recognised cloves growing in the Moluccas. This prompted European nations to find a way to cut out the Arab middle men who traded the valuable spices overland. The Portuguese were the first to monopolise the clove islands, but in the seventeenth century the Dutch chased them out and limited all clove production to one island, Amboina, destroying crops grown elsewhere and executing anyone who threatened their control.

The French, until this time not associated with the search for spices, eventually broke the Dutch monopoly. Governor Poivre of Mauritius and La Réunion encouraged the planting of cuttings on these French-controlled islands. From there they spread to Madagascar, Zanzibar (today a major source) and the West Indies, Grenada in particular.

Medicinal and other uses

Cloves have antiseptic properties, which make the oil extracted from them (eugenol) useful to dentists. The Indians chew them with betel nut as a breath sweetener.

The world's major consumers of cloves are the Indonesians, who use them in the manufacture of a flavoured cigarette, Kretek, a breathtaking smoke along the lines of menthol (peppermint-flavoured) cigarettes. Kretek accounts for 300,000 tonnes of cloves a year.

Thyme is an essential herb in European cooking, not only for its intense, appetising perfume, but also for its medicinal properties. Its Greek name means 'to burn sacrifice', which immediately evokes memories of sprigs of thyme smouldering on a spit roast or barbecue, the acrid fumes bringing tears to the eyes or dry Mediterranean hillsides, where you can recognise its sweet, pervasive smell from a distance.

What does it look like?

Thyme is a small, shrub-like perennial that grows to about 40cm with grey-green leaves and purple flowers.

How do you use it?

The perfume of thyme is its outstanding appeal but, as a flavour, it creates warmth and a sense of well-being, and it goes with everything including meat, poultry, fish and vegetables, especially tomatoes (a feature it has in common with oregano).

Thyme is an effective dried herb. Powdered, it is mixed with other spices in Jordan and the Yemen to make a spice mix called *za'atar* (see page 78), which is spread on hot flatbreads as a regular snack. They use a particularly pungent form of thyme, which they call Persian thyme (*za'atar fars'i*).

Where does it grow?

There are hundreds of cultivars of thyme, the most accepted being lemon-scented, but there is also orange-scented, and it is possible to find thymes which are scented with pine, caraway and even nutmeg.

Medicinal and other uses

From the sixteenth century thyme has been embraced medicinally, used as a mouthwash, a gargle and in cough medicines. Its essential oil thymol kills staphylococcus and fungal infections. Like lemon juice it also kills salmonella, so the two in tandem, stuffed into the interior of a chicken for roasting, not only improve the flavour but help ensure it's safe to eat.

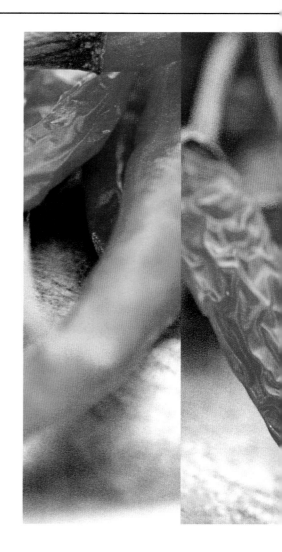

A member of the chilli family, paprika is one of the world's most traded spices, highly valued in the food industry, especially in food processing.

What does it look like?
Paprika is a small, bush-like plant that grows to about 1m in height. The pods or peppers resemble red peppers but they have thick, leathery flesh you can hardly chew.

How do you use it?
The Spanish and Hungarians compete gastronomically for the most ingenious use of the spice. By volume the Hungarians are way ahead, using a vast 10kg per person per year. This sounds unlikely, but virtually every dish in Hungary begins with instructions to melt some lard and fry 2 tablespoons of paprika until it develops its flavour, before adding fish, goose, chicken or meat. If it knows no other, the world will know one paprika dish: the red, soupy meat dish goulash (see Goulash Soup, page 118).

Where does it grow?
Paprika was developed largely in Europe, especially in Hungary. Israel grows it for export, and Spain has its own, which is called *pimenton* (made from a smaller cultivar). Between them, they supply a hungry commercial market, where paprika is used as much for its cosmetic effect on food as for its dry, earthy, bitter-sweet taste.

Unfortunately, 50 years of political upheaval have drawn a curtain across Hungary's gastronomic history. Paprika dates its import from the New World in the sixteenth century – via Turkey, when it was known as Turkish pepper. Under Turkish occupation it was more or less illegal to grow it, but so much did the Hungarians love it a black market grew and it flourished secretly.

Today the growing and drying of paprika is very much a cottage industry in the hot, southern plains around Szeged. After picking, the peppers are strung up to dry against whitewashed walls in the late summer sun. When the wind shakes them and the seeds rattle, they are ready to be milled. Millstones, like those in a traditional flour mill, are used, each set grinding the powder finer and finer.

Grades of paprika
There are five main grades of colour, flavour, sweetness and heat: *kulonleges* (delicate), *edesnemes* (delicate noble sweet), *feledes* (semi-sweet), *rozsa* (rose-coloured) and *eros* (hot).

Spanish paprika
Spain has just as long a history of using paprika (*pimenton*) and it is the key spice in the preparation of *embutidos*, the generic name given to cured sausages such as *chorizo* and *salshichon*. *Pimenton* gives a deep, brick-red colour and an agreeable sweetness to the mixture of minced pork and pork fat, controlling the flavour.

Spanish smoked paprika is a gourmet choice, made in Extramadura, and this is another cottage industry, the drying patiently carried out over wooden grids, using charcoal from the nearby woods.

Medicinal and other uses
Paprika has often been used for healing. In Spain it was mixed with alcohol and cucumber juice as a cure for upset stomach and cramps. In Hungary it was added to fruit brandy to cure a cold or fever.

Turkish boy selling sacks of colourful spices at Fethiye, on the Mediterranean coast.

Arguably the most effective spice in the world, chillies are inexpensive, and magically bring life to such plain staples as rice, beans and lentils. Since the chilli was brought from the New World in 1492, it has revolutionised global eating habits. Can you imagine Indian food without chillies (although the Indian taste for hot food was well established before the arrival of chilli, as India is the world's largest source of peppercorns)?

What does it look like?

Chillies vary in size from the ample pimento-sized *poblano*, used for stuffing, to the bird's-eye chilli, a fraction of the size, and smaller than the bird chilli universally used in Southeast Asia. Some chillies are rich and raisin-sweet like *pasilla*, others are dry and sharp like the Tabasco chilli.

How do you use it?

Cookery writers often advise on removing the seeds to reduce the heat but this is not strictly correct. The seeds actually contain the lowest concentration of capsaicin (bite on one and you'll see), but the white membrane to which they are attached has the highest: twice as much as the pod itself. So, to reduce the heat, scrape out the membrane.

Dried chillies feature in many spice mixtures and pastes, none so renowned as the north African *harissa* paste (see page 98). They are also used in Tabasco sauce in the USA and in *berberi* in Ethiopia (see page 96), and the chilli is a primary ingredient in all Indian and Pakistani cooking.

Where does it grow?

Mexico is the home of chilli and hundreds of cultivars flourish there. More than 30 kinds of chilli, fresh, dried and smoked, large and small, are to be found in a Mexican market every week, and no cook would dream of cooking without a choice of five to ten in the house, many of them rich in tropical flavours. Those which are dried and smoked have extra complexity.

Associated with a hot climate, they are also happy to grow anywhere in the world under glass. At Dean College in West Sussex in the UK, over 200 varieties are grown under glass: red, yellow, green, purple and blue, long and thin, short and round and bulbous, including: *anaheim*, *ancho*, banana pepper, *cascabel*, cayenne, *fresno*, *guajillo* (and *mirasol*), *guindillo*, *habanero*, Hungarian wax, jalapeño

(chipotle when smoked), *pasilla* (*chilaca*), *peperoncini*, *serrano* and *tabasco*.

How hot is hot?

Chillies range from the hottest *habanero* or Scotch bonnet (up to 300,000 units on the Scovell scale) to the mild Californian pepper *anaheim* at around 1000. *Tabasco* is a fairly hot chilli at 70,000. The Scovell scale is a measurement of the active agent, capsaicin, a substance used in medicine, cough mixtures and heat treatment to relieve muscle pain.

In food, capsaicin initially causes burning in the mouth to which the brain responds by producing endorphins which trigger a feeling of well-being. Hot curries can become addictive, as consumers increase their tolerance and eat them hotter and hotter without undue discomfort. However, capsaicin can 'burn' you, as you will find if you put your hand to your eye after handling a cut chilli.

Medicinal and other uses

Chilli peppers were used by the Mayas to treat asthma, coughs and sore throats. The Aztecs used them to relieve toothache. Today chilli is even being used to spice up beer! In Poland there is a chilli vodka.

A little girl walks over chillies drying in the sun in a Nepalese village.

The most famous of chilli powders, cayenne pepper is the quickest route to putting a kick into food.

What does it look like?

Cayenne is a shrub-like plant that can grow to 60cm. It has leathery, dark green leaves and flowers that produce pods or peppers ranging in colour from green and yellow, through to orange and red when finally ripe.

How do you use it?

Until the world woke up to the possibilities of using fresh or dried whole chillies, powdered chilli was the only choice. Unfortunately, it is raw in flavour and a real mouth-burner, so the tiniest amount, on the point of a knife, is sufficient to flavour a batter, say, to cook devilled whitebait.

In most countries it is understood that you must temper the raw powder, heating it first, then frying it in a little oil or fat to reduce its crudity.

The alternative to powder is one of the many chilli sauces, usually from the Caribbean. One of the best, Tabasco, from Louisiana, is made from ripe red chillies preserved in salt then aged in barrels for three years before being ground and diluted with vinegar. But many West Indian pepper sauces are on a par. No table in Brazil is without a small bottle of *malagueno* chilli sauce: tiny chillies steeped in oil or vinegar. The Chinese use chilli sauce freely as a condiment.

Chilli powder is used in numerous spice blends, famously in the American *chile con carne* mix, with powdered cumin, cloves and garlic powder.

Where is it grown?

Authentic cayenne originates in the island of Cayenne off Venezuela, but these days dried chilli powder from numerous sources is substituted.

Medicinal and other uses

It is believed to help settle the stomach and relieve headaches. For centuries herbalists have suggested rubbing red pepper on to sore muscles or joints.

mangifera indica (mango)

An acid, fruity powder obtained from dried unripe mangoes and used as a flavouring in India. In Persia you can buy dried grape powder and dried lime powder, which are similarly used to add a tart flavour to dishes where vinegar might be used in the West.

What does it look like?

The fruit vary in length from 5 to 25cm and can be almost round in shape or long and slim. They grow in clusters on a tree, which can reach the height of an oak, and they make a loud cracking noise as they ripen and fall to the ground. To make mango powder, unripe fruit are harvested, the stone removed and the fruit cut into slices. The slices are left to dry before being ground to a fine grey powder.

How do you use it?

The mango not only provides luscious sweet fruit when ripe but is useful to the cook all year round. When green it is used in pickles, chutneys and *sambals*, and in some *nam priks*, the hot, sharp relishes which are the basis of so much Thai cuisine.

Mango powder is sour and tart with a subtle taste like resin. In northern India it is used with ginger, coriander, cumin, garlic, red food colouring and natural yoghurt to make a seasoned paste for *tandoori* cooking. The paste is spread on meat, chicken or fish, left for several hours, then roasted in an extremely hot *tandoor* or oven. Mango powder helps to tenderise the meat. It is also used with vegetables, often instead of tamarind.

Where does it grow?

Native to India and Southeast Asia, mangoes are also grown in Brazil, Mexico, the West Indies and north America.

Medicinal and other uses

The mango appears in many myths and legends. It became a status symbol in India at the time of the Moghul rulers and Akbar (1556–1605) is said to have had an orchard with 100,000 mango trees.

The most universal condiment in the West for hundreds of years, pepper, made by grinding peppercorns, placed with salt on every table. The view that hot spices, like peppercorns, were used to mask off-flavours in days when refrigeration was unknown, is now challenged. People used peppercorns because they simply adored the aroma and bite of pepper.

What do they look like?

Peppercorns are the fruit of a climbing vine. Black peppercorns are whole green berries which have been dried in the sun until they wrinkle and turn black and brown. White pepper is made from the fully ripened red berries, which must be soaked in water so that the skins can be rubbed off. The white seed inside is dried in the sun.

How do you use it?

Pepper should be ground from the whole seed when required. Once ground, it loses its flavour, and white pepper completely spoils a dish when it is stale. You can usually detect it in cheaper commercial sausages.

Compared with chilli, the heat from peppercorns is gentle and warming, and they are ground for use in the warming Indian spice mixture, *garam masala* (see page 31), which is added at the end of cooking. When you use pepper in cooking, the flavour quickly diminishes, but it adds a keen edge to meat, poultry and fish stocks. Because heat drives off the piquant volatile flavour oils, a Peppered Steak (see page 128) can be smothered in 40 or 50 crushed black peppercorns before grilling and still be palatable.

Where does it grow?

Peppercorns grow on climbing vines in the rain forests of southwest India. The plant clings to palms and mango trees, producing strings of beautiful green berries which ripen to red, shining like jewels along the bright green, pointed leaves.

The Romans developed the trade in pepper and brought it to Europe. It was so valuable, it often passed for currency. A few peppercorns could buy you a slave. Indeed, towards the end of the Roman empire, when the Goths surrounded Rome, a ransom was paid in peppercorns to save the city; Alaric the Goth demanded 1350kg of pepper to spare Rome. In England, too, the expression 'peppercorn rent' has passed into the language, meaning a comically small rent. But it had not always been regarded like this. Even before the Norman Conquest, King Ethelred demanded 4.5kg of pepper as part of a tax on merchants.

Until Columbus brought back chillies from the New World in the sixteenth century, pepper was the uniquely hot spice of the Old World, and nowhere more so than in India, its country of origin. It reached Southeast Asia more than 2000 years ago and has been grown in Indonesia and Malaysia since then. Nowadays it is cultivated also in Thailand, Vietnam, China, Sri Lanka and Brazil.

Medicinal and other uses

Pepper has traditionally been used for stimulating the appetite and also for the relief of nausea and vertigo. It is carminative and laxative, and can be used to treat fevers and chills. In east Africa it is said to help repel mosquitoes. In Nepal it is used to keep leeches at bay.

tamarindus indica (tamarind)

Tamarind is the sour fruit of a giant, beautiful tropical tree. It is known also as Indian date.

What does it look like?
The seed pods resemble conkers or chesnuts. When broken open, they have soft, sweet-sour fruit pulp inside, with several large, black stones.

How do you use it?
Eaten fresh it is delicious, but it is usually semi-dried, losing its appetising, fresh mouth appeal. It is sold in lumps, for the cook to soak, squeezing out the stones. It also comes ready-prepared in jars, the ghost of the fresh product. Given the choice, Indian and Sri Lankan cooks utilise the fresh fruit which ripens around January. It is an essential ingredient in the numerous soupy, sour *sambal* sauces. which accompany starchy food on the subcontinent, such as *appari*, the breakfast pancakes of Sri Lanka.

Tamarind is more widely used in the West than might be expected, a prime ingredient in many proprietary fruit sauces found stacked on the tables of lorry drivers' câfés, including HP and Daddies' sauces. It's an important ingredient in chutneys, too, and it makes a refreshing long drink for summer days.

Where does it grow?
Tamarind is the fruit of a giant tree with spreading branches and a thick, straight trunk that grows in India, tropical Africa and the West Indies. Little boys throw sticks up to the high branches to knock down the seed pods, with their sticky sweet fruit inside.

Medicinal and other uses
Tamarind has been used as an astringent and antiseptic, as a laxative and to help ease stomach pains and biliousness. It has been used to destroy worms in young children and externally as a wash for sore eyes and ulcers.

Vanilla is one of the world's most loved tastes, accounting for the flavour of over 90 per cent of all ice creams consumed. Its name means 'little bean' in Spanish; the name given to it when first encountered by the conquistadores in Mexico. It is the second most expensive spice after saffron.

What does it look like?

Vanilla is a long, thin, brown-black seed pod shaped like a French bean. It comes from an orchid with a modest white flower, the least glamorous among the thousands which comprise this dazzling, show-off, technicolour family.

Vanilla pods set out for sale on newspaper in Sri Lanka.

How do you use it?

Vanilla is the most important spice for the world's pastry cooks, who use it in desserts which contain cream, milk and eggs, such as *crème brûlée* and Pavlova (see pages 148 and 150). Combined with almost any other flavours, it overpowers them with its irresistible perfume. It has the capacity to smooth over rough edges and fill in gaps, like snow blanketing an alpine scene. Because it is so expensive, the real thing is widely substituted by artificial vanilla flavouring – which the law no longer permits manufacturers to call vanilla essence, as it bears little resemblance to the original.

Where does it grow?

Vanilla is native to the rain forests of Central America, a climbing vine that produces a long green bean that takes three years to mature on the plant.

The green beans are picked and spread out to dry in the sun. Each day they are soaked in boiling water and drained. The process is continued until the enzymes are neutralised and tiny white crystals appear on the surface of the bean as it darkens, a sign that the perfume and flavour have developed. By now the beans are hard and brown and almost black.

Early explorers to Mexico hoped to harvest vanilla in other lands but were frustrated when most of the plants resisted germination. The French, who had not competed with the British, Spanish, Dutch and Portuguese for control of the spice roads in the sixteenth and seventeenth century, were the unlikely beneficiaries. Thanks to research by a Belgian botanist who discovered that vines were pollinated by certain bees and hummingbirds, he deduced that the flowers could be pollinated by hand. A 16-year-old African slave on the French island of La Réunion in the Indian Ocean was first to put the idea into practice and the island became famous for producing the world's best vanilla, sold as Bourbon. Their skills were passed to Madagascar, then a French dependency, which is now the world's largest producer.

Medicinal and other uses

Since Aztec times vanilla has been used as an aphrodisiac and a cure for impotence; it is also used to bring down fever.

Coconut is almost an essential ingredient in the cooking of Southeast Asia and Brazil. Along the sandy strands of Copacabana and Ipanema beaches in Rio de Janeiro, young, green coconuts are sold at stalls as a refreshing drink. The top is hacked off with a machete and the nut served with a straw to extract its liquid.

What does it look like?

A fibrous, hairy, wooden shell, with indentations on the top resembling smiling eyes and mouth, hence its name, from the Spanish *coca* – meaning 'grinning face'. It has a lining of thick white flesh.

How do you use it?

As a flavouring, coconut is available in several forms: grated and dried (desiccated), powdered (like instant coffee), in waxy bars, or as canned coconut milk. Coconut milk is not the liquid inside the coconut but is made by grating the flesh and soaking it in boiling water, then straining it to produce a mixture of 'cream' and 'milk', the thicker part containing more of the saturated oils (and therefore high in calories). A can of coconut milk contains both, but for maximum flavour buy fresh coconut whenever possible.

Brazil boasts many hundreds of sweets, as a result of the culinary skills brought to the colony by Portuguese nuns. Most are made with eggs, sugar and grated coconut, which was substituted for the original almonds of their homeland. Coconut is also grated on to seafood dishes, or roasted and sprinkled on other dishes, as a nutty garnish.

In the Caribbean coconut rice is one of the most loved dishes, as it is in Indonesia. In Malaysia coconut is used to moderate the fierceness of hot chillies in soups and stews.

Where does it grow?

A plant of Malaysian origin, it has colonised the tropics, from Asia to Africa to the Americas, growing easily and cheaply on poor sandy soil. It provides coconut fibre, timber and a saturated oil used in industry and in the food world. The main producers are Indonesia, India and the Phillipines.

Medicinal and other uses

The liquid inside the coconut makes a cooling drink.

ferula assa-foetida (asafoetida)

The most contradictory of spices, asafoetida is foul-smelling yet enhances every dish it flavours. Its smell initially masks other strong odours but then magically disappears in the cooking. It is an essential ingredient in south Indian vegetarian dishes, imparting a savoury, meaty flavour.

What does it look like?
Asafoetida is a brown gum collected from the roots of a giant fennel plant. Rolled into small balls, it is dried in the sun until hardened.

How do you use it?
It has to be grated before use, then heated in a pan to release its pungent, sulphurous odours. Some liken the smell to rank garlic and leek. Use with discretion, obviously. For some dishes, Indian cooks do no more than rub a cooking vessel with it, just as the French will rub a salad bowl with cut garlic to give the merest hint of flavour.

Where does it grow?
The plant originates in Afghanistan and Iran where it was an essential flavouring in food ('what pepper was to the Chinese', wrote one early historian). Alexander the Great discovered it in Afghanistan, which was at the limits of his Persian Empire and, because of its similarity to sylphium (an early spice now extinct), he brought it to Europe.

Greek cooks loved it and later introduced it to the Roman kitchen where it became a significant ingredient. Half the recipes in the Roman cookbook by Apicius included it. It disappeared from the European table after the fall of the Roman Empire.

Asafoetida was enthusiastically adopted in India, where it's known to the Hindus as *hing*. Their poets called it the nectar of spices but its repellent odour prompted Westerners to dub it devil's dung.

Medicinal and other uses
Highly regarded as a means of promoting appetite, as a digestive and as a cure for wind. Eating a tiny piece the size of a match-head with a splash of juice of ginger (once every two days) was thought to promote sexual activity among those of failing powers.

One of the world's most sought-after spices, nutmeg is prized for its versatility and is the essence of what a spice ought to be. Its dynamic personality, glowing with warmth, lights up everything it touches. It has a resonance that simply makes anything milky or creamy sit up with shock. It is like a lantern that lights a warm fire inside you.

What does it look like?

Nutmeg is the nut of a fleshy green fruit, which resembles a walnut. The tree is a most sensual thing to encounter, the leaves and bark also impregnated with nutmeggy perfume. The flesh of the fruit used to be candied in sugar as a sweetmeat and exported. When the flesh is stripped off, it reveals an reddish-orange cage called an aril (see mace, page 204) and beneath it the hard brown nut that must be dried in the sun.

Buy whole nutmeg and grate when needed – you don't even need a grater: you can take off shavings with a sharp knife.

How do you use it?

Nutmeg has many uses. Chaucer refers to it as both a flavouring for ale and a spice to fumigate a clothes chest. Byzantine monks sprinkled it on their pease pudding. It puts life into mulled wine mixtures and rum punch. In India, they use it as a warming ingredient in spice pastes and in powders sprinkled over food just before serving.

In the Caribbean, it is often included in jerk pastes used to marinate pork, goat, chicken and fish (see page 115). In Europe, nutmeg is the very spirit of Christmas, included in Christmas pudding (see page 132) and mince pies. It is also used with cheese and milk dishes: added to a dull cheese sauce, it transforms it to a thing of startling interest; added to a drink of hot chocolate, it makes it zing.

Where does it grow?

Nutmeg is native to Indonesia but is now grown around the tropics, especially in the Caribbean, Guadeloupe and Martinique. In Grenada, the world's largest source of the spice, they categorise nutmeg by weight. Thrown into a water tank, those nuts that sink, known as sinkers, go to the food industry. Floaters are sold for medicinal use.

Medicinal and other uses

Nuns believed that nutmeg purified the senses and lessened evil humours. Nutmeg is a rare spice in that it is, in large quantities, a narcotic with hallucinogenic properties. This won't affect your cooking unless you're thinking of grinding more than two whole nuts into a dish.

Mastic is a resinous flavouring in the Middle East, moderating the sweetness of milk in blancmanges, junkets, semolina and rice puddings. It was so sought after in the fifteenth century that it was listed as one of the valuable spices on Christopher Columbus's shopping list for his voyages to the New World, along with peppercorns, cinnamon and nutmeg.

What does it look like?
Mastic is a diamond-bright, hard gum, like pine resin in flavour, extracted from trees.

How do you use it?
Mastic crystals provide flavour and give a chewy texture to ice cream and Turkish delight (see page 76). Mastic is also added to some bread doughs to make them more elastic.

Where does it grow?
Mastic comes from trees of the pistachio family growing wild on hillsides in the Middle East. It has resisted cultivation except in one small area of the Aegean island of Chios, tucked into the Turkish coast.

Prized in Greece and Turkey for 2400 years, it was considered very precious in the Topkapi royal court in Istanbul during the Ottoman Empire, where it was used as a breath sweetener and chewed all day by the ladies of the harem. The Turks protected supplies in Chios, building fortified watchtowers in the dozen small towns which cultivated it.

Mastic is harvested by slashing the trees with a knife. They duly 'bleed', producing transparent teardrops. These are collected and washed, initially with soap, and repeatedly rinsed until they sparkle like clear glass. It is the work of old women with pails to gather up pieces which fall into the dirt and stick to the leaves, collecting and washing them like gold prospectors.

Medicinal and other uses
Mastic has been used as a stimulant and diuretic, and to cure diarrhoea in children. It is used to sweeten the breath and help decaying teeth. In the East it is used in sweets and cordials. Sometimes it is mixed with the anise-flavoured Turkish spirit *raki* to make it denser. Before the discovery of chewing gum, mastic had a very special place in society as a breath sweetener – it could be chewed for hours.

Along with vanilla, cocoa is one of the world's two most important and valuable flavourings. Curiously, its success as chocolate is due to processing which minimises the essential properties of the raw product. Its rich oil (cocoa butter) is removed, and its intense bitterness is diminished by heavy concentrations of sugar and, in the case of milk chocolate, with milk powder.

What does it look like?

The cocoa tree grows to a height of 4–5m with bright green leaves, small reddish flowers and red fruit. It produces large pods shaped like ridged rugby balls. When the large seeds (beans) are ripe, they rattle in the capsule (each capsule has about 25 seeds). The seeds are scraped out with their pulp, laid in the sun to ferment and dry out, then roasted and ground to a fine powder.

How do you use it?

The cocoa bean is used as a bitter ingredient in savoury cooking. In Mexico it is combined with chillies and sometimes vanilla in some traditional stews (*moles*, see page 101), a taste combination which predates its use in the post-Columban world, when it was mixed with sugar.

The Belgians, Swiss and British have done most to develop modern chocolate culture, but the French and Italians have monopolised the gourmet end of the market, treating the best harvests as *grand crus*. And, uniquely among Europeans, the Italians are comfortable using chocolate in savoury dishes, with meat, poultry, game and even octopus.

Where does it grow?

Cocoa originates in the rainforests in the north of South America (now Venezuela, which still produces the world's top-quality beans).

Originally cocoa was made into a stimulating and refreshing drink (like tea, it contains caffeine). The Mayan people introduced it to present-day Mexico, where it became a cult drink with the Toltecs and especially the Aztecs, who gave it commercial status, using the beans as currency.

By the time that Hernando Cortes, first of the *conquistadores*, arrived at the Aztec court in Teochtitlan in 1519, cocoa was considered a drink only for a king, the emperor Monteczuma drinking it from a gold cup. It was consumed unsweetened, which accounts for the name *choclatl*, considered to translate as 'bitter water'.

Columbus identified it on his fourth voyage to the West Indies, but Cortes was the one who promoted it in his homeland, where the Spanish were the first to drink it with sugar and cinnamon rather than chillies. They managed to keep its import secret, and English pirates, finding the thick paste on a captured Spanish galleon, tipped it into the sea, dismissing it as 'sheep shit'.

Medicinal and other uses

Oil of theobroma or cocoa butter is used as an ingredient in cosmetic ointments and for coating pills. It is also used to soothe chapped hands and lips. It has a diuretic effect and has been used to treat high blood pressure.

Slabs of chocolate savoury dishes, suc *moles*, piled high o Mexican market sta

menu planner / menu planner / mer

soups

Borscht (Russia) **118**
Callaloo soup (Jamaica) **106**
Chicken noodle soup (Vietnam) **38**
Country chicken soup (Southeast
   Asia) **51**
Florida bean soup (USA) **121**
Ful mesdames (Egypt) **93**
Goulash soup (Hungary) **118**
Hot-and-sour soup (China) **34**
Laksa soup (Singapore) **48**
Lentil and rice soup (Yemen) **66**
Noodles with togarashi (Japan) **34**
Saffron carrot soup (Australia) **142**
Shellfish soup with lobster wontons
   (Australia) **138**
Spicy vegetable soup (Indonesia) **48**
Tom yam kung (Thailand) **52**

appetisers, side dishes and snacks

Aubergine in tomato sauce
   (India) **18**
Black-eyed bean fritters (Brazil) **102**
Chicken satay (Indonesia) **52**
Chickpeas and potatoes (India) **21**
Chilli crab (Singapore) **55**
Cottage cheese (India) **19**
Crispy duck (China) **37**
Crispy fried puffed patties (South
   Africa) **85**
Dhal lentils (India) **22**
Falafal (Egypt) **91**
Grilled chilli prawns (Indonesia) **51**
Guacamole (Mexico) **103**
Marinated herrings (Denmark) **121**
Mussels stuffed with spicy rice
   (Turkey) **72**
Peas and cottage cheese (India) **19**
Poppy seed roll (Poland) **122**
Pork terrine with quatre épices
   (France) **127**
Potato samosas (India) **14**

Potatoes stuffed with almonds
   (India) **16**
Potatoes with cheese sauce
   (Mexico) **102**
Raw tuna with goat's cheese
   (Australia) **145**
Sesame spinach (Japan) **36**
Spiced cauliflower and potato
   (India) **15**
Spiced fish kebab (India) **25**
Spiced okra (India) **19**
Spiced paratha flatbread (India) **14**
Spiced potato cakes (India) **21**
Spicy crab in filo pastry (India) **25**
Spicy gram cake (India) **29**
Stewed red cabbage (Australia) **142**
Stir-fried spicy rice (China) **44**
Stuffed aubergines (Turkey) **68**
Stuffed chard leaves (Turkey) **67**
Stuffed courgettes (Turkey) **67**
Sushi (Japan) **41**
Sweet potato fritters (New Zealand)
   141

main courses

Aubergine moussaka (Greece) **124**
Bean purée (Mexico) **105**
Beans in the pot (Mexico) **105**
Bobotie meat loaf (South Africa) **93**
Bokoboko beef porridge
   (Zanzibar) **90**
Bredie lamb stew (South Africa) **89**
Chicken tagine (Morocco) **88**
Chicken tikka masala (India) **28**
Chickpeas and potatoes (India) **21**
Chilli-roast spare ribs (Vietnam) **43**
Chilli-spiced chicken stew
   (Mexico) **108**
Cold noodles with sauces
   (Taiwan) **36**
Crab, chilli and lime spaghettini
   (Australia) **141**
Crusted lamb biriani (India) **26**
Curried goat (Jamaica) **112**
Dhal lentils (India) **22**

Fillet of beef marinated in rendang
   (Bali, Indonesia) **56**
Fish stew (Portugal) **122**
Green curried beef with noodles
   (Thailand) **58**
Grilled chilli prawns (Indonesia) **51**
Grilled spiced snapper (Mexico) **104**
Indian risotto with chilli prawns
   (India) **16**
Jerked pork (Jamaica) **112**
Jewelled rice (Iran and Turkey) **70**
Lamb and red bean stew (Iran) **74**
Lamb in a creamy yoghurt sauce
   (India) **28**
Louisiana jambalaya (USA) **125**
Masala fish steaks Cape Malay
   (South Africa) **95**
Midwest spare ribs (USA) **129**
Minced lamb kebab (Turkey) **71**
Mixed vegetable casserole
   (Balkans) **124**
Paella valenciana (Spain) **128**
Peppered steak (France) **128**
Pepperpot (West Indies) **109**
Pickled pork with sauerkraut
   (Germany) **129**
Pork with soy sauce (Malaysia) **54**
Prawn and chilli salsa (Brazil) **105**
Prawn in tamarind sauce (Iran) **72**
Rabbit with mustard (France) **127**
Red chicken curry (Sri Lanka) **22**
Red chicken curry with noodles
   (Thailand) **58**
Roast pepper cervena
   (New Zealand) **145**
Saffron chicken (Iran) **74**
Salt fish curry (Tanzania) **94**
Savoury spiced pork (Malaysia) **57**
Seven-vegetable couscous
   (Morocco) **90**
Slow soy-stewed pork with
   mushrooms (Malaysia) **61**
Sosatie lamb kebabs (South Africa) **86**
Soy-braised beef with turnips
   (China) **43**

conversion charts / conversion charts

UK WEIGHTS

5g	1/4 oz
15g	1/2 oz
20g	3/4 oz
25g	1oz
50g	2oz
60g	2 1/2 oz
75g	3oz
100g	3 1/2 oz
125g	4oz
150g	5oz
175g	6oz
200g	7oz
225g	7 1/2 oz
250g	8oz
275g	9oz
300g	10oz
325g	11oz
350g	11 1/2 oz
375g	12oz
400g	13oz
425g	14oz
450g	14 1/2 oz
475g	15oz
500g	1lb
625g	1 1/4 lb
750g	1 1/2 lb
875g	1 3/4 lb
1kg	2lb
1.25kg	2 1/2 lb
1.5kg	3lb
1.75kg	3 1/2 lb
2kg	4lb

UK MEASUREMENTS

5mm	1/4 inch
1cm	1/2 inch
1.5cm	3/4 inch
2.5cm	1 inch
5cm	2 inches
7cm	3 inches
10cm	4 inches
12cm	5 inches
15cm	6 inches
18cm	7 inches
20cm	8 inches
23cm	9 inches
25cm	10 inches
28cm	11 inches
30cm	12 inches
33cm	13 inches

UK OVEN TEMPERATURES

110°C	225°F	Gas 1/4
120°C	250°F	Gas 1/2
140°C	275°F	Gas 1
150°C	300°F	Gas 2
160°C	325°F	Gas 3
180°C	350°F	Gas 4
190°C	375°F	Gas 5
200°C	400°F	Gas 6
220°C	425°F	Gas 7
230°C	450°F	Gas 8

UK LIQUIDS

15ml	1/2 fl oz
25ml	1fl oz
50ml	2fl oz
75ml	3fl oz
100ml	3 1/2 fl oz
125ml	4fl oz
150ml	1/4 pint
175ml	6fl oz
200ml	7fl oz
225ml	7 1/2 fl oz
250ml	8fl oz
275ml	9fl oz
300ml	1/2 pint
325ml	11fl oz
350ml	12fl oz
375ml	13fl oz
400ml	14fl oz
425ml	3/4 pint
450ml	16fl oz
475ml	16 1/2 fl oz
500ml	17fl oz
575ml	18fl oz
600ml	1 pint
650ml	1 pint 2fl oz
750ml	1 1/4 pints
900ml	1 1/2 pints
1 litre	1 3/4 pints
1.2 litres	2 pints
1.5 litres	2 1/2 pints
1.8 litres	3 pints
2 litres	3 1/2 pints
2.5 litres	4 pints
3.6 litres	6 pints

US WEIGHTS

¼ oz.	7g
½ oz.	14g
¾ oz.	21g
1 oz.	28g
2 oz.	57g
2½ oz.	71g
3 oz.	85g
3½ oz.	99g
4 oz. (¼ lb.)	113g
5 oz.	142g
6 oz.	170g
7 oz.	198g
7½ oz.	212g
8 oz. (½ lb.)	227g
9 oz.	255g
10 oz.	283g
11 oz.	312g
11½ oz.	326g
12 oz. (¾ lb.)	340g
13 oz.	369g
14 oz.	397g
14½ oz.	411g
15 oz.	425g
16 oz. (1 lb.)	454g
20 oz. (1¼ lb.)	567g
24 oz. (1½ lb.)	681g
28 oz. (1¾ lb.)	794g
32 oz. (2 lb.)	908g
35 oz. (2.2 lb.)	1kg
44 oz. (2¾ lb.)	1.25kg
48 oz. (3 lb.)	1.34kg
54 oz.	1.5kg
56 oz. (3½ lb.)	1.56kg
62 oz.	1.75kg
64 oz. (4 lb.)	1.79kg
71 oz. (4.4 lb.)	2kg

US MEASUREMENTS

¼ inch	5mm
½ inch	1cm
¾ inch	2cm
1 inch	2.5cm
2 inches	5cm
3 inches	7cm
4 inches	10cm
5 inches	12cm
6 inches	15cm
7 inches	18cm
8 inches	20cm
9 inches	23cm
10 inches	25cm
11 inches	28cm
12 inches (1 foot)	30cm
13 inches	33cm

US OVEN TEMPERATURES

225°F	110°C	Gas Mark ¼
250°F	120°C	Gas Mark ½
275°F	140°C	Gas Mark 1
300°F	150°C	Gas Mark 2
325°F	160°C	Gas Mark 3
350°F	180°C	Gas Mark 4
375°F	190°C	Gas Mark 5
400°F	200°C	Gas Mark 6
425°F	220°C	Gas Mark 7
450°F	230°C	Gas Mark 8

US VOLUME MEASURES

½ fl.oz.	15ml
1 fl.oz.	30ml
2 fl.oz. (¼ cup)	60ml
3 fl.oz.	90ml
3½ fl.oz.	100ml
4 fl.oz. (½ cup)	120ml
5 fl.oz.	150ml
6 fl.oz.	175ml
7 fl.oz.	205ml
7½ fl.oz.	225ml
8 fl.oz. (1 cup)	235ml
9 fl.oz.	265ml
10 fl.oz.	300ml
11 fl.oz.	325ml
12 fl.oz.	350ml
13 fl.oz.	385ml
14 fl.oz.	415ml
15 fl.oz.	445ml
16 fl.oz. (1 pint)	475ml
17 fl.oz.	500ml
18 fl.oz.	530ml
19 fl. oz.	560ml
20 fl.oz.	600ml
22 fl.oz.	650ml
25 fl.oz.	750ml
30 fl.oz.	900ml
32 fl. oz. (1 quart)	945ml
33 fl.oz.	1 liter
50 fl.oz.	1.5 liters
64 fl.oz. (½ gallon)	1.9 liters
68 fl.oz.	2 liters
96 fl.oz. (¾ gallon)	2.83 liters
128 fl.oz. (1 gallon)	3.77 liters

photographic acknowledgements

Key: IPL – Impact Photo Library; FL – Francine Lawrence; MWS – Marcus Wilson-Smith; PdV – Patrice de Villiers.

All photographs by Steve Baxter except the following:
page 3 (left) Dominic Sansoni/IPL; page 7 PdV; page 12 Wally Santona/IPL; page 13 Dominic Sansoni/IPL; page 15 David S Silverling/IPL; page 18 PdV; page 31 Charles Coates/IPL; page 33 (top) MWS; page 33 (bottom) Mark Henley/IPL; page 41 PdV; page 47 FL; page 49 PdV; page 55 MWS; page 59 PdV; page 63 Jonathan Pile/IPL; page 64 Robin Laurance/IPL; page 65 Alan Keohane/IPL; page 70 PdV; page 80 MWS; page 81 Ben Edwards/IPL; page 84 FL; page 88 PdV; page 94 MWS; page 99 Ray Roberts/IPL; page 100 Mark Henley/IPL; page 104 PdV; page 108 PdV; page 115 FL; page 123 MWS; page 132 MWS; page 134 MWS; page 137 MWS; page 163 FL; page 181 FL; page 197 Daniel White/IPL; page 198 Caroline Penn/IPL; page 211 FL; page 216 Piers Cavendish/IPL; page Christophe Bluntzer/IPL; page 224 FL; page 232 FL; page 234–5 PdV